T0367841

MASTERY
MIND-SET

*Doing the Impossible
in Martial Arts*

Craig R. E. Krohn

Edited by Jeff Morgenroth

iUniverse LLC
Bloomington

MASTERY MIND-SET
DOING THE IMPOSSIBLE IN MARTIAL ARTS

iUniverse books may be ordered through booksellers or by contacting:

iUniverse
1663 Liberty Drive
Bloomington, IN 47403
www.iuniverse.com
1-800-Authors (1-800-288-4677)

ISBN: 978-1-4917-1459-1 (sc)
ISBN: 978-1-4917-1461-4 (hc)
ISBN: 978-1-4917-1460-7 (e)

Library of Congress Control Number: 2013920835

Printed in the United States of America.

iUniverse rev. date: 12/05/2013

For my mother, who taught me courage and faith.

Contents

Preface

There was once a time when I believed that there were distinct boundaries between the possible and the impossible, especially in the martial arts. Fighting five people at once? Impossible. Absorbing full-power kicks to the knee? Impossible. Knocking someone out with a tap? Definitely impossible. It was only later, after I trained with several martial arts masters, that my eyes were opened. There is a simple truth that belies the lessons I had learned up until that point: these impossibilities were artificial limits I was placing upon myself.

In the world of martial arts, many things look amazing, but the reality is that they are not. Jump kicks, while being very impressive athletic and acrobatic feats, require an opponent to move only a few inches one way or the other to avoid the blow. I've even been full-on jump kicked in the face by a black belt, and it did nothing more than produce a fat lip. I've seen people deliver lightning-fast kicks three times to the head. Again, this is an impressive athletic endeavor, but when I asked the person to kick me in the head at full power, he couldn't down me. I didn't even block or move. It wasn't a pleasant feeling, but in spite of the kicker's agility, the result felt like a slap. Had it been a tournament, he would have won. Had it been a real fight, his arts would have been unsuccessful.

I once knew a man who performed kung fu competitively in China. He was an exceptionally gifted athlete, and his technique kept spectators on the edge of their seats. And yet, he ended up in the hospital after a bar fight one day. Even though his arts looked amazing, he failed to gain practical insight into how his arts function in real situations. He trained for performance, not self-defense.

Conversely, there are things that look simple in martial arts, yet are exceptionally complex. My karate sensei once placed his hand on my chest and made a fist, sort of like the one-inch punch that Bruce Lee made famous. He hit me, but this punch did not make me move. Instead, it sent a vibration to my heart, and I felt blood squish upward through the arteries in my neck. I almost passed out. The room was spinning, and I had to hold on to a wall so I wouldn't fall over. My sensei told me that he only used 5 percent power, because he didn't want to kill me. Seeing how nonchalant he was with such a devastating punch, anyone would have believed him. This was real martial arts and this was real power, and yet this sort of thing looks impossible to others.

You may have started your training in martial arts with a specific goal in mind. That goal may have been to simply get in shape, or it may have been to become better at self-defense. There may have been a picture in your head of that ideal person you would like to become. Perhaps there was a mentor in your life who you wanted to emulate, or a movie that you saw that stuck in your mind. Martial artists tend to dream about having power and wisdom that come with great sacrifice, dedication, and discipline. "The devastating punch can be mine," we say, "if I only work hard enough to achieve it."

I grew up being beaten down by bullies a number of times. I never wanted to feel that shame again, and so I took up martial arts to learn how to fight. At first I had to hide this practice from others because I was afraid of persecution. But as time wore on, martial arts became a passion for me, and the original reason for joining was transformed. I now pursue a different and—in my opinion—logical direction in my training. I want to advance the arts further than they are now. This is a lofty goal and one that might be scoffed at by others, but such individuals do not concern me. I have already accomplished a great deal in my training that I myself thought was impossible only a decade earlier. This leads me to believe that there are other sorts of magic out there that seem equally impossible, and yet are undiscovered only because we haven't dared ourselves to go looking for them.

Gravity was always here before we "discovered it." Radio waves were always present before we discovered how to hear them. The power of electricity was always available to us, but we needed to understand it. What other forces are out there in the world that we have not yet tapped into? What are our minds capable of? ESP? Telepathy? Telekinesis? Our knee-jerk reaction to these things is that they are impossible, but that's what the critics of the Wright brothers thought about the airplane.

I'm not saying I know magic, nor am I claiming I can cast fireballs from my eyes and lightning from my fingertips. These types of skills seem like fantasy, but it is my hope to share with you how you can attain real "magic" within the martial arts. By developing a mastery mind-set, one can achieve genuinely amazing abilities.

If you are looking for corner-store martial arts, you can find them at any strip mall. To find mastery-level martial arts, you must go in search of them, because the places that teach at such a level are not on every corner. It is these kinds of mastery arts that I am going to discuss in this book, and hopefully help you in opening yourself up to the challenges and power that can only come by practicing them. Regardless of whether you have been studying martial arts for a lifetime or are a new student, you can achieve a greater understanding of your art to do the impossible. First, though, you must recognize false boundaries and limitations that you may perceive to be real and be open to the concept that the impossible is possible. You will be amazed at what imagination and determination can unlock within ourselves.

Acknowledgments

Throughout this book, I make mention of many teachers whom I have studied with throughout my martial arts career. I am keeping their identities confidential, as several of them would not like being mentioned in a book. All of these teachers are exceptionally humble, and all of them would feel it distasteful to be referred to as a "master," which I frequently do in these pages. I can call them masters because all of them have decades of intense devotion to the martial arts, and each has exceptional abilities.

Therefore, it is out of respect for my teachers that I have not added their names, but they know who they are, and they know the great gifts that they have freely shared with me over my life. I owe much of my understanding of the arts to each one of them.

For years I have refrained from formally documenting these teachings out of respect for my teachers' wishes. They feel that martial arts can only be truly imparted from teacher to student directly. While in general I agree with them, my views on this changed in 2012, when I taught a seminar in Missouri. One of the students who attended remarked (I am paraphrasing), "There are many terrible martial arts books. It would be a shame to have the real arts lost in this noise. You need to write this book." Because of this, it is my sincere hope that my teachers forgive me for expressing these lessons in writing, and understand the great benefit for others that I hope will come from it.

Many martial artists practice what I refer to as "sport martial arts," that is, arts designed for tournaments. These types of arts are beneficial in many ways, but do not foster the mind-set of a master. Real fights are not scored with points, and an attacker will not stop striking you while you are on the ground. When I was a child, I often played guns in the forest. I would feign shooting at other kids, who would say, "You missed!" The same could hold true for tournament fighting. I have received points in tournaments for techniques I know were insufficient to down my opponent. Likewise, I have had people throw kicks and punches at me that were weak and powerless and sometimes a foot off target, and yet they received points for these hits. If you are in a real fight, try saying, "Nuh-uh, you missed," to your attacker.

Sport martial arts are designed to teach techniques that look good in tournaments, rather than determine real fighting prowess. Many people will disagree, but I'm betting these same people are not masters. The older ways of martial arts were about winning fights through exceptional skill. Real arts show you the deeper understanding of how to create, dissipate, and transfer power. Sport arts do not teach these lessons, though sometimes they are learned accidentally or by aggressively trying to figure them out. I spent a decade doing sport arts before I realized that I was not really fighting. At the time, you couldn't have convinced me otherwise; I was practicing full-contact karate, and I thought this was as real as it came. I was wrong.

This led me to find masters of both karate and aikido who could help me solve the puzzle between fact and fiction in the martial arts. Once I learned their lessons, it felt as though I had thrown away that decade of practice, but my karate sensei said to me, "You had to go through that (sport training) in order to appreciate the real karate."

I did not want to do sports. I did not want to do tournaments. I don't care about scoring points, and I don't care about fancy or flashy techniques that may not work in the real world. I wanted to be the best martial artist that I could be, and I wanted the magic that the masters had. I wanted to do the impossible. I wanted to get kicked in the solar plexus and not flinch. I wanted to punch with minimal effort and bring a huge man down to his knees. I wanted a throw that was effortless, yet brutally efficient.

Masters of martial arts do not care about points in tournaments; they have their minds fixated upon improving every single thing that they do. Masters diligently move forward and ignore the noise and haste around them. Following their wisdom and tireless examples, I have dedicated my life to understanding the arts and making the impossible possible. It is my hope that you will too.

Introduction to the Impossible

The majority of my training has been in karate, aikido, and kenjutsu, although I have also practiced jujitsu, nan quan kung fu, wushu, and judo. My bias is clearly for Japanese art styles, and so this is where the majority of my direction is coming from. I have met Chinese masters of kung fu who were just as capable and as effective as the Okinawa masters whom I trained with. This is one of the first lessons we should learn about the martial arts: it doesn't matter what style you practice. I do not dwell upon external forms, but rather focus on internal methods by which we can make amazing things possible.

I once considered myself a skeptic about most things, especially when it involved martial arts. I viewed the world with a prove-it sort of attitude after I became discouraged by seeing many things in the martial arts world that simply weren't true. In the town that I grew up in, I knew of a fifth-degree black belt who was beaten up severely during a convenience store robbery. In an interview afterward, he said that he couldn't fight back because there wasn't enough room to do his kicks. If you are a fifth-degree black belt, understanding the spacing needed for your arts should really be the starting point of your training. Clearly this man did not practice real martial arts; he practiced kicks.

I've seen students promoted to sixth degree at the age of twenty. I once met a teenager who had a "mastery certificate" in his style of kung fu after only a few years of practice. I've met people who had been doing martial arts for thirty years yet could not take on a fourteen-year-old. Watching these martial artists perform, one might think that they were not half bad, but they clearly decided it was time to stop learning because they were already "masters." Their certificates said so.

I've met instructors who said they could knock me unconscious with a slap, and when they tried and failed, they simply remarked, "Well, it works on my students." Once I heard a man claim he knew the best technique for any situation; he called it the jammer or jacker or something just as silly. I didn't have the heart to tell him it was an aikido technique—done poorly. I've seen a martial arts demonstration where child black belts all wore tie-dye hakama and spun their swords in their hands like little Conan the Barbarians, proceeding to do jump kicks and then call it swordsmanship. There are people promoted to high ranks that I would fail for green belt. There are others who win tournaments that should not have even received a participation trophy.

There is a lot of bullshit in the martial arts.

I used to look at this as a horrible thing that discredits practitioners of the "real" arts, but I've matured some, and now I think that these guys are doing me a favor. I do not teach flashy jump kicks, flying dragon strikes, or acrobatics. I'm interested in teaching effective martial arts that can be used right away. These same arts, if practiced over a long duration, can lead to mastery-level understanding in a way that sport martial arts can't. Arts that require speed or flexibility can only be done when one is young, therefore losing their sustainability. Arts that require youth diminish over time, and therefore I no longer teach these practices. I've been able to see and accomplish a lot of amazing things over years of diligent training by eliminating sport practices.

I've been sent flying after being lightly punched by Okinawa masters. I've been struck in the calf by a strike that exploded my veins. (I still need vascular surgery in my left leg.) I've seen people be tapped in the forearm and almost vomit. (They had to stop to heave.) I've had my sword disarmed from me so fast that it seemed to disappear. The sword sailed over my shoulder and landed twenty feet behind me; my teacher's sword was at my neck before I could blink. I've been thrown so lightly and landed so hard that I saw the sky and both feet in front of me before I hit the ground, headfirst. I got up with no injury, but the muscle spasms took ten minutes to fade. I've been thrown offstage during demonstrations, emerging unscathed as I landed. This was not magic. This wasn't a fairy tale. This wasn't a movie set with wires and special effects. All of these examples are real, and were accomplished by people who held great understanding of the arts and could thusly do the impossible.

If you have doubts about the reality of what I am about to convey in this book, I welcome your skepticism; however, I ask that you hear out the message in its entirety and try it out for yourself, rather than immediately dismissing it as fiction. One may find many fictitious things in the world of martial arts, but the skills I outline in this book are not fairy tales. They are real, and what makes them truly amazing is that anyone can do them with enough practice and mental conditioning. Try each exercise that I outline with a partner from your school, whatever discipline you may practice. I wanted to make this book style-neutral so that we can look at internal principles that make anything possible.

If you are already a martial artist, either aspiring, retiring, or perhaps one who was like me and seeking answers to ancient questions, this book will serve you well in taking your arts further than you may have ever thought genuinely possible. If you are not a martial artist, my hope is that I inspire you to seek out arts that interest you so that you can begin your own fantastic journey of self-discovery.

Martial Arts Tradition

You will often hear the term *traditional* in the martial arts world thrown around by just about everyone. Many traditions were born out of the post–World War II era, when Japan feared that the American occupiers would forbid martial arts. They changed their combat arts into sports so that these arts could survive. This transformation gained popularity and spread to other styles. What many think of as martial arts tradition was simply born out of this desperate move to preserve martial arts.

If your club uses colored belts, know that this tradition only goes back to the 1940s, when Jigoro Kano, the founder of judo, standardized a ranking system. This ranking system was later adopted by other arts.

If your karate dojo uses long stances like *zenkutsu dachi*, this tradition only goes back to World War II, when *shotokan* became popular and standardized many training practices. If you practice high kicks, spinning kicks, or jump kicks, this tradition again only goes back to World War II. So exactly what constitutes martial arts traditions? Who made these traditions? Just because something is old doesn't make it valuable. A snake-oil salesman in the 1920s was just as shifty and useless as a snake-oil salesman of today. Traditions that precede World War II are difficult to discern because many of them have been lost and there are no practitioners who remember them. Many of the traditions and secrets were never written down, and so they vanished.

Both my aikido sensei and my karate sensei were born and raised in Japan. My aikido sensei once remarked that he liked to hear what beginners thought the philosophy of aikido was, because they seemed to know more about it than he did. My karate sensei would sometimes laugh at the start of class when he saw us bow-in and follow it up with basics. He thought this tradition was rather American as he never practiced in this way. My sensei would often just come in and start practicing. No warm-up, no bow-in, no line basics, just circle up, learn a technique, and pair off to practice it. He mocked the formalities that we tried to put in the arts! "Where did you learn that?" he asked.

During the occupation of Japan, many American soldiers studied karate, judo, and other Japanese arts. Some of these soldiers came back stateside and opened up schools even having only a year or two of experience. I admire their enthusiasm, because they were pioneers of their time, but with such little experience, it is no wonder that martial arts became an exercise in the telephone game. Many "traditions" were simply made up, or were based on assumptions. Typically the Japanese were careful in what they taught foreigners, which meant that secrets were often deleted. Even if no arts or secrets were deleted, two years is not enough time to learn all of the details of one form, let alone an entire martial arts system. Some techniques take decades to master.

I've seen *kata* (a sequence of martial arts movements or forms) taught several different ways by the same teacher. My karate sensei was notorious for performing our principal kata, sanchin, three different ways. Other students of his perform it in yet different variations. When I asked my teacher why these forms were different, he became agitated and said that the form did not matter. The lesson was not in the pattern, but in the structure and posture of your body. The pattern was an afterthought, and almost meaningless. And so, it is easy to see that if you only practiced with a particular teacher for two years, you may have only seen one variation; you may not be aware that the technique is *not* the pattern of a kata's movements. One variation may become tradition in one school, and another variation may become tradition in another school. Who is right?

Once during an aikido demonstration, my sensei went onstage with a sword and did a kata that I had never seen before. I scrutinized his form and tried to commit every movement to memory. When he got offstage, another student asked, "Wow, is this the third form for sword?" My sensei shrugged and said, "I just made that up." He had gone onstage, in front of hundreds of people, and simply made up an entire kata on the fly. It looked flawless, as though he had practiced it for decades. I was shocked. He was so good at what he did that he could just do whatever came to mind, but he made it look as though he had practiced it a million times.

This is part of the power of mastery: making improvisation appear as intentional action. Masters of bowling could bowl with their off-hand and still score consistent strikes, even though they may have never practiced that way. The understanding of body movements and how they connect to your mental attitude is a key part of doing the impossible.

Martial arts tradition means very different things, and it is almost as diverse and controversial as religion or politics. The older ways of doing things were much simpler. If something worked, you adopted it. If something hindered you or proved to be less effective for you, you discarded it. Too many martial artists are overly concerned with keeping their arts pure. In the strictest sense of tradition, there is no such thing as purity. You kept learning by adopting new ideas. If you intentionally block new ideas from entering your training regime, then really you are not studying in the traditional manner: you're simply preserving what came before you.

Studying vs. Preserving

Teachers of martial arts might fill your mind with ideas that simply are not true, even though they may have your best interests at heart. They may tell you this way is better or that way is better, but they may not even know! Or a certain way may be better suited for them, but that doesn't mean it is necessarily better suited for you. They may be teaching you skills that they learned from their teacher without even knowing why. Much of this misdirection comes from the poorly chosen emphasis on preserving arts.

I don't like the idea of preserving the arts. *Preserving* sounds like something you do with old paintings or homemade jelly. Preserving sounds boring, and boring does little to inspire you to do greater things in life. Preservation of the arts sounds like blindly following what you have always been doing, yet we always seem to want different results. If you cannot punch someone unconscious with your "preserved" technique, you need to work on your punch. If your art's lineage doesn't allow you to absorb power from a kick, you need to assess whether it's lineage or effectiveness that you care about. Preserving the arts may mean that you are actually retaining bad habits that someone else has taught you. Therefore, I prefer the term *study the arts*.

You might think that *studying* also has negative connotations or is just as boring as preserving. Studying martial arts is not like studying for the SAT or cramming for your midterm exam. If your automatic response is to scoff at the idea of studying, then you'll never achieve more than you have now. I want you to fall in love with the idea of learning. It is this pursuit of knowledge that can make average people extraordinary. A persistent and relentless spirit will reward you greatly.

By studying the arts that you already know, you can unlock a lot of mysteries that are inherent to all systems. This is because there are always better and more efficient ways of doing things. This improvement is not necessarily an external trait of the art; in fact, it is more often an internal trait. Some styles punch with a vertical fist, and other styles punch with a rotating fist; some styles hit with the index-finger and middle-finger knuckles, while others hit with the pinky and ring-finger knuckles. I don't care to argue these kinds of points, because they are simply external issues. If your style of punching works for you, then use it. If it doesn't, then figure out why and change it. It really is that simple. Just because someone told you a certain way was the best way doesn't make it true. It may be the best way for *the person who told you*, or it may be the *only* way that person knows. This doesn't make the person a horrible teacher; it simply makes him or her an inexperienced teacher. Most teachers will try to impart the knowledge that they know, but by studying your arts, you will begin to become your own teacher.

For example, I personally practice four different styles of punching, each of which is emphasized in a different kata, or style of martial art:

- ikkyo (aikido)
- naifanchi (shurite)
- sesan (tomarite)
- sanchin (nahate)

For the first ten years of my practice, I made no distinction between many of these forms. At that time, punching was simply punching. However, I noticed that some high-ranking black belts broke the rules and punched in nonstandardized ways. I even saw one man who was five feet ten inches tall knock a man out who was six foot five with a weak-looking jab. It was unorthodox, but it simply worked. It was then that I realized that there isn't one true way to punch. There are many ways to create power, and I intended to study this further. Naturally I sought out guidance from martial artists more experienced than I. To my amazement, many people simply did not know how they generated power and could not explain sufficiently for others to replicate what they were doing.

For me, then, studying became a series of experimentation in breaking the rules. I had an aha moment in my backyard practicing reverse punches. I found that if I stepped forward several times in rapid succession during a reverse punch, I was unable to twist my hips. I was taught to always twist my hips when punching to create power but found that my punches were stronger when I didn't. Later, when I met several Okinawa masters, they stated that twisting the hips was not necessary. I had found the answer before it was taught to me!

By having different methods of generating power and different thought processes for striking, I find that I am more diversified as a teacher. If one method does not work for a student, then I encourage the student to actively seek out a method that resonates better for him or her. For self-defense, one only needs a single, reliable method of punching. After a while, all these methods appear the same, because the internal feeling is the same. Studying what works best for your own body is the key to success. Do not rely on what works for other people; it may not be the best choice for you.

Internal power used in martial arts is easily understood from posture and the placement of one's body weight. If you punch someone while your weight is on your heels, you will bounce off that person because your center is behind you. If you place your weight in front of you, your fist will match the direction of your body weight, and consequently your punches will have more power. Likewise, if you try to throw someone with your weight on your heels, you will likely fail. If your weight is in front of you, it is much easier to lead someone to unbalance. If your current training has you punching or throwing mindlessly, or if you never considered your placement of weight before, it is likely that you are not getting the full amount of power that you are already capable of. This is why studying your arts is exceptionally important. I will explain ways that will help you study internal power in later chapters.

As you begin to study your arts, keep in mind that you will create more dramatic changes if you focus on the internal, rather than the external, elements of your style. For example, you shouldn't be too concerned about fiddling with where your left foot goes or the angle of your fist. You should create images in your mind, planting them in your subconscious, to change your results. You are then in a position to find the correct way of doing things because you are creating those changes for yourself, rather than just repeating what your teacher demonstrates. You then become your own best teacher. You know exactly if you have correct balance and posture. You can sense when a technique feels right or when it feels off. Technique should flow freely from you and not be squeezed out through tremendous effort. Power is created in your mind and then expressed through your body. Feel it, know it, anticipate it, and it will happen for you. If you only concern yourself about the exterior appearance of your arts, you will inevitably miss the larger lesson.

A fun analogy might be comparing martial arts to the great pyramids of Egypt. We can focus only on their majestic appearance from a distance, but as we get closer, we can see that their beauty is actually ragged and weatherworn. Ignore the interior, and you miss out on all the gold and riches that the treasury contains. The same is true for our arts. Focus on the outside, and your technique will always be superficial and will wear away with age; focus on the inside, and you'll find riches that will stay with you forever.

Consider this: no matter which art you are pursuing, that art will be degraded if you do not surpass your teacher. If your students do not surpass you, then the art will further be degraded to the point where it probably should be abandoned entirely. You must endeavor to become better than your teacher. That way those arts will continue to improve generation after generation. Strive to find the treasure within your arts, rather than fight the losing battle of preserving the superficial aspects of it. The mind-set of preserving is a disservice to the arts and serves only to make things worse.

This doesn't mean that you should change your kata or your techniques. I'm saying you should always study the internal connection for all of these movements and never preserve something that doesn't work simply because your teacher's teacher said it was important. Often one of my karate teachers would stand in nonkarate stances and insist he was standing in sanchin. When I would point out that he was not standing in sanchin, he would punch me and say something to the effect of, "This is sanchin!" I understood this to mean that the position of his feet was irrelevant and that he internalized the feeling of sanchin, which allowed him to manifest its power in any stance. Formlessness might not help you as a beginner, but experienced practitioners should heed this lesson well.

I once worked with a student who was up for his black-belt promotion after twenty years of practice. Because of some bureaucratic restriction, his teacher was not allowed to promote within his system, so this student came down to test with one of my teachers. I was surprised just how terrible his arts were. I worked with this man day and night for about a week to prepare him for his test. He harbored some serious misconceptions about the arts that would get you killed in a real situation; in fact, each technique he did needlessly turned his back to his opponent. I asked him about this, and he looked very confused. He really believed he was doing the right thing, and in some cases he could not see the difference in the technique he employed and the ones I was showing him. He hadn't bothered to really study his arts. He just copied what his teacher was doing and never thought twice about it. It was very clear to me that his teacher had no clue about how to perform these arts either, and so he passed down a flawed form to his students. Maybe he lost his way or discontinued his pursuit of the martial arts. This is really sad to me, because in his mind, he ceased following a joy for learning about the arts.

In the beginning of a martial artist's training, the first five years or so, it is absolutely the teacher's responsibility to make sure his or her students are all on the right track for success, whatever that means to them. In this period, it is imperative for the teacher to take a solid role in the development of the student, and any failing here falls squarely on the teacher's shoulders. After the first five years, students have enough knowledge to begin experimenting and really learning the arts. They have likely done a significant amount of basic movements and can now apply these basics to a multitude of purposes. During the middle period of study, that is five years to twenty years or so, motivation should come from both the teacher and the student to continue pursuing higher learning. After this period, the students now become the teacher and have the sole responsibility for making sure that they have not strayed from the path. To do so, the teacher must continually study the arts as well.

I never want to feel that I'm doing my students a disservice. I wish to bestow upon them my knowledge to the best of my ability. I strive to make sure that each day I practice I become better, so that I can make others better. I don't want to remain better at my arts than my students—I want them to be better than me. The only way that this can happen is if I am actively studying the arts and pursuing different methodologies of teaching. This is how a teacher cultivates the mastery mind-set.

At times I come up with ideas for practicing the arts, and I try them out in class. Sometimes this falls flat, and it is clear that it is a wrong direction. If this ever happens to you, abandon what you are doing and change focus immediately. This may sound like a gamble, or even a waste of time, but if you never try to do this sort of exercise, then how will you get better? Playing it safe will only ensure the status quo. Experimentation can be very rewarding.

Making the conscious decision to passionately study your arts—to always look for better ways to do something—will fuel you with enthusiasm and excitement. Use this energy and inspire others along the same path. This will not only lead you to mastery of the arts, but also to perform what you may have previously believed impossible. Once you successfully perform something that you once considered impossible, your mind will open up to unlimited wonder of how much more there is to discover. We got to the moon by mastering the laws of math and science, so imagine what else we can do when we put the power of thought into action. Imagine what other natural laws are out there that we have yet to uncover. It was once believed that the world was flat, but now we know better and snicker at those who still cling to outdated ideas.

How many other things might we find in our arts that we consider to be impossible? What sorts of things have we taken for granted as fairy tales and fiction, when in reality they are quite real and attainable? What impossible things can the study of our internal spirit make possible with our ceaseless and overwhelming drive to make the impossible possible?

Why Do the Impossible?

The path of least resistance makes all rivers, and some men, crooked.—Napoleon Hill

Some may still ask the question, "Why attempt the impossible? What good will mastering anything do for you? Is mastery worth the years of dedication and effort that it takes to achieve it? Why even bother?"

Why not master something? Why not bother? The electric lightbulb was impossible until Thomas Edison made it possible. Flying was impossible before the Wright Brothers made it possible. Putting a man on the moon was impossible until NASA made it happen. Ask yourself, How old will you be in twenty years? How old will you be in twenty years if you master something? We will get older no matter what, so you might as well master a skill in the time that was given to you.

Many of us have very unfulfilling jobs, which is unfortunate. Many of us may believe that our window of greatness is gone, usually because of work or family obligations. But I argue that this does not need to be the case. If we have enough time to brush our teeth each day, we have what it takes to learn a new skill or get better at an existing one.

Do you really want to be known for the work you do at your day job? For those who do "important" work, this may be a moot exercise, but I know many professionals who are underemployed. Many highly educated people who once dreamed about changing the world and making a difference now stay in comfortable jobs just to earn a paycheck. While there isn't anything intrinsically wrong with contributing to the workforce, paying bills may not have been your childhood dream, let alone the legacy that you want to be remembered for.

When we were ten years old, we imagined ourselves as doctors, lawyers, secret agents, astronauts, or whatever. But once we reach certain milestones in life, those idealistic doors seem to close one by one. If you are over thirty, have never been in the military, don't have a degree with high honors, and are not in top physical condition, you will never be an astronaut. But that doesn't mean all your dreams are dead—it's just time to make some new ones.

Often when I teach martial arts, I will ask this question: "Who here is a master at driving?" Usually no one responds, probably because they think it to be a rhetorical question. Then I ask people how long they have been driving, and for some, their answer is more than twenty years. If you have been doing something consistently for twenty years and you are not a master of it, I think there is a problem. This means people are not paying attention when they are driving, and are instead going on autopilot. After graduating from driver's education, did you not learn anything more about driving?

If you are interested in self-defense, you should be a master at driving. Why? Because if you are going to get killed accidentally in this country, the chances are you will be driving when it happens. Driving is dangerous, even though we are very accustomed to doing this activity daily. Treat driving like fighting; keep your eyes on the road and on everyone else. Would you answer a phone call when fighting? Would you text your friend while being mugged by three assailants? Why would anyone do these things while driving? Just as with an everyday skill like driving, we do not want to go on autopilot for our arts. We do not want to coast by and develop an attitude that we are done learning. We want to become masters.

To develop your mind so that you are always training, practice your arts for ten minutes a day. You can master any skill by practicing in this manner given enough time. If you tell yourself to practice for two hours a day, you will likely find excuses not to practice, and your self-discipline will diminish as a result. Create self-discipline and a new habit by practicing for just ten minutes. You may find that you will practice more than ten minutes once you find your groove, but do not tell yourself you will go longer than this period of time. The idea is to make this a habit so even when you do not want to practice, you will still do it because the time is so brief.

Once learned, this simple strategy will help you master martial arts or any other skill by creating good habits that will last a lifetime. First, however, we must journey inside ourselves and understand who we are and what is preventing us from greatness.

You may find yourself getting into a slump in your life, or even in your martial arts training. Hitting this plateau is the signal that it is time to change something. Yet seeing these signals can be challenging. Because of this, we begin to let stagnancy become the norm, just like we do with our driving, and as a result we stop pursuing our desires or goals. We then become agitated and angry; we may not even know why we are feeling this way!

I have found that when I have promoted students to black belt, many of them quit. They had a goal, and they completed that goal; their goal was never mastery. Their goal was to get a degree but not master the skill. This is a very Western concept, and a difficult one to eliminate. We go to high school, and regardless of our grades, graduate and receive a diploma. Then we go to college, and good or bad grades, we can graduate and get a degree. The level of skill is irrelevant; the piece of paper is what matters. I've known brilliant people who dropped out of college, and I've known dunces who finished despite being able to barely tie their shoes. Mastery is a lifelong journey, not instant gratification or a piece of paper. If you are bored, then you have stopped learning, and this is the first sign that you are either in a slump or heading for one. Continuous improvement is never boring.

Do you dismiss achieving mastery and even doing the impossible as unachievable? Be honest with yourself in your reflection. Do not allow false visions of your achievements or your failures to trick you into thinking that you can't attain the mastery mind-set. You may find that you yourself are the biggest naysayer and blocker of dreams in your own life.

Sadly I see this happen to many people whom I encounter in daily life, not just in the dojo. Many people who are nearing forty complain of knee pain, back pain, and how getting older sucks. You are only forty! My teachers are in their late sixties and don't complain as much. If you are looking for an excuse, you will find one. Look for solutions, and you will find those instead.

Do you complain a lot? Not just to others, but to yourself as well? Do you make justifications for your lack of self-discipline? For example, do you reward yourself with ice cream and cookies because you worked hard today? Do you have more drinks than normal because of stress? Do you try to find excuses to avoid certain tasks or encounters that might be difficult? Or do you find solutions for all things in your life? Are you blocking yourself from achieving the goal you desire the most?

Examine yourself and ask yourself critical questions about your arts. Do you practice things just because someone told you that you should, or because *you know* that you should? For example, I knew a fantastic martial artist who would only work out if he could get in two hours of practice or more; anything less than that, and he felt as though he wasn't giving it 100 percent. He thought it was better to go extreme or not at all. Later in life, he became very busy with work and family obligations, and it was difficult for him to find those two-hour blocks of time he was used to. Instead of working out for a half hour, he stopped working out completely and eventually gave up practicing altogether. His preconceptions of what was "right" blocked him from getting better.

I have a friend who is a video-game addict. He sits at work for nine hours a day, and then goes home to sit until late into the night. Then he complains about knee and back pain. I've offered many times to help him get in better shape, but he would rather stay at home and play his games. There is nothing wrong with playing video games or other entertainment like watching TV, but activities that consume vast amounts of time can become the block that prevents you from accomplishing your life's goals or aspirations.

You may have similar habits that could interfere with you being able to achieve the impossible. These habits may have been learned from your parents, other family members, teachers, spouses, TV, movies, or seemingly anything. Regardless of where your habits came from, we don't need to dwell on them because what is in the past is already done and there is not much we can do about it. We may not be able to change or dictate everything that happens in our lives, nor can we truly ever change others—the only thing we can do is change ourselves. The first step to do this is to reflect on these questions, and then look to the future. Changing our current path is perhaps the only real power that we are gifted with.

Forgive your past self for blocking your success. Your subconscious had your best interests at heart when it told you not to do this or that because of X or Y reason. That part of your mind came to a logical conclusion, and it told your creative mind to shut the hell up. When I became a live-in aikido student, I had very little time to practice karate. I still practiced, of course, but to a much lesser degree and I had to keep it secret. Karate techniques are frowned upon in art forms that are considered "soft" arts. I felt unfairly judged by my involvement in karate, and so I kept this part of me hidden. At the time, I thought I was protecting my own best interests, but in reality there was a chunk of time where my arts suffered as the result of this type of negative thinking. I allowed the opinion of others to interfere with how much I enjoyed practicing martial arts. Once I understood this about myself, I reversed it immediately.

You have been protected thus far by your logical mind, so don't beat yourself up for lost time. It took you this long to get to a point in your life where change can freely flow through you in a way that you can truly appreciate. Now that you can realize this, suspend logic for a moment as we journey deeper into our spirit.

Choose the Impossible

> **We come this way but once. We can either tiptoe through life and hope that we get to death without being too badly bruised or we can live a full, complete life achieving our goals and realizing our wildest dreams.**—Bob Proctor

You have two choices in your approach to the mastery mind-set: you may choose to believe, or you may choose to disbelieve. I have seen things that I once thought were impossible, but seeing becomes believing. At this point, you shouldn't be surprised to hear that it came when I was punched by one of my Okinawa teachers. I began to laugh because this was one of the most eye-opening and awesome experiences that I have ever felt. My sensei thought I was laughing at him. He hit me again, harder. It picked me off my feet and sent me into the wall, where I hit my head. I continued to laugh, which sounds crazy, but the joy of feeling that this type of mastery was even possible was a liberating experience. My sensei continued to hammer on me, like the character Agent Smith did to Neo in the *Matrix*. After a dozen hits, I fell to the ground. At this point I couldn't laugh, not because I didn't feel compelled to, but because I couldn't breathe. I can absorb power from punches and kicks to my solar plexus by most black belts that I have encountered, but these punches were on a completely different scale. It was like my sensei brought a tank to a knife fight.

When we hear the term *faith*, we typically think of the religious kind of faith. But there is another faith, which I believe is the power that you already have locked inside of you. This may sound corny, but true power begins with faith in yourself. Believe you can do something, work hard, and it will happen for you despite adversity. When I first discovered how to absorb power from punches, I practiced relentlessly for months until I got it right. My sensei would come to class and want to work on other things, but I always redirected him to the topic of absorbing power. He got annoyed at me from time to time, but he continued to teach me the same thing over and over until I finally got it right. I could see and feel how he was making this skill happen, and I had faith that if he could do it, so could I. I held on to that mental picture I had of my sensei performing this skill and planted it firmly in my mind until I made it real for myself.

Do not listen to the naysayers who live in a world of cynicism and complacency. They want to drag you back to their world so they can be made comfortable again. Everything is possible in the mind; the mind has no boundaries save those we manufacture or allow others to manufacture for us. If we allow the opinions of others to influence us and we follow the easy and familiar path of least resistance, then our paths can become crooked, meandering aimlessly.

Open your mind to the impossible, and set aside the skeptic that may live inside of you. To perform the impossible, you must have faith in the impossible. To drop an opponent with a tap used to be fantasy for me, but now it is reality; absorbing a front kick to my solar plexus or even to my leg was once unthinkable, but now I show these arts as part of my regular teaching routine. What other things lie out there in the universe waiting to be discovered or rediscovered, and how can cultivating a mastery mind-set not only improve your martial arts, but your entire life as well?

Understanding Energy

To fully understand the concepts I will outline in this book, you must first understand what I mean when I use the word *energy*. Ignoring this important concept will prevent you from developing the power to perform the impossible, such as rupturing internal organs with a fist or sending someone flying with an effortless throw. If you look at your hand, or any other physical object, your mind perceives it as being solid; however, through physics we know that all matter is composed of atoms, which in turn consist of electrons and protons (which in turn are composed of smaller particles). These particles vibrate at a very fast rate, yet our impression is that they are solid matter. Knowing that all matter vibrates is a key factor of creating and diffusing power, as well as other things that look impossible to the uninitiated.

So consider this: if we are composed of atoms, and atoms are energy in a constant state of vibration, then we are simply beings of energy that see ourselves as solid matter. We perceive the world around us as solid due to the limitations of our bodies. This was likely an evolutionary design to help our ancestors survive in ancient times. The solid world is thus an illusion, and a powerful one, because we cannot perceive this vibration without training.

If our bodies are energy, our minds and even our thoughts are energy too. Wouldn't this then make thoughts physical things? Do thoughts have the same substance as what we perceive as matter? Perhaps we have yet to discover a technology useful in perceiving thought energy. This debate might only be proven by neuroscientists, but for our arts, picturing thoughts as energy can become exceptionally useful in our development.

Thought energy is our most powerful ally, becoming as useful as a suit of armor, a trusty sidekick, or an army on our side; but remember: these allies only manifest if we create positive energy within our minds. I feel that everyone has an important choice to make: you can tell yourself that you are not good enough to achieve the mastery mind-set, or you can believe in yourself and discover that you are capable of doing extraordinary things. If you decide well, then the energy created by your thoughts will take you to amazing places.

A common misconception about thought energy is that it is the same thing as intelligence, but this is not the case. If knowledge alone were power, then the world would be ruled by librarians, because they are sitting upon a wealth of knowledge. It is people who discover the context of knowledge who achieve mastery. The same holds true for your arts. You may know the textbook method of blocking a punch by studying a reference manual on martial arts; however, if you have never practiced such a technique with an opponent, you will likely be unsuccessful in a real situation. We must convert what we know in our minds, and apply it in the real world. With this understanding of energy and our knowledge of the arts, we are able to create true power accomplished through applied knowledge.

This relationship between energy and knowledge leads us to one of the most important aspects of applied martial arts: understanding how an opponent's thought energy creates vibrations that we can sense. If we are attacked, an opponent's power, and therefore energy, can only come to us in a finite number of ways. First of all, because we are the target of the attack, we know the power's destination. Secondly, if we are paying attention, we can see the origin of the attack, be it the human staring us down or the one sneaking up on our flank. Third, I'm assuming you are being attacked by a human and not a monster or an alien, so the attacker only has two arms and two legs at best. Since the attacker only has four limbs and not sixteen tentacles, it isn't that difficult to see what your opponent is doing, particularly if he or she is untrained. A blow from an opponent can come straight down, straight in, up, or angled, but no matter what, the energy behind the intent creates vibrations. Our understanding of energy will allow us to sense this the moment we encounter someone who wishes to do us harm. At that point, we need only apply our knowledge of the arts and how it interacts with the opponent's energy. Once you've mastered the timing necessary to interact with the opponent's energy, your strikes, blocks, throws, and composure will push the boundaries of what you thought possible. To fully understand how to achieve this sensitivity to the vibration of others, we must delve into what it truly means to be aware.

Awareness

I once asked my aikido sensei how I could improve my awareness. His answer boggled my mind. He said, "Allow yourself to space out, almost force it, and you will see more things." Well, it wasn't the answer I was looking for, but I decided I would go ahead and try it out anyway. I went to a bar that night and made it my goal to space out on purpose. To my surprise, this actually forced me to relax, and as a result I was able to see things I would not normally have been paying attention to. By doing this technique, I could sense that one of the waitresses was behind with her orders and this was causing her anxiety. I noticed one man at the bar who was wearing a weapon concealed under his shirt. I felt anger from another man one booth over, whom previously I had ignored because he was older. My sensei wasn't crazy!

It is a common theme in martial arts books and other sources that awareness is the first element to self-defense. I agree with this, but I think it is important to understand how we can develop this awareness within the context of our arts and our opponent's energy. If we don't, we will forever just be paying attention, and not doing the impossible. Have you ever seen street signs that say, "Use Extreme Caution"" What does using extreme caution look like exactly? Does that mean you scrunch your face up and continuously shift your eyes left and right? Do you lick your finger and hold it to the wind every hundred feet? What is it? Is it telling us to simply pay better attention? What a dumb sign!

To me, awareness is being tuned into other people's emotional and energy vibrations. For example, you should be able to tell when someone is mad or sad without any martial arts training. These are very powerful emotions, because they echo out into our perceptions, and if you are paying attention they are very loud. Fortunately, aggression is an especially loud emotion and can be felt easily. The gray area of emotions is harder to detect because concentration can be mistaken as anger and sleepiness can be mistaken for sadness. We don't have to be telepaths or psychics to detect this; we can pick up on the distant early-warning signs of impending danger through what most people will call intuition. Remember that attacks are emotional issues; if a person is calm and at ease, he or she isn't going to be attacking. Therefore, identifying people who are projecting negative thought energy can be the best self-defense technique one need learn.

I like to practice a simple exercise between two students that allows us to examine our intuitive power of sensing hostile intentions from others. I have one student stand and close his or her eyes. Then I ask another student to approach with either a feeling of hostility or a feeling of friendship. The hard part here sometimes is generating a sincere desire to cause harm, as we all tend to be friends in the dojo. So to make this a bit easier, I let the person approaching make a fist if he or she wants to harm the other, or open his or her arms as if going to give the other a hug to create friendly thought energy.

The person with closed eyes then holds up one finger if he or she feels hostile intent or two fingers if he or she feels friendly intent. What I have found over the years is that people have a significant chance of correctly sensing the emotional energy. Even if they get confused and raise the wrong finger, they always stop the person in a hostile mind-set before he or she gets too close. This is usually about six feet away.

This tells us that there is an emotional perception that we all have. I'm not talking about sounds from footfalls, because these sound the same in both situations. I'm talking about something unseen, but very much felt. Most of us have experienced this on at least one level or another. Have you ever walked into a party and then felt an overwhelming urge to turn around and leave? Was there a vibe that you could not exactly understand but made you uncomfortable nonetheless? Have you ever suddenly noticed someone in a crowd of people and thought that you needed to cross the street to avoid him or her?

These hostile or aggressive examples should be easy even for those with no martial arts training to pick up on, but for those of us pursuing the mastery mind-set, a higher level of intuition should be practiced. Doing so is easier than you might think. We can hone awareness by actively listening to others and being more emotionally involved with our daily interactions. Very often we may feel as though we are listening to others, but how often have you been introduced to someone only to forget his or her name after a few short minutes? You can listen to people and not hear them because you are simply not emotionally involved in the conversation. By practicing connecting with people, you will naturally gain insight into subtle cues that people give away. The other person might not know that he or she is projecting an emotional energy at all.

When I was going through a divorce, I had gone to advanced class at the dojo and was in a back room adjusting my uniform. I was so full of sorrow, anger, and such a mix of things that I felt like a swirling vortex of emotions. My sensei entered the room, walked past me, and stopped about ten paces away with his back to me. He had not seen me because of where I was standing when he entered the room; he did not hear me because I was motionless. He turned around and asked, "Are you okay?" The look of concern on his face was very sincere. "Hai, sensei!" I responded. He squinted and gave me a long hard look, and for a moment we just stood there and stared at each other. "You sure?" he asked.

I nodded, but I couldn't manage to get any words out the second time. He took in a deep breath, nodded in return as if to acknowledge what I was thinking without words, and proceeded to go into his changing room. At that moment, I felt as though I were under an extremely large magnifying glass; I could feel my sensei look into my soul. He perceived me by the vibration I was sending out through my emotions. I have witnessed him do this dozens of times with me and with others, so I know that his perceptions weren't just lucky. He had truly mastered the impossible; it was like being around a magician.

This energy is all around us, and if we open ourselves up to it, we can tell a lot about others even in brief encounters. I once witnessed a conversation my aikido sensei had with someone who was new in the dojo. This person was disruptive to class, but was also somewhat distraught for unclear reasons. The sensei patiently listened to the person, and then made a remark that seemed totally random to me: "I'm sorry your father was never there for you." The man gasped, and clearly the sensei had hit the nail on the head. Then he added, "Time is such a thing, that when things come to pass, we must say good-bye."

The sensei was able to see the problem, long before I could have, and said comforting words in a way that was genuine, yet at the same time ended the conversation. Students can sometimes take up a great deal of class time with personal conversation, and the sensei handled this brief interruption to class in a sophisticated, yet personal, way. This was aikido with words. This was a powerful lesson for me, and one that I will never forget. Many times conflict can be resolved with words and not with fists. Resorting to fisticuffs should be our last line of defense, when all attempts of diplomacy have failed.

There was one time at the dojo when a homeless man interrupted class and started yelling at everyone. Many of the students chatted among themselves and formulated a plan on how to kick this guy out and what strategies we might need to employ to ensure he stayed out without anyone getting hurt. The belligerent man flailed around and shouted threats. My sensei approached him calmly and said, "No one hears you here." There was a moment of silence, and the man left the dojo. My sensei saw what needed to be done and just did it. There was no hesitation or violence in his words. He cut through the other's negative energy in microseconds, yet his demeanor was calm and compassionate. He did not challenge the other with words or with physical prowess. He was aware enough to know what the man needed to hear, and he let the man defeat himself. The silence was deafening.

Think about examples in your own life when you have witnessed people who could seemingly read your mind. You may have experienced an event where your spouse knew instantly what you were thinking about. I once looked sideways across a room, without moving my head, but my wife saw what I was looking at. She looked over her shoulder, spotted a woman standing among a large group of women fifty feet away, and said, "So you think the blonde woman with curly hair is good-looking?" My infraction was tiny, but my wife could pick out of a crowd of good-looking people who had actually caught my eye. She had the advantage of knowing my type, but it was much more than just prior knowledge. There were plenty of other women there who were attractive and who fit the description, but she could feel the curly-haired woman's vibration overwhelming the crowd and my reaction to it.

It is much easier to tune in to people you know, and as a matter of practice, you should already be doing this. For example, you should know exact social cues for when your spouse wants to leave a party. He or she should never have to tell you—you should be able to pick it up. This is often easier said than done, because close relationships can be very convoluted and emotions can be easily confused. However, if you are able to do this, you will notice the added harmony it will bring to your life. The same holds true for all of our human interactions, be it with parents, boss, fellow practitioners at the dojo, or an assailant on the street—though harmony here transforms into safety for yourself. I had one aikido sensei who would muse on occasion that his method of self-defense was to allow his opponents to "harmonize" with the ground when he threw them. Partly a joke, but his throws demonstrated how truly sensing an opponent's vibrations can give you total control of the situation.

With a look, you should be able to communicate simple things like, "I'm hungry," "It's bedtime," or "It's time to leave." By practicing tuning in with your spouse and close friends, you will get into the habit of trying to connect with people you interact with. This will have a great benefit for you in understanding human relationships, both loving and hostile, as well as how emotions precede actions. This leads to true martial arts awareness. Beginners look twice before walking into a dark alley, while masters sense hostile intent as if they had a sixth sense.

Outside-In Approach

With our understanding of how the energy of others is manifested and how we can detect it, we must now assess the energy we can create ourselves. There are different ways that the martial artist can create energy, but not all methods lead to the mastery mind-set.

Most martial arts are taught from an outside-in approach. That is, most of us learn from our teachers where to place our hands and our feet and how to position our bodies in order to understand the techniques. Everyone wants to learn cool moves that they see in the movies, and imitation seems to be the obvious way of achieving that goal.

Each style of art has a reason for all that it does. This might be a particular stance that is favored, or a particular hand position that is optimal for its techniques, or whatever. Some of these reasons are sound and have real applications, while others are better suited to tournament-style fighting and do not offer much real-world application. Each style will boast that it is the best and will enthusiastically demonstrate why. This isn't a bad thing; in fact, I believe it to be a good thing. If you do not believe your art is the best, then why would you practice it?

When you know nothing of the arts, you've got to start somewhere, and often using an outside-in approach is a sound stepping-stone. It can be used to build the framework of any art, and gives the novice clear direction for practice. Vague instructions are often confusing and too open-ended for new students to understand. So an outside-in approach makes more sense in these terms, at least for the first few years of practice.

One of my karate teachers would often point to his feet and say, "This is sanchin." But he was actually standing in *shikko dachi*, a very different stance. What he was talking about was not his feet placement, but where his weight was in relation to his opponent. Now, I could see this because I'd been practicing a long time, but the beginners in my class were outright confused and could not understand the lesson. At this point, I had to take them aside and say, "Just do sanchin stance."

Beginners need a concrete way of doing something, with very clear instructions. In this sense, an outside-in approach is a very powerful tool that builds confidence and skill for the novice. New practitioners need to form a foundation for their arts, so that they can gain some basic understanding of what they should be doing. If you have no experience with fighting, violence, or martial arts, you can find yourself being completely lost by the unique terms of your art and new things your mind is telling your body to do. For example, you may feel as if you have no idea which foot to have forward or where you should put your hands. This is why it is important for beginners to simply copy their teachers at first. Failing to do so can sap your mental energy and desire to continue practice. By mirroring what experienced practitioners are doing, you can attain a firm starting point that will foster positive energy that can fuel your efforts for your first few years. So if you have no idea where to start, simply become a sponge and absorb everything. Just remember that when it comes to your techniques, nothing is sacred and traditions should be scrutinized to see how effective they are in the real world.

There have been times when I believed I was practicing and teaching techniques correctly, only to find out years later that what I was doing was "wrong." I put wrong in quotation marks, because it was simply less correct than what my teachers later showed me. I had to copy what they were doing at first, so I could absorb the lessons fully. After I sat with these new techniques and studied them like crazy, I made them my own; I made them work for me by making changes. If this studying doesn't take place, the outside-in approach will fail you. You will become so fixated on mastering the superficial that you will not be able to sense the thought energy of others, or even create your own energy beyond the whimper of pride you feel for having "perfect" form.

These disadvantages to the outside-in approach may not be evident for the first twenty years of practice. Once they are, these downsides can cause devoted martial artists to lose the desire to practice, their minds no longer capable of creating the positive thought energy once gained through perfecting form. Once you start getting older, you will begin to realize that you cannot move as fast as you once did. Techniques that were once easy to do may simply become unfeasible, or even dangerous, to practice. I used to be able to shin kick anyone to the head, but age has robbed me of the flexibility and the speed to do this as effectively. If your mind is stuck on a certain idea of how a technique should be but your body can no longer obey your commands, you may become injured when performing it. Alternatively, you may become overwhelmed by frustration and simply quit. I no longer kick high, and I now use low kicks and solid punches from a much more stable position. The kata in traditional Okinawa karate never really showed high kicks anyway, and this is likely to be the reason why; the outside-in approach is simply unsustainable.

Having an outside-in mentality can sometimes lead you to dangerous assumptions, and even dangerous situations. I once sparred with a practitioner of another style, whom I punched in the face. I did not hit him hard, yet he got very upset with me and said that punching to the face was not permitted—never mind that he was a guest in my dojo! He made no effort to block my attacks and refused to practice any further with me because I was not playing by his rules. His mind was so fused with his style that he could not think outside of the box. He was so used to an outside-in approach that he became confused when someone didn't follow the same rules. As martial artists, we need to expect to get punched in the face when fighting—this is the whole point! The head is perhaps the only real target. People strike for the face because that's the part they are angriest at. If we spoke with our elbows or thighs, then these areas would become the prime targets.

Another time I had a student who full-on front kicked me to the chest, who then lost balance and fell to the ground. He got up, laughed at me, and said, "Ha! I got you." I cocked my head to one side and said, "You are mistaken, for I am standing and you were on the ground. Your kick did nothing." He tried again, kicked me square in the chest, and fell over, but still he claimed to have bested me. I corrected him a second time, so when he tried to kick me yet again, I punched him in the forehead, wanting to demonstrate just how vulnerable he really was (aside from him continuously falling over, which we can assume would be a problem in a real fight). Again he fell over, but he did not understand why it was a problem. Further explanations I tried proved to be futile; he never showed up to class again.

Both of these men had ideas of martial arts that hindered them. Just because you place your foot on an opponent's chest does not mean you did anything other than play foot tag. Fighting is not for points, after all, and I hardly see falling down from your own kick as a useful skill. The other gentleman refused to acknowledge that punches to the face would even happen in the real world. How can someone like this learn to achieve mastery? These paradigms are crippling because they either kill one's thought energy or weaken it so an attack's vibration literally bounces off its target. This is why I much prefer an "inside-out" approach to learning martial arts and feel that it is the true path to pursue the mastery mind-set.

Inside-Out Approach

Every martial art has stance work. Each stance, you will be told, is for one reason or another. Stance work is critical in the beginning stages of development because some arts can be very confusing to beginners. It is therefore imperative to impart a sound foundation for learning that focuses on basics. This emphasis changes over time. Some of my karate teachers were so good that all of their stance work blended together in such a way that one could not tell what stance they were in. To a novice this might be seen as sloppy or even confusing. However, these masters could generate amazing power from their punches and their kicks in these sloppy-looking, non-karate stances. They could even receive full-power blows to their bodies and knees without injury. But sloppy stances are not a good method for beginners, and having a basics class that teaches "proper" form is essential. I put proper in quotation marks because the meaning of this idea will vary drastically from style to style, from dojo to dojo, and from person to person.

For black belts, stances should be less of a concern. Sure, you need to be able to practice the form for your art, but do not let your mind get stuck on what foot should be where. At some point, you will need to let all of that go so that you can develop a different mind-set: a mind-set that is not bound by the constraints of style or rules that someone else made. Your mind is as free as you make it. It doesn't matter if you dream big or if you dream small, because both dreams require the same amount of energy. So you might as well dream big.

When I first started martial arts, my mother read some pop-culture article on the subject. She remarked to me, "When the student is ready, the art form will be his or her own." I thought this meant that the student was creating bad form by not listening to the teachers and instead making it up as he or she went along. I thought this was a terrible idea. But now, many, many years later, I see this in a different light, and the statement holds some truth to it. If you have been practicing martial arts for a long enough time, there is no such thing as stance work any longer. Wherever your feet are is where they are, and that's it.

I sometimes see my students struggle with how to make certain arts work. I see how awkwardly they move their bodies, and I can see their frustration on their faces. I want to tell them not to worry about it because before too long, they won't need to worry about any of that minutiae. With a proper understanding of how to distribute your weight to your advantage, your feet can be in any position. With a proper understanding of how to create vibration, it won't matter what your fist looks like.

For longevity of practice and for a deeper understanding of any art form, we must adopt a different strategy to achieve spectacular results. I call this method the "inside-out" approach.

Working from the inside-out means that you are developing a mental picture of what it is you wish to accomplish, be that a punch, kick, block, throw, choke, or whatever. By first seeing this image of success, you can activate things in the future with less concern about where your left foot is or where your right hand should go. With a focused mental picture, you can develop amazing power, even from awkward circumstances, and perform arts that look physically impossible. You should be able to punch from any position, even while grappling, and apply the same amount of power as if you were standing. Many times, to demonstrate how insignificant your stance can be, I will stand on one foot, put my arms in ridiculous poses, such as scratching both armpits, and then I will strike a black belt in class with what looks like something that shouldn't do a damn thing. I delight to see their eyes bulge from their heads when they realize the amount of power that has been transferred to them!

With an outside-in approach, the only way to be ready for an attack is to have a physical plan for each scenario beforehand, which is practically impossible. With an inside-out strategy, we can imagine ourselves successful no matter what sort of predicament we find ourselves in.

We can do amazing things simply because our minds are working to make our visions a reality. This is perhaps the most powerful application of thought energy. If you simply dismiss this, you will never understand the power your own mind plays in your personal development, nor will your arts ever surpass where they are today. If you are experiencing a slump in your growth as a martial artist, you could train harder through forms, drills, and whatever, but you may never climb higher than the plateau preventing you from the next level. This slump you might be experiencing is likely from a culmination of an "outside-in" paradigm. If you continue to practice the exact same way you do now, you will continue to get the exact same results. To truly get out of a rut in training, you have to change your paradigm; you have to harness the thoughts of a master.

In order to change our results, we must change our subconscious minds. The subconscious is where our expectations and paradigms live, and it can become a powerful tool at our disposal. What you put into the subconscious is what you will get out of it; it cannot reject anything you feed it. So if you constantly think about how bad your arts are, you will continue to produce bad results because this is what is fed to your subconscious. We must feed our subconscious positive images so that we may begin to see positive results. Strive to only put positive language on your tongue and power images in your mind so that you may naturally set a course to your new future. Fill your mind with images of successful techniques and meditate on these images; hold them in your mind's eye every day until you can accomplish whatever it is you set out to do. This is the first step toward training with the inside-out approach.

Allow yourself the joy of imaging perfect technique, perfect execution, and perfect results. This sort of positive thinking takes great discipline because we are always our own biggest critic. Stop this self-defeating behavior and endeavor to enrich your training by filling yourself with images of success rather than beating yourself up with criticism or frustration. Try to surround yourself with like-minded people to further enhance your powers of positive thought. I recommend lectures and books by Bob Proctor and Napoleon Hill.

Guard your thoughts. It is very easy to slip into old patterns and old routines. If you believe that success can only be made through tens of thousands of repetitions, then you will be caged by this paradigm and bored by your practice. If you create images of power, accomplishment, and skill, your training will not only become more effective, but fun as well.

If you truly understand a technique, you should be able to perform that action immediately. Let me repeat this. If you learn a technique, you should be able to do it exactly how your teacher did, right then and there. If you cannot, then you do not understand the art, and most importantly you do not have the correct image. Now, you may trick yourself and think, "I understand this in my head, but my body can't do it." This is simply a lie you tell yourself. If you can understand something in your head, you can do it. If you can solve the equation 2+2 in your head, then you can do it on paper. It really is that simple.

If you are unable to do something immediately, it means that your mental picture is wrong. You may have made an assumption about the technique, such as where your hips should go, or perhaps you have been held back by a subconscious glutted on boredom and self-defeating thoughts. Either way, your mental image is flawed. Examine your mental image for all of your arts, and you will soon see that there are vast portions of your mind filling in the blanks and you don't understand the techniques that well after all. It's these blanks that are holding you back from being able to perform your arts with efficiency and clarity.

I once had class with my aikido sensei, and he had me throwing a fellow student for an hour using the same technique. About every ten minutes, I would quizzically look at my sensei, and he would only stare back at me in response. After a while, my partner got very tired; he couldn't even fall. No matter how hard I tried to throw him, no matter what sort of pain I gave, my partner refused to fall. At this point, I turned to my sensei and said, "This throw does not work if my partner is unwilling to fall."

"Ah," my sensei said, "and why is it that he does not wish to fall?"

I felt a lot of shame in that moment. I understood the words my sensei was saying, yet I could not make the throw work at that time. It was years later that I realized that the image in my mind about how the throw was supposed to work was incorrect. The one thing I thought was correct was the exact thing he wanted me to fix. I had changed each element of the throw with the exception of that one assumption. You must be careful then about what you assume is correct, because that very thing may be what is holding you back from true understanding.

Your old habit may be to just practice more—to do more push-ups and more sit-ups or whatever, but practicing more with a bad image will just reinforce bad habits. The result will be that you still won't be able to do the technique right, and this will cause frustration and aggravation, and eventually you will give up. You may resign yourself into believing something is impossible because you yourself are unable to do it. You may have thought you tried with all of your might, but if you have consistently placed your attention into the wrong area, then nothing will change. Often the problem is not your effort; it is your mental image that needs to be corrected.

When I teach punching to students, I sometimes ask them to imagine that their fists are bursting with flames or electric energy. Upon striking, imagine this fire or electrical current leaping instantly into the target. We may not be able to conjure flames or electricity (yet), but this image can often help people gather an internal feeling for their arts. Sometimes I will hold both hands open, as if holding a basketball; in my mind I'm imagining a ball of blue light growing in intensity and power as I manifest it into existence. I will rotate the ball as if passing it to my training partner, striking with an open fist (that is, I'm hitting with my punching knuckles and my wrist is in alignment with my forearm, but my hand is open). This mental projection can have devastating effects on an opponent. Do not underestimate your imagination.

I often show a technique called *tenchi nage* (heaven and earth throw). I will use an open hand and catch my opponents lightly on the jaw, as if I were softly caressing their cheek. I then scoop their head and bring them down to the mat before they realize they are being thrown. The throw is so gentle in terms of my physical contact with the opponent, and so passive it seems impossible. People do not brace for impact because the touch is so disturbingly light that it does not warrant the need to fight back. By the time I've moved my opponent's head off-line, he or she is off-balance and essentially trip themselves. While performing this art, I imagine my opponent is a river rock, and I am the river. The river does not want to destroy the rock, but the water is going up and over that rock no matter what the rock thinks. The use of this imagery greatly aids in the execution of this technique.

When I demonstrate chokes on students, I gently coil around their necks and allow them to breathe for the duration when I am getting into position. When I go to choke, I imagine that my arm is a boa constrictor that has decided it is time to kill its prey. Immediately I coil up, but in a manner that is relaxed, yet constricting to my opponent. They do not resist because, again, the touch is deceptive. A harsh entry may make your opponent fight more, but a gentle touch catches your opponent off guard, and the choke has double the effect in half the time.

How could visualization and imagination help your arts? What sorts of images can you conjure to make your strikes more powerful? You do not have to tell anyone you are doing this if you feel silly playing make-believe. You can keep this fantasy to yourself, and use it as a powerful training tool to aid you on the road to the impossible. If at any moment you discover how to send fireballs or lightning bolts from your hands from nothing, please do not hesitate to call me because I want to learn how to do this as well!

By cultivating an inside-out approach to our training, we can relax our minds to let go of our formalized regime of training. We can loosen boundaries of what this stance is supposed to be and where this hand is supposed to go. We can then foster images in our minds, and these images will be fed to our bodies. Desiring to do something is the key to success. If you desire a strong punch and continuously imagine your punches as being strong, while also reinforcing positive ideas that your punch is strong, then naturally your punch will become strong. Your subconscious mind cannot reject any idea you give it, and by overflowing it with ideas such as these, you will see tremendous results. Remember that mental images are simply energy, and we can use this energy to inspire us to discover deeper power in our arts.

Aging and the Inside-Out Approach

When you get older, your strength and your speed will deteriorate. When you've reached your forties, you may even feel as if you lack the energy to practice. If you train like a twenty-year-old when you are fifty, or even forty, you have missed an important lesson in martial arts. If you continue to train from an outside-in approach when you are old, then you will become discouraged when you find that people can move faster and train longer than you. But, while our bodies weaken as we grow old, our minds become stronger, and it is this mental acuity that can lend us great power, even greater than when we were young.

I no longer train speed drills, spinning techniques, or high kicks. I used to love to do these things when I was younger, but now they no longer interest me. For one, I hit harder now with my fists, so why even worry about training my legs to strike the head? I can do more devastating techniques simply with my hands. Concentrate then on things your body can easily handle in the long run, rather than things that will run it down prematurely. This will create sustainable power for you. We want our arts to get more powerful as we age, not less powerful. I have removed all the "young man's" arts from my system, replacing them with arts I can do well into old age. To me, these are the true arts; the rest are just distractions I teach the kids and young adults. For them, these arts are useful and should still be taught to them because they may find value and joy out of practicing these things. Just remember that you should always consider sustainable arts so you can continue practicing as you progress in years. This will allow you to use your life's pursuit of the mastery mind-set in effective applications of your arts.

For sustainable striking arts, I recommend concentrating about 80 percent of your effort on hand techniques and 20 percent on foot techniques. Hand speed will not change over time the way leg speed will, and thus hand arts have a sustainable nature to them. Practice a variety of punches and focus on creating energy vibration through your opponent, rather than using pushing-style punches. You want your opponent to drop, not to be pushed back. For leg techniques, concentrate on legs and groin as targets. Low kicks do not require as much athleticism as a younger person's head kick, and yet are insanely difficult to block and are loaded with power. I will discuss ways to learn and apply all of these techniques later on.

Roundhouse and front kicks are the easiest of kicks to transfer energy to an opponent with. I have deleted all high kicks and spinning kicks from my arts, and almost completely abandoned side kicks. In one class, my karate sensei asked me to break his knee with a side kick. At this point I had about twenty years of karate experience, and could easily break boards with this kick. I never practiced full-on to someone's knee before that day because I always thought that this was too dangerous. I kicked him with full power, trusting that he had a trick, over and over to his knee. Not only did it do nothing to him, but he didn't even flinch. He did not move, and he did not block; he simply absorbed all of the power from my side kick. "This kick is useless; do not bother practicing it," he said to me. Ever since then, I have all but removed it from the system we teach.

I really liked side kicks for many years, and it was a bit heartbreaking to see that I could do nothing with this kick to my sensei. I had thought this kick was powerful, but as it turned out, it was a high-risk and low-reward technique. Now, granted, he was a master at absorbing power, but it did show me the futility in this kick that I had not previously been witness to given my paradigm. It is therefore important not only to see what is better, but to *be* better. For me, this meant deleting this kick and practicing other arts that were more universal.

By using an inside-out approach, we can dream big and create a different type of magic to transform our art; this thought energy is a gift to your future self. By creating images in our minds, we no longer need to do ten thousand repetitions to gain the same amount of benefit. As we age, we need to be kinder to our joints and connective tissues, as these things take a longer time to heal when we are older. Practicing a young-person's arts when you are old is a recipe for self-destruction. Do not brutalize your mind by trying to keep up with the twenty-year-old version of yourself.

If you are young, you should train hard and not worry so much about what you are going to do when you are older. That time will come on its own. When you are young, your body can heal quickly, so I recommend doing as much as you can to gain experience. Practice your techniques a lot, stay after class and practice, and practice when you get home. By doing this, you can make up for your lack of experience through sheer volume of enthusiasm. When I was a teenager, I would come home from school and then go immediately to karate class. I would come home late and crawl into bed and pass out. Waking up was difficult, but by noon my body was fully ready to take more punishment.

One of my senseis, who was in his sixties at the time, would stand next to me, flop out his arms in front of him, and then pull his hands back to his chest. He asked me to mimic the movement and try to beat him at speed. I couldn't, even though he was over twenty-five years my senior. He said, "Craig San, I am old, and yet our hand speed is the same. This is how I beat you!"

There is a great bit of wisdom here. Masters never have to chase anyone, nor do they have to compete with a younger person's speed. Because his hands were the same speed as mine, the advantage of youth disappeared. Moreover, thought energy can only increase with experience and wisdom, which is the true advantage of the master. We must concentrate then on arts that make our rhythm and energy better, rather than just speed alone. Speed will go away in time, but rhythm is something that grows with maturity. Look at the old jazz musicians, who've increasingly gained in skill and prowess over the years. The same holds true for martial arts, if we have the correct mind-set.

If you put your faith in your muscle, you will eventually be betrayed by it. If you put your faith in speed, again your body will betray you. Put your faith in your mind, as this is the only thing that grows stronger with age. Two of my senseis are in their sixties, and neither one shows a lack of energy. Both of them have vibrant enthusiasm that is contagious. This type of energy does not grow old like your muscles do. Your body may lack energy, but your mind should never lack energy.

Here's a metaphor that might inspire your creativity in approaching the inside-out method of training. Imagine that our thoughts are like water, with our minds being the vessel. Water will take the shape of any container we place it in, be it a jar, fountain, or toilet. If kept within that vessel, water will only accomplish a limited effect. Let loose the water, and it can fill in any cracks in the earth, carve out canyons, flood cities, or quench the thirst of billions of people. Water can dissolve anything given enough time, put out fires, and expand and contract under heat and cooling. Water, just like our thoughts, can seemingly accomplish the impossible. If you limit your container (your mind), your thoughts will fill that container and accomplish the equivalent of scrubbing a toilet or watering the daisies. If you change your paradigm, you can break down the barriers of the vessel and allow the water to run its true course. Thoughts are powerful, like water, but what you decide to do with that power is your choice. Choose to cultivate power from your inside-out, and you will begin to do the impossible.

Principles of Internal Power

The first time I was punched by a master, my chest caved in, and I fell to the floor. His punch didn't even look like an attack at all; it looked like he was simply reaching out to touch me. He caught me in the sternum, and the power reverberated inside of me in a way that I could never have imagined. Had I only witnessed this punch connecting with someone else, say, another student in class, I would have thought the reaction to the hit was phony. This power didn't come from muscles, as this master was smaller than me, nor did it come from overall fitness, as the man had a bigger belly than me. No amount of weightlifting or push-ups could create this kind of power; this power was internal, an awe-inspiring application of the inside-out approach to generate energy.

Many martial art styles use either internal or external forms. For example, karate and judo are considered to be external, while aikido, tai chi, and chi gung are considered to be internal. This is an oversimplification, but this generalization is the common focus of these art forms. External arts often call upon physical speed, power, and endurance. Internal arts require calmness of action, smoothness of movement, and a definite mental purpose.

I argue that all martial arts have both internal and external means of expression, just like we as humans do. After all, we all have minds that we think with and bodies that we live in. If you pay attention only to your body, then you will miss important issues of the mind. Likewise, if you intellectualize all of your arts, you will not be physically capable of performing them. We must balance our external and internal powers so that they work in harmony with one another. Focusing on one or the other exclusively will not get us positive results. You may sit upon a mountaintop and meditate, but your body may wither away; likewise, you may work your body day in and day out to become a physical titan, but you may still be afraid of the dark.

Learning to use internal power will bestow new ways to look at all of your arts. Internal power has helped me create a devastating punch, a fear-inspiring kick, and impossibly light yet overwhelming throws. Moreover, by understanding internal power, we can take more skills with us into old age than we could with just understanding those that emphasize external strength.

In the course of my study, and with the help of many of my teachers, peers, and my business partner, I have developed three principles for understanding how to create internal power. These are

- be centered,
- be relaxed, and
- be present.

I call them the "Three Bs." I use bullet points instead of numbers for a reason: none of these principles takes precedence over another. Without each principle supporting the others, none of them truly works. If you are truly centered, you will be relaxed and present, and vice versa. From each of these principles, we can derive many lessons about internal power.

Be Centered

Our center of gravity is roughly two inches below our navels. In meditation, there are often many centers in the body, but for martial arts, this focal point near the navel is the most important because it involves our physical balance. Think of this point as your mental center too, because if you are spaced out, it is easy to lose balance. Someone who is mentally present is simply harder to push over than someone whose mind is wandering or whose eyes are looking the other way.

To find this focal point, you can start by standing normally. Then, rise up on the balls of your feet, and then gently place your heels on the ground without shifting your weight onto them. This forward feeling is very useful in martial arts because if you are relaxed and centered, you are more difficult to throw or be caught off guard. Likewise, you must first have good balance and control over your own body if you wish to unbalance your opponent. Touch your center that is two inches below your navel and let this focal point be both your physical and mental centers for mastering balance.

Maintaining this posture throughout our daily lives is our goal. To be centered is to be ready for anything. This requires us to be consciously aware of our mental state, and to correct it should we find ourselves out of alignment. Looking forward and to the horizon helps us remain centered; looking down while we walk produces the opposite effect. We already know where the ground is—we don't need to look at it.

Be Relaxed

When most of us think of relaxation, we think of peaceful waves at the beach or perhaps of lounging in a chair sunning ourselves. Relaxation is not lounging around like a limp noodle. Relaxation in martial arts is a physical and mental state that is ready, but not tense. If we are standing, we should stand tall and be ready, rather than slouch. If we are attacked while slouching, we must first center ourselves to react, be that move away or into an attack. This momentary loss of time to simply ready yourself will probably make your response too late. Too much relaxation is no good; if you don't believe me, try staying in bed for two days solid and see how you feel. Likewise, too much tension will kill you. Again, if you don't believe me, try stressing out over everything in your life and see how long it takes to have a heart attack (I would recommend not testing this).

Relaxation in the martial arts means a readiness without excessive tension in the body's muscles. If you are simply standing in place, you do not need to raise your shoulders or tighten your abdomen. This tension wastes energy that you may need. Being relaxed allows you to find the minimal amount of power necessary to perform any action. If you give 100 percent to something and it doesn't work, then there is no such thing as adding more. You gave it your best! If you give only 10 percent yet that is enough, great. You've accomplished what you needed to and are not exhausted. If that 10 percent wasn't enough to get the job done, fine; you still have reserves to add.

Being relaxed has additional benefits as well. Relaxed people are pleasant to be around, and this can be contagious. Relaxed posture allows blood to better circulate throughout the body and promotes good health. Excessive tension can lead to chronic headaches and pains. Practicing being relaxed in all situations will prepare you for any challenge you face in your life, and we must be diligent to protect ourselves from these hidden opponents if we truly want to understand all aspects of self-defense.

Be Present

When you look at people, they may be mentally present, or they may be thinking of the sunny beach in Hawaii; it can sometimes be hard to tell. What's more important, however, is that you are able to know if you are mentally present. Being tuned in 100 percent of your waking life is not realistic. After all, spacing out is natural and should not be seen as an evil thing; dreaming about positive goals in your life also isn't evil. The issue we face as humans is that most of us space out too frequently and have no idea that we are doing so. How many times have you been driving behind someone who has left his or her car's blinker on? How often have you been in a line when the person ahead of you had no idea that the line had moved up? As martial artists, we should not be consumed by distractive thoughts. When we realize that we are spacing out unintentionally, we must take the opportunity to do something about it and pay attention. Just as everyone gets angry and everyone gets sad, spacing out should be seen as natural as long as your thoughts are focused. Spacing out habitually over nonrelevant thoughts should be avoided by martial artists.

Awareness should be your primary method of self-defense, not a specific martial arts technique. If you see a threat coming while practicing these principles of internal power, then you can leave or otherwise get away safely. If you are not paying attention, bad things can happen to you.

When we test someone's posture for proper structure, we are also testing to see if he or she is mentally present. People who are spacing out will lose balance easily, while those who are present will not. Since we cannot push on someone's mind (not yet anyway), we must push on their bodies. If mind and body are truly one at this moment, the student will demonstrate good posture. If your mind is wandering, you will lose your balance from a light push.

Another thing that can sometimes rob us of mental presence is the replaying of negative emotions, such as getting down on ourselves for past failures during practice. Do not let past defeats rob you of success in the present moment, in or out of the dojo. What is in the past should stay in the past; each moment is a new opportunity to turn your life around. You have already paid the price for past failures, and so there is no need to keep paying for them. Having a mind that is in the present moment allows you the ability to notice things that many will not see. A relaxed and present mind is open to infinite possibilities.

The Three Bs of internal power (Be centered, Be relaxed, and Be present) are the basic principles that can help you take your arts to the next level, no matter which style you practice. This power is capable of amplifying conventional muscle strength by allowing us to master the energy vibrations within our bodies and our opponent's. Moreover, the principles of internal power bring benefits to daily life. If you see that you are off-center, correct it. If you see that you are tense, relax completely. If you are aware that you have spaced out, come back to the present. By constantly reinforcing these principles through daily action, we are practicing both on and off the mat. If you are centered and relaxed, you are ready for anything that life can throw at you.

Holding Ball

One of the primary training tools for developing internal power is a standing meditation called "holding ball," derived from karate's naifanchi kata. Some martial artists, such as chi gung practitioners, call this practice "hug the tree," but by any name, it is one of the most powerful and fundamental tools in our training arsenal. It is also a very efficient practice, because the skills that it develops can be applied to virtually all karate techniques. Practiced correctly, holding ball uses the Three Bs by developing centeredness, relaxation, and mental focus. Through the exercise of holding ball, we begin to understand structure and relaxation. These two principles are inextricably linked, and in a sense, you cannot correctly apply one without the other. This simple practice will give you the tools you need to develop a powerful block and a devastating punch.

Specifically, holding ball is used to develop

- *balance*, the ability to maintain it, but with the ability to make subtle adjustments.
- *stability*, for both delivering and receiving power.
- *connection to the ground*. By smearing your feet into the floor, you can more easily absorb power.
- *linking body joints*, essential for structure as well as proper movement.
- *heavy hands and feet*, to increase the power of strikes and blocks.
- *elbow-out fixation*. By feeling as though there is an outward pressure on your arms, like an expanding balloon, you will be better suited to absorb power from strikes.
- *isolation of the hips*. By rotating left and right, without moving the hips, we utilize our back muscles, a fundamental in naifanchi-style punching.

Holding-ball practice should be done daily for as long as you can stomach standing in horse stance. When practicing this technique, feel your weight sink downward and do not try to resist being there. That is, do not have an upward sensation that is felt when you try to move away from the pain. Relax your body, and pay attention to how this sensation feels on your feet. We are trying to develop a connection from the ground up so that we can create seemingly impossible power to absorb attacks and deliver devastating strikes of our own.

Holding ball is primarily a static exercise; you do not move while you hold this position. Yet there are several ways to practice it so that you can maximize its use for you.

Solo Practice

- Stand in horse stance at a reasonable depth. It is actually counterproductive for this practice to go so low that your thighs are parallel to the floor.

- Create solid, but relaxed, structure in the stance. Imagine yourself as being carved from a solitary block of stone.
- Extend your arms as if holding a giant beach ball against your chest.
- Imagine that your arms are an unbroken and unbendable iron ring.
- Create a "circuit" of connectivity in your entire body:
  - Feel the connection from the fingertips of one hand connecting through your arms and back, all the way to the fingertips of your other hand.
  - Feel the connection from the ground through your toes and one foot, connecting through your legs and hips, all the way back down to your opposite foot.
  - Feel the connection from your right hand through your left foot, and vice versa.

Once you feel comfortable performing holding ball from a motionless posture, you can begin making it more dynamic by rotating your torso from side to side. When you do, still pretend to hold a ball, and pay special attention not to move your hips or change the size of the ball. By isolating the hips, we learn how to do the naifanchi punch, which when performed well, possesses a stunning amount of power. Hip twisting is not used in this style of punch; focus rather on the large muscles in your back. When stretched, these muscles want to bounce back to their original position. This will be very useful when doing multiple attacks, as your body will come back to a neutral position without you having to twist your hips to make it happen. Think of this like a coiled spring. When you punch, the spring is compressed, and when you let go, the spring returns to its original shape.

If you are able to, practice the holding-ball technique with a training partner. Have one person assume the position, while the other person tests the connections created by pushing at various angles for several seconds each. For example, if you push on one hip, the power of the push should go to the opposite foot; if you push on one of the arms, again, the power should go to the opposite foot. The person testing should not deliberately be trying to push the other person over. Push on your partner so he or she can feel where the power is going so that he or she can direct this energy. At first, push lightly, but as you get more confident with this, you can apply significant pressure. We are not trying to make the person fail; we are trying to make him or her understand how to hold the stance and absorb power.

A poor angle of a push may cause the person to lose balance even with good posture, so testers should push so that the power can be absorbed properly. Naifanchi stance (horse stance) is weak front to back. If a tester were to stand in front of a student who was standing in horse stance and push on the chest toward the back, he or she might lose balance. This isn't a bad thing, though, because this is not how this stance is used. This stance is used at a particular angle to your opponent, more like a front stance.

Partner Practice

- Perform holding ball and resist while your partner gently but firmly pushes and/or pulls from different angles:
    - Bend one arm, then the other.
    - Push one knee in, then the other.
    - Pull the knees together.
    - Push through the side of one hip toward the other hip.
    - Push through the shoulder at a downward angle toward the opposite foot.
    - Push through one shoulder toward the other.
    - Push at a 45-degree downward angle through the chest.
    - Push straight through the chest toward the spine.

For advanced practice, the tester should punch the one performing holding ball. Punch him or her at such an angle that he or she does not have to move an arm to block. The person practicing holding ball should be able to block the blow by body structure alone, not having to move the arm to intercept at all. Of course, the angle of this punch has to be very specific, but it proves that correct posture is all that is needed to block a blow. You don't have to add anything to a block in order for it to work; your body just needs the correct structure. When done well, it makes your blocks effortless. I practice punching my training partner with two targets in mind: the head and the floating ribs. For the floating-rib target, your partner should be holding the ball low. For the head target, your partner should be holding the ball high.

This exercise takes time to master. Just as you wouldn't expect to be able to pay off your mortgage after a single day's work, you shouldn't expect to do this exercise once and figure it out immediately. If you are not getting it, simply go through the exercise daily and think about it more. Reread this section until you make it part of you. This is one of the "secrets" often shared by karate masters. They believe, as do I, that this is a fundamental exercise to understand internal power.

Exploding Ball

Another exercise I do is the exploding ball. With this exercise, I start in horse stance like the holding-ball practice. From here, though, I hold my hands in front of me as if I were holding a soccer ball. Then I move my hands rapidly outward to the holding-ball position. It is like the soccer ball suddenly exploded. With this technique, we can develop another type of block that creates an explosive feeling. When your hands move outward to the large-ball position, make sure that they stop without shaking. This should not create a reverberation within you; your energy must travel into your opponent.

Imploding Ball

The reverse of exploding ball is imploding ball. In this exercise, we start with the holding-ball position, and then rapidly move our hands to our center, as if we were catching a soccer ball. This exercise is a way to absorb power from a punch or kick. We follow the shock wave our opponent is creating and guide that wave to our center; in doing so, you will rob your opponent of power. To practice this, have your training partner punch you in the solar plexus, but do not try to block the punch. Instead, have one of your forearms "surf" the punch in toward your stomach. This simple touch destroys the integrity of the shock wave your partner is trying to make. The result is that the punch becomes feeble and useless.

For both exploding- and imploding-ball exercises, it is important to receive feedback from your training partner. Dial up the power of incoming blows when you feel confident that your technique will work. Do not shy away from the incoming punch, but remain steadfast in your position. By using these exercises, you are developing your internal power. The more you practice them, the more confidence you will see in yourself, and the better all of your arts will be.

Impossible Techniques

Now that we are beginning to understand the fundamentals of energy and internal power, let us look at the various "impossible" techniques that you can learn and use for yourself. For the most striking style of martial artists, the first thing you should learn is how to absorb and dissipate power. Once you understand how to take a punch without blocking, a whole new world of possibilities opens up. Once you free your mind of the paradigm that you have to expend energy to defend yourself, you may then concentrate on finer details of the arts that you may have previously missed or put off for later.

Impossible arts go far beyond being able to take a punch, though. With a keen understanding of energy, we can use our body to transmit internal power efficiently to another. This transference of energy creates shock waves within our opponent and can have dramatic effects with very little physical effort. In fact, if you ever have to force any martial art technique, I would have to say that you are doing it incorrectly. Water flows downhill, not up, and likewise we do not want to combat others with arts that require tremendous effort. There will always be someone stronger, and so we must get into the habit of finding better ways of employing the arts.

To use the techniques I will outline in the following chapters, you do not have to quit your dojo and find another style to practice. You can simply consume this information and apply it to what you already know. As I have said before, I am not that concerned by the outward appearance of any art. You will find that the techniques I offer in subsequent chapters can be easily integrated with whatever system you currently follow. Many people would like to argue that there is a best stance to use or what the best hand position is. These arguments are pointless. I have seen masters use whatever footwork or hand position they want and still create amazing effects, even if in absurd or ludicrous positions. Do not be overly concerned with how something looks. The first time I saw my karate sensei do kata, I thought he looked sloppy! But there was no denying that he could punch harder than anyone I'd ever met, in addition to being able to take full-power kicks without flinching. Who cares if it looks sloppy? I care that what he did looked magical, and I wanted that magic.

To begin, I would like to talk about how to absorb power from blows, as this is often our first line of defense. If we fail to see an imminent attack in time to block it and are unable to absorb the opponent's power, there may not be the chance for utilizing any other techniques.

Absorbing Power

Upon learning how to absorb power from punches and kicks, you will instantly become less frightened of any unarmed opponent. If people cannot seriously harm you with their fists or their feet, then you have absolutely nothing to worry about should you have to fight them. In fact, you could spend the entire fight standing there taking punches and doing nothing. I have a fifty-eight-year-old student who once got into a fight with a twenty-five-year-old. The young man struck my student repeatedly in the face and body. My student said he was too shocked to retaliate, but instead he stood there and took the punches like we did in class. The younger man got tired, puzzled that his punches did nothing to my student. Eventually the attacker gave up and left.

Sometimes it is important not to fight back, and simply take a few hits. Maybe you're being attacked by a drunk friend or are being chewed out by someone whose parking spot you just took; either way, we don't want to unthinkingly dial the energy up to ten in these situations. This could turn us into the bad guy. You aren't going to die from a couple of punches from people who know nothing about how to hit. If you are practicing correctly, your peers in your own dojo will have hit you harder than anyone can on the street. *Absorbing power from any opponent is the single most valuable asset we can achieve in the martial arts.* By learning to absorb power, we remove the fear of being injured by others. If you can do this, the rest of your arts are almost extraneous. The true skill is nullifying the source of power from anyone wishing to do you harm.

When I was a child, I saw a kung fu demonstration on TV where they performed "iron shirt." A man would stand there in horse stance while people punched, kicked, and bludgeoned him with sticks. They punched him in the throat and even kicked him in the groin. I seem to remember that they even placed a spear at his throat and tried to jab him with the spear. All attacks had no effect on the man. I was too young to know if this was fake or real, but it set a chain of thoughts in my mind that would dominate my thinking in martial arts. Whether this demonstration was fake or real no longer mattered; it was real in my mind, and I intended to attain this skill for myself.

I joined a kung fu school at the age of fifteen, being excited by those images. I asked my sifu about the validity of the iron shirt and other such superpowers, but he was very dismissive, quickly passing them off as fairy tales and cheap tricks. It was not until much later that I realized that absorbing power from punches or kicks was a real thing, and something that could be learned like any other skill. While learning to absorb power from blows is intimidating at first, it is achievable if you have faith in yourself, persistence, and a strong mental image. The biggest obstacle is disbelief; if you disbelieve in yourself, all energy leaves you.

Because we are made of energy and energy is always in motion, even when we stand still, we remain moving. On a micro level, blood and lymph circulate through our bodies as our chests expand and contract with each breath. We have cellular activity and digestive activity— everything is in constant motion. On an atomic level, all of the atoms that we are built out of are also moving and vibrating. So in a sense, we carry these vibrations with us. Let's use them to our benefit.

When we are attacked, we can use this vibration to absorb blunt trauma, from fists, elbows, feet, shins, or whatever. Since our opponents are also composed of energy, we can synchronize our vibrations to theirs, thereby nullifying the effects of their attacks; making their strikes suddenly feel like pillows.

There may be a way to absorb power from blades or bullets, but I haven't figured out a way to do this yet. Both of these practices are significantly more dangerous than absorbing power from fists, and testing out ways to accomplish this safely needs further study. I hesitate to call these sorts of things impossible, because I've been shown several times that my skeptical assumptions of what a master can accomplish have been proven wrong. However, my logical mind steps in and prevents me from trying any of this out. Perhaps that is a good thing.

Knives and guns aside, I can absorb full-power kicks and punches to the body, arms, and legs with no aftereffect other than a bit of pink skin. Absorbing power from attacks to the head is possible, but concussions are usually the result, and so this is not recommended for any practice. This is why I recommended covering the head very well while fighting, and leaving the torso obviously open to attack. This will invite your opponent to strike in the area that looks unprotected, when in fact you are fully protected. Let him or her beat upon your chest futilely, while you have your hands free.

I once asked a student to punch me in the chest as hard as he could. The man was six foot two and weighed about 280 pounds. I assumed that he would punch once and stop for the demonstration, but he didn't stop with one punch; in fact, he proceeded to beat on my chest like a drum, with both fists going full power for twenty-five or thirty punches. This caught me off guard, but I absorbed the power of each of his blows, relaxing to conserve energy. After a time, he realized his punches were having no effect, and he became exhausted. I then said, "Okay, it's my turn." The student turned white, and I struck him lightly only once in the solar plexus, and he collapsed to the floor.

The human body is composed of mostly water; we know this to be true from high school chemistry class. I would like you to consider this: if I had two drops of water and moved them together, what would happen? They would move together harmlessly and become one drop! Since we are composed of mostly water, we can use the vibration of that water to dissipate energy from another person, who is also made primarily of water, just like two drops gently contacting. This may be a bit of a stretch for most people to see, but I want you to know that there is logic to all of this madness. This is how the impossible can become possible through careful study, analysis, and physical experimentation.

There are two major factors for dissipating power from an opponent: psychology and physical structure.

Psychology

Most people fixate on a superficial approach to absorb the power of a blow, that is, they focus on how they should look, rather than how they should think. In actuality, it has more to do with what's within your mind than how you hold your body. To develop the ability to absorb all power of an attack and receive absolutely no injury, you must first have faith in yourself. You must see in your mind a picture of yourself completely still and unmoving. Flinching, moving away, or trying to dodge an attack will aid your opponent's attempt to damage you.

By flinching, you will actually increase your opponent's power, as he or she can adapt to your body's momentary weakness. Running away from your opponent's energy will encourage your opponent's desire to do you harm, making you receive much more of his or her energy and increasing the likelihood of injury. Do not become the sheep before the wolf; become a wolf right back, or better yet, a bear. Be confident and unyielding. Stand in the midst of adversity and deny any entry.

I like to practice an exercise where my opponent does nothing but repeatedly punch me to the stomach. For safety reasons in the dojo, we don't go to the head for beginners. I then move forward and continuously push my opponent back, using his or her shoulders or biceps (again, for safety reasons only). I do not yield one inch of ground; in fact, I force my opponent backward. Typically this will spin my opponent to face away from me, and I can get a few free shots to the back if I want. This constant pressure of pushing makes it insanely difficult for your opponent to get one blow in, because your opponent's weight is all the way behind him or her. If your opponent kicks, he or she often will fall down when pushed. This is why this sort of technique is illegal in sport martial arts; you can simply push your opponent out of bounds in seconds, and then rinse and repeat.

This unyielding nature does two things. First, it demonstrates a lack of fear, and your opponent will instinctively wonder what is wrong with you. When the blows land and do absolutely nothing, your opponent will begin to doubt himself or herself and will more likely want to leave than continue fighting. We want to take away our opponent's mind, which is his or her most powerful weapon, because without mind, the attacks are useless. Disarm your opponent's mind with unwavering confidence.

With the mind now in doubt, we will take away his or her physical weapons, to be discussed in a later chapter. For now, know that it is imperative that you become unyielding in your practice so that you develop a keen sense that there is no reason to defend yourself—because nothing can really hurt you anyway. At times when people come to punch me, they simply stop midway. People don't even know why they are stopping the attack; they just sense it is futile. This is the power we want to develop. This is the source of our strength. This is the center of all martial arts. We should be nonviolent people, but not shy away from violence; we stare it down and do not yield to weaker-minded aggressors. With this power, you can stop fights before any blows are even thrown. Allow your opponent to do the monkey dance, but don't dance with him or her. (The term *monkey dance* was coined by Rory Miller in the book *Meditations on Violence* to describe the human dominance ritual. It is a deliberately ridiculous name for a pattern of behavior that young men are conditioned to follow.)

Make the mental decision that you are going to stand your ground and not move. Look straight at your opponent and do not waver in your posture. Allow your posture to speak for itself; become the wolf and not the lamb. Once you have the correct image in your head of how you are going to use your opponent's attack energy, you can diffuse this through your own body and down into the ground. When someone decides to strike you, he or she first has to make a conscious mental decision. With enough awareness training, this moment becomes obvious. This gives you all the time you need to mentally prepare for being struck.

Practicing Absorbing Power

A friend of mine was a bouncer who was once cornered and beaten up by two men after the bar had closed. My friend put up a valiant effort to thwart their attacks, but he became exhausted after what he claimed was more than twenty minutes. They beat on my friend until both attackers could no longer move, at which point they took turns, like a wrestling tag-team match. One would sit and rest, while the other would beat on my friend. Eventually the attackers had enough and left. You may say that my friend lost the fight, sure, but he suffered no broken bones or serious injuries, just a few bruises and scrapes.

It may not be romantic to have your strategy be to be beaten up. However, if you get to go home to your family at the end of the day, does it really matter? Relaxing and absorbing blows may be your best defense in certain situations.

To practice absorbing blows to your chest, you do not need washboard abs, nor do you need to be able to bench four hundred pounds. This has less to do with strength than you may believe, instead having more to do with how you receive power from a mental standpoint. If you "resist" the power, it will hurt you. If you "accept" this power, you can then absorb it and use it. You must welcome this energy to you, and then you can simply send it through the ground and be done with it.

There are many ways to approach this sort of practice, but all of them involve being struck by an opponent. It is not enough to intellectualize violence; we must practice violence in order to be its master. You can read all you want about fixing automobiles, but if you don't get your hands dirty in an engine, you will not be a good mechanic.

Your partner should start by tapping you in the chest with a fist. I encourage people to punch to the solar plexus. As we know, the solar plexus is a sensitive area roughly in the center of our chest. If we stand tall, this area has an open sort of feeling to it, and any blow received here will likely make you double over or cough. If we allow ourselves to relax, this area will be closed off (more on this in following chapters). By closing off the solar plexus, we become immune to blows to this area, as if we were wearing armor.

It is important when receiving blows that we do not wince, tense up, move away, or otherwise show any discomfort. Start out slow and with low-power punches to get used to the idea of being struck without blocking or moving away to avoid it. This can be very challenging for beginners, but the emotional rewards for early success here can be very gratifying, as well as eye-opening to further impossible techniques.

A straight shot to the solar plexus is better for learning this technique; we can throw curveballs in later. For now, punch straight, and dial up the power consecutively. When starting out, don't have your partner hammer you with full power and then deny that this works. You wouldn't go to the gym as a novice and put five hundred pounds on the bench press, would you? You have to exercise your mind in the same way you would work out your biceps. Start with low weight and a lot of reps.

Create a Mental Image

Create an image of a pebble that is dropped into a still pond. See those concentric rings expand outward like a shock wave. Use this image to create your own shock wave that starts from your center and expands outward infinitely. Since we are dealing with the speed of thought, your wave can hit your opponent's energy instantly. This outward feeling makes you feel forward, by just a tiny amount, and this is ideal for absorbing power.

This is where holding-ball practice can come into play. As your opponent punches low, have your arms on top of his or hers and expand outward in your mind, as though your arms were creating a shock wave. This might feel like a conventional block, but avoid the temptation to move your arms to meet with the attack of your opponent. The attack is coming to you, and as long as your angle is correct, the attack cannot penetrate. For the purposes of practice, the person punching should strike on the angle that makes this "block" the most effective. This is to practice absorption of power without moving, not blocking practice.

If you are in the correct position and have the correct mental image, then you don't need to block anything, because there is no energy to block. It is all dissipated. Hold the stance, hold your arms in this position, and don't physically move. Allow your mind to move. Keep the holding-ball image in your mind, and then you will be closer to understanding that you don't need to defend yourself, because no one is capable of hurting you without your permission.

Physical Structure

I define proper structure as a relaxed posture that is balanced and stable and facilitates movement. You must be capable of withstanding energy without collapsing, as well as delivering powerful blows through minimal effort. If an accidental push can disrupt your balance, then you are in no position to receive a deadly blow, and in no position to return that blow. This is less about where to put your feet than you may think; it has more to do with the proper alignment of your spine and orientation of your body weight. Too much weight on your heels, and you will be pushed back; too much weight on the balls of your feet, and you can crumple forward with impact. Much like how the size and mass of a tank provides a stable firing platform for its big cannon, proper structure provides the necessary stability to project your weight and power behind your attack.

This structure, when used correctly, allows us to block punches and kicks without moving. We can also decide how much power we wish to use. In practice, I often try to find the minimum amount of power necessary for performing any action. That minimum serves as the baseline, allowing you to always have the option of adding more power to it. Having the proper alignment of our bones makes us capable of deeds that look impossible to the novice, but these techniques can actually be learned quickly. You must first have faith that your structure is enough to block a blow; this faith should keep you from feeling like you have to move off-line or evade in any manner. We build this faith in our structure by practicing our form and providing each other with feedback. Later on, we can work on getting off the line of an attack. That is, if an opponent is coming straight toward us, it may be to our best interest to move to one side or the other, especially if the opponent is significantly larger than us. There are times when we do not want to absorb the power of an attack, particularly from a weapon. Moving off-line from a stab is preferable to standing there and trying to diffuse the power of a knife.

My sensei always used to say, "We punch bone on bone, never muscle on muscle." This is the feeling that you should have when creating proper structure. This "bone on bone" feel should be relaxed and fixing you to the ground. My sensei would demonstrate this by pointing to his foot, and say that your foot bone is connected to your calf bone and your thigh bone; your thigh bone is connected to your pelvis, which in turn is connected to your spine. The bones in the arm and in the hand must have this connection running from the ground into your punching arm. Even though there are many joints located throughout the body, the term "bone on bone" means that we think of this chain of bones as one solid structure upon impact.

Often my sensei would punch us by first leaving his fist out in the air, and then make a twitching motion that would hit so hard you would land on the floor. It looked impossible. But he was connecting all of his body weight and slamming it up into you via his knuckles. His "bone on bone" connection, from hand, to arm, to shoulder, to spine, to hip, to thigh, to calf, to foot, made it feel like the entire floor just leaped up and crashed into you. It might look stiff and rigid, but the muscles themselves are actually relaxed. When done well, it should seem that we are merely holding our bones in the correct position.

To absorb power, we utilize the same "bone on bone" feeling to bring the vibration through us and down to the ground. Tense posture opens you to your opponent's power, thus causing more damage to you. Moreover, tense muscles expend energy rapidly, sapping your strength before your fight is done. An overly relaxed posture that stands like deadweight makes us more like Jell-O or wet noodles, and does not serve us well when we need the full capability of our minds and bodies. We hope that real fights take only seconds, but should they last longer, we must master the art of proper structure and relaxation to create the maximum effect with the minimum effort.

Once you have employed this mental and physical structure, you will begin to witness that most people are unable to harm you with their fists or their feet. This will instill you with a great sense of confidence, and then you can really begin to learn the arts because you no longer have to defend yourself. By not being afraid of injury, you are free from the most crippling enemy: fear. Once you are no longer afraid of injury from other black belts, what could a guy on the street possibly do to you?

This is why contact training is important at higher levels of martial arts. Being familiar to the sensation of being punched and kicked is a complete discipline in itself. No one on the planet can punch or kick me the way my teachers have. Therefore, any adversary I meet will be a lesser opponent than my teachers. If you are an instructor, you must instill this in your students so that if they get into a real fight, then they will be overprepared.

A friend of mine whom I've trained with for almost two decades is one of the best martial artists I've had the pleasure of knowing. His brother—I'll call him Bob—is much bigger than he is, but only has a few years of martial arts training under him. Bob got into a fight one day and was struck repeatedly by his opponent. Bob then laughed at the guy and pointed out that his brother hit harder than he did, and he proceeded to throw the attacker through a window.

Now, I don't recommend people fight, ever, but this situation made me feel my friend did his job well. His brother Bob could take a punch, because he had taken hits from one of the best.

Creating Proper Structure

The basic concept behind creating this physical structure is to relax your body enough to become like a sponge that absorbs blows using the correct amount of muscle to have an unyielding posture. Too much muscle, and you will be pushed over. Too little muscle, and you will collapse like a house of cards. Do not actively engage your muscles, but instead, hold an image in your head like a river rock, which has a constant stream of pressure applied to it and yet remains motionless as the water rushes over it.

We want to redirect all incoming power through our bones down to the ground. This grounding is best utilized when you are still, though it is possible to maintain it while moving. For the novice, it is suggested that primary practice be done without moving. After all, if someone wants to cause you harm, he or she has to approach you, and during this approach you are free to do all sorts of things. Retreating gives your opponent power, while staying still and denying him or her entry robs your opponent of power. Imagine an internal frame throughout the body, using skeletal alignment and mental intention to keep it in place. This connection starts from the ground and transmits through the body, linking bone to bone from head to toe.

Sometimes practicing these concepts might look silly. Just imagine a bunch of tough-looking martial artists concentrating on how to simply stand still! Isn't it more fun to practice breaking boards or spinning kicks or something? While we all know how to stand, ask yourself honestly, can you take a full-power punch or kick to the solar plexus and not flex your abdomen? If the answer is no, then you have not learned the correct posture as taught by the masters. If you have been studying karate for twenty years and you still cannot do this, I feel your pain, as you have probably been taught sport karate versus original karate. Sport martial arts are designed for scoring points, not for severely injuring an opponent; mastery level of any martial art should be designed to survive real-world self-defense.

Shutting Off the Solar Plexus

The solar plexus is a very vulnerable part of our chest area when it is not "shut off." If we stand tall, our solar plexus is in an "open" position. That is, you can poke someone in this area with a finger, and he or she will experience a disruption in breathing (you are poking the diaphragm). In a proper karate fighting position, this area will close, and no amount of force from hands or feet will be able to penetrate it.

Imagine you are wearing two five-inch-wide bands of steel armor around your chest that encircle your body, like a breastplate that was cut in two horizontally. One band of armor will wrap around your upper chest and the other band around your abdomen. In between these bands is a two-inch gap, which is obviously unprotected and vulnerable. We need to close this gap so that we are better protected.

Stand in a short stance with one foot forward (sanchin works best). Make sure your body is square to your opponent. Remove the natural curve in your lower back by tucking your tailbone slightly, and then with your upper body hinge downward with your solar plexus by about an inch or so. Do not hunch over, and do not force it. Relax, and have your weight slightly forward. This will close the gap between the bands of armor and thus give you better protection. Even though we are not made of steel, our rib cage can cover our solar plexus so that it cannot be struck.

Standing at attention opens the solar plexus and it is vulnerable.

Hinge your body (without slouching) at the solar plexus to protect it.

With enough practice, this should be a natural movement and not a painful or tight feeling. If you relax your upper back and flatten the small of your back, this moves the top plate over the bottom plate and thus closes this vulnerable gap.

In this position you have

- *skeletal alignment,* made anatomically strong through a bone-to-bone connection. Think of a house: it needs a frame for structural integrity.
- *mental intention.* Your physical shape plus your own awareness of the connection to your joints creates strong posture. Our houses are wired for electricity, and we must turn the electric current on.

The connection is made without muscle tension; we use the minimal amount of power to hold a position. Make this mental connection inside as well as out; connect to your opponent.

Standing Posture

Although it is possible to absorb power from any stance, some stances make this concept easier to manifest in the body. Aikido postures are used for movement and not for absorbing power, because they typically have us standing upright. This is because aikido arts came from armed arts, where moving away from swords, knives, and spears is a better idea than trying to absorb the power of a full swing. Karate postures are primarily for unarmed fighting, and are very useful for absorbing bludgeoning power.

The kata sanchin, and the stance of the same name, is the starting point for understanding how to absorb power within our bodies from punches and kicks. A common misunderstanding about sanchin comes from the position of the knees. This stance is often called the hourglass stance, and many practitioners bend their knees to appear like the center of an hourglass. The center of the hourglass should be your waist and not your knees. Placing your knees in this awkward position makes them susceptible to injury both from being struck and from long-term wear on tendons and connective tissue. Your knees should always be directly over your feet to ensure you do not get chronic knee problems through practice. I've met many old karate practitioners who failed to learn this early, and as a result, can barely walk. If you would like to walk when you are sixty, then take this lesson to heart.

When practicing sanchin stance, remember to do the following:

- Smear the feet into the ground, rather than gripping with the toes.
- Put your knees directly over the feet.
- Tuck the tailbone to remove the natural curve of the lower back.
- Hold the spine straight.
- Put on your iron shirt by shutting off the solar plexus (this is like a hinge in the middle of the chest).
- Seat the shoulder by having slight downward pressure.
- Keep your head in neutral position while tucking the chin.
- Weight is 2 percent forward.

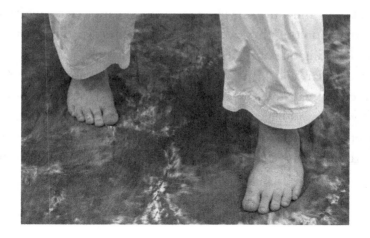

After a while, this stance will become more natural, and you can then relax more, which will help you absorb even more power. Work with a training partner to develop this physical structure to the point where you no longer have to worry if you have the right position or not. In the beginning, placement of the feet is critical, but please note that your mental attitude is much more important than your physical position. You should be able to absorb blows to the body easily even while grappling.

Other stances also work for absorbing power, but they need to be short stances. You can shut off your solar plexus with a regular standing posture, a cat stance, a short fighting stance, or a narrow horse stance, as well as sanchin. Back stance and a long front stance will tilt the pelvis in the wrong direction and will actually make your solar plexus more vulnerable to attack. This also holds true for a long and deep horse stance. A long front stance and back stance did not exist in old Okinawa karate, though they are often utilized today. This is why front stance and body punches are often employed in sport martial arts. It is easy to lightly hit one another and cause disruption to the solar plexus to cause a "point." It is likely these arts were chosen to discourage face contact during tournaments.

Do not be discouraged if you are unable to absorb power from punches or kicks for the first three or four months of practicing this.

Start out slow, and build up your confidence. Learn to relax while being hit and maintain this physical structure. This effort is both physical and mental; ignoring one of these will destroy the whole.

Once you are confident in your ability to absorb power from proper structure, you can then experiment with other stances and positions so that you always have the ability to absorb energy, no matter where your feet are. Try even ridiculous positions to see what you need to do to absorb anything. Learn the rules, study the rules, and then break the rules!

Impossible Blocks

Of all the impossible techniques, blocking is the only one that's so easy that sometimes I forget to mention it. Attacking by punching and kicking may be a very unnatural paradigm for some students to overcome, but blocking is instinctive and requires little training to get the hang of. I can often get students to perform correct blocks within a few classes, while it might take a few years to get the same student to punch with power. That being said, there is a difference between narrowly deflecting an opponent's blow and blocking with such efficiency and power that it makes the attacker want to give up before you even strike back. These are the impossible blocks.

Impossible blocks are blocks that do not look like blocks at all. A master can block a punch by poking it with an index finger; in fact, my sensei would often do this to prove a point, and it was maddening. My karate sensei would also block using his breath. That is, you would punch him in the face, and he would breathe inward and avoid the blow. This sounds outrageous, but no matter how hard I tried to punch him in the face, he could avoid it with this breathing technique. Sometimes my karate sensei would belly-block punches and kicks, that is, he would expand his belly out so that it looked like a beer gut for a brief second, then he would suck it back in to make your punch meet with nothing. Other times he did a technique he called "read book." He would look into the palm of one hand, and then as you punched him in the face, he would look into the palm of his other hand, evading the blow. All of these I would have considered laughable arts, mocking or dismissing them as hocus-pocus entirely. But when you are the one punching and you meet with nothing but air, your mind is changed in a big hurry.

To understand impossible blocks, we must first begin with regular blocking philosophy. Sometimes beginners have problems creating a functional mental image of what blocking looks like, and these images need to be corrected immediately or there will be painful consequences. The basic rule of blocking is to make sure you do not get hit by redirecting the force away from you. One would think that this is logical and obvious, but sometimes it needs to be pointed out. Those of us who have been training a long time can see this easily, but those new to training must take these first blocks slowly, and with great focus.

A perfect example happened to me one day. A student who had been practicing diligently for about four years asked me to punch her full power in the face. I declined, stating that she was not ready and that this seemed like a really bad idea. She insisted. So I punched her to the forehead because I did not want to cause her any harm. I hoped that the worst that would happen would be that she would have a pink mark on her forehead and a bit of embarrassment.

At the moment of my strike, she redirected the blow from her forehead—into her nose. Since I intended to hit her, it was too late for me to pull the punch. Her nose snapped at the bridge, and the bone broke through the skin and penetrated my hand between the knuckles. I remember the feeling of bone penetrating my body; her bone shards sliced my hands pretty badly, but her injury was much worse. A huge pool of blood splashed on the floor. I asked her if I could take a look at her nose. She opened up her hands like double doors. Blood shot out of two holes near her eyes in squirts. I said, "I'm not a doctor, but I think we should go to the hospital." She agreed and we left.

Others in the dojo were stunned. I heard a scream from the bathroom when she got a chance to look in the mirror. The trip to the hospital was not fun. With her broken nose and my split hand, some men in the waiting room looked like they were going to jump me after we left. Fortunately for me, she was a good sport, and the doctor even did some nice plastic surgery for her that she had always wanted. I later offered to cover anything else she needed fixed, but she respectfully declined.

We must endeavor to practice safely because what we are doing is inherently dangerous, and once you begin to quadruple your power through the methodology I discuss in this book, these arts become even more dangerous. I once tapped a man to show that he had an opening while we were lightly sparring (mostly I was letting him hit me), but as it turns out, I broke two of his ribs. I didn't even form a full fist because I didn't intend on hurting him. Another time I blocked a punch with an open hand while my thumb was hitchhiking (sticking out). My thumb caught on a uniform and was consequently torn backward and touched the back of my hand the way a thumb shouldn't. This was a beginner mistake, occurring because I got lazy with my arts.

As a beginner, it is good practice to learn to perform a block in the correct direction: away from you, rather than performing a counterattack. This allows beginners to focus on each skill and develop it when they're ready. The problem is that very advanced practitioners, and even capable fighters, still fight with a "one-two" mind-set. That is, blocking an attack and then launching a counterattack. This method is a training tool to help beginners learn and is not necessarily how one should fight. A more efficient method of blocking and counterattacking is simultaneous, not one-two.

Move Your Hand First

A blocking fundamental that sometimes fails to be mentioned is the need to move your hand first. Regardless of which style of block we chose, we must endeavor to move our hands first. What I mean by this is that we must get into the habit of making sure the block lands before we move our bodies. By moving your body first, you run the risk of stepping directly into the strike. Moving your hand first ensures that you first deal with the attack before anything else. Also, by moving your hand first, you can encourage your body to come along with you if you want. Sometimes when we are scared, our legs do not work well, and by moving our hands first, we can encourage them to move.

To practice moving your hand first, stand with your feet shoulder-width apart. Have your training partner step in with a lunge punch to your chest. Without moving, block this attack with whatever block you choose. You should be able to do this with 100 percent success. You should not have to move your feet, your body, or your head, nor should you have to dodge in any manner. Make sure you move only your blocking hand (your other hand can chamber on your hip if you want) and make no attempt at escape. If you are getting punched, you need to work on your timing. If you are moving out of the way, you have to train this instinctive reaction out of your practice.

For more advanced students, try the same blocking practice, but instead have the target be the head. Make sure you move only your hand to block, and make sure you do not move your body or your head in an attempt to escape. Train your mind to stand your ground. Have faith that your blocks will work.

Inside Blocks vs. Outside Blocks

Different martial art styles classify the same blocks in different ways. For example, an inside block in one style might be called an outside block in another style. If a block starts from the outside and moves inside, it might be called an outside block from where it originated. Or it might be called an inside block to where it terminated.

Okinawa style names the block by the relation to your opponent. If you are "inside" your opponent's guard while standing (that is, your arms are between your opponent's arms), then this is referred to as an inside block regardless of the blocking technique employed. If your arms are on the outside of your opponent's arms, then this is called an outside block regardless of which hand or which technique is used to block.

Outside blocks are more advantageous, as they make it difficult for your opponent to rapidly attack you with his or her other hand. The problem with outside blocks is that they are difficult to perform if your opponent is very close to you or if your opponent has a rounded attack like a hook punch. An inside block is often faster and easier to use in close-quarters fighting, but often leaves you open for another attack if you fail to break your opponent's balance upon blocking. Inside blocking is also easier to do if you are unable to move your legs for whatever reason.

Neither inside nor outside blocks are the "correct" method, because ultimately the decision rests on how your opponent attacks, so practice both of them well so that you're ready for any situation. That being said, the best blocks are those that are so versatile that they can be used for almost any attack, without thinking. Begin by honing your blocks so that they become another reason for you to feel invulnerable from attack. Once you've reached this level, strive to have your blocks lead into your attacks so naturally that they simply become one technique.

Blocking Procedures

Blocks should be either hard like a hammer-and-anvil (*ra-ka*) or surprisingly soft (*ryu-sui*) or have an uprooting nature to them (*kushin*). Anything in between isn't good enough. A block that was meant to be hard but turned out mushy doesn't disrupt your opponent. Likewise, a soft block that simply slaps your opponent achieves the same result as a failed hard block. All receiving techniques are designed to break your opponent's posture, whether they are hard or soft techniques. These concepts are seen in Japanese and Okinawa karate, but are essentially universal to all arts. Aikido and jujitsu tend to focus more on ryu-sui movements, but hard blocking techniques still exist in those arts as well. Typically these hard blocks utilize cutting motions from sword arts and can be used with the sword or without it.

Many different types of blocking procedures exist, and most people don't believe me about the power of soft techniques unless they have directly experienced them, so I teach them how to block hard first. In karate, this is referred to as ra-ka.

Ra-Ka

Translated from Japanese, *ra-ka* means "dropping flower." This is a hard technique used to crush your opponent, and can be used in both strikes and in blocks. In fact, all karate blocks can be used as strikes. Low blocks can be used as strikes to the groin or inner thigh, rising blocks can be used as elbows to the face or neck, and middle blocks can be used to break arms by the elbow. As an aside, many karate kata end in "blocks," but it is my opinion that these techniques are actually strikes or throws and not blocks at all.

Ra-ka has a dropping effect, like that of an old flower falling from its branch. While it sounds romantic, it isn't; it is very painful. Your power doesn't go up or sideways; it just drops without preparation and puts your full weight and power into the target.

Practicing ra-ka is excellent for beginners, as it demonstrates how easy it is to cripple an opponent's arm or leg with minimal effort. Ra-ka is best performed when relaxed, so that the body can move swiftly and easily. Upon impact, focus and lightly squeeze your hand into a fist to ensure that shock travels through you and to your opponent. This is sometimes referred to as "making sushi rice." Sushi rice is squeezed in the hands by sushi chefs. Too much power, and all the rice squeezes out of the palm. Not enough squeezing makes the rice not clump together properly. This is the same sort of squeezing feeling we want to have when we block. Our arms are relaxed right up until the point of impact, and then we squeeze lightly to make that shock happen. To create shock in our opponent, we must first create it within ourselves. Creating shock will be discussed in a later chapter.

When performed well, ra-ka blocks possess devastating power, so much so that some attackers will lose the stomach for fighting just because you can punish them so badly for attacking you. They can't imagine taking any more of this pain.

Ryu-Sui

In Japanese, *ryu-sui* means "flowing river current," and it is a soft blocking technique. Don't let the word "soft" confuse you. Just because we haven't crushed our opponent's outstretched arm doesn't mean we are not strategically placed to deliver a devastating blow. A soft block should not feel rushed, nor should it create an opposing force that slaps against your opponent. A soft block should have a guiding feeling that gently moves the attack away from you. Typically students will learn hard techniques before advancing to softer arts, so that they gain the confidence that they have the ability to block a blow with force if they need to.

Ryu-sui is a subtle art that requires more attention to detail. A harsh block stops your opponent from continuing toward you, which is often a good thing; but while a harsh touch is easy to resist, a gentle touch is difficult to struggle against. With ryu-sui, we want to encourage our opponent to overreach with the attack so we can guide him or her to further imbalance and take away the ability to fight, often by throwing. When you block an attack using ryu-sui, your opponent will naturally enter closer to you while you guide his or her attack away from you. For one thing, your opponent will believe that he or she has already struck you. Secondly, your opponent now is in perfect range for you to launch your counterattack. You don't even have to reach out; your opponent has come directly to you!

Ryu-sui may be employed to confuse an opponent. For example, if the opponent thinks he or she is going to hit you and suddenly you direct the blow away from you while simultaneously moving away, he or she will find nothing to measure himself or herself with in space and time. In this instant, we position ourselves in a superior spot so we can deliver power to our opponent, while he or she is unable to hit us. This may appear like we suddenly teleported to another location somehow. Usually when I do this technique, my opponent anticipates making contact with me, and he or she will trip slightly when I move away. This places all of my opponent's weight forward in a predictable manner, which can then be exploited.

Kushin

In Japanese, *kushin* means "down up." With kushin, we use the weight of our entire bodies to affect that of our opponents. We move down first, and then on contact, we rise upward slightly, with the intention of uprooting our opponent, not simply blocking his or her strike. This has an immediate and dramatic effect on our opponent. Kushin will displace a person from his or her stance and often make him or her spin slightly so that your opponent's back now faces you. Kushin is performed with the legs, so power comes from your thighs, not from your arms. The arms lock in, like a rising block, and the legs do the majority of the work. The thighs are much stronger than the deltoid muscles, and therefore have an easier time moving an opponent.

The advantage of kushin is that your opponent no longer has the power to ground himself or herself to the floor, which will make your opponent's punches and kicks less effective. After performing kushin, I sometimes ask my partner to punch me, to show that his or her power is 10 percent effective at best. Kushin is also very good at getting your opponent to move away from you. Once uprooted, you can chase your opponent by continuously pushing. Once your opponent is in this defensive mode, it is difficult for him or her to retaliate by striking. Often you can push so that your opponent faces away from you, and then you can punch him or her freely anywhere in the back or in the back of the head.

Kushin is an excellent choice if you happen to be significantly smaller than your opponent. Your thighs are capable of pushing more weight, and so you can move people who are much larger than yourself. I had a student once who was six foot six and weighed over 330 pounds. I myself am six foot and weigh two hundred pounds. By using kushin, I was consistently able to thwart any attack he was able to muster, and I kept him constantly on his heels and unable to punch or kick effectively.

During these push matches, you have plenty of opportunity to strike or throw, should you feel like it. When done well, kushin will make your opponent feel completely useless and suddenly on the defensive, which will rapidly deteriorate his or her resolve for fighting.

Sashikae

Sashikae, translated as changing block, is a more advanced practice of blocking. This is where we block first to the inside, and then rapidly change positions to be on the outside of our opponent. This requires good timing, as the moment to pull this technique off is very slim. This is not accomplished by speed alone, but is aided by deception. We use deception to make our opponent believe we are striking. At that moment, we move to a better position, instead of striking. For example, if your opponent steps forward and punches you to the chest, you can feign a hard inside block. Before your block lands, switch your feet and switch your hands, so that now you are on the outside of his or her outstretched arm. Endeavor to keep your head height the same to avoid detection. After the change block succeeds, a counterattack is encouraged before your opponent recovers. A simple practice one could do for sashikae is to have your opponent step in with a low lunge punch. As he or she steps forward and attacks with his or her right, move to block with your left, then rapidly change your feet and instead block with your right hand. The result is that you are now on the outside of your opponent, and when done well, your opponent will feel like you suddenly disappeared, only to reappear in a stronger position to counterattack.

Unbendable Arm

To get a stronger understanding of how structure plays an important role in blocking, I employ the use of the "unbendable arm" technique.

Unbendable arm is a concept derived from aikido that describes good attack and blocking form for any striking-based art. For example, if you use tension to block a blow, your arm utilizes opposing muscles: the biceps that contract and the triceps that extend. This is an oversimplification, of course, but we can agree that the arm has these two basic functions near the elbow. If you employ both of these muscle sets, the bicep will aid your opponent in breaking through your shield. By relaxing the bicep, we can focus our minds upon only using the triceps and connective tissue, which allow anyone to create a very powerful block that is practically impenetrable

One way to train unbendable arm is to first do it the wrong way, and then compare it with the right way. First make a fist and tense up your arm. Your training partner can then place one hand on your bicep and one near your wrist and try to bend your arm the way nature intended it to be bent. Try to resist your opponent's bending of your arm with all the strength you can muster. You'll find that you usually lose this contest easily, unless you are supernaturally strong. Even if you can hold it, you are exerting much more energy than is needed. This is because it is easy to bend an arm that is tense, because opposing muscles are being used.

The wrong way

Now practice the correct way. Extend your arm out, open your hand, and relax your whole body. Imagine your arm is a fire hose and that water is gushing forth from it and spraying the far wall across the room. Focus on this spot, and don't allow yourself to be distracted by what's on TV tonight. While you have this image in your mind, ask your training partner to try to bend the fire hose. It should be much more difficult to bend an arm in this fashion. This is because we are concentrating our minds outward, rather than toward ourselves; in doing so, we use the correct muscles and connective tissue to hold this position with very little effort. Once you've mastered this technique, you won't flinch nor have any muscle tremor in your arm; your opponents will think that they're trying to bend a statue of solid stone.

The correct way

If your angle is right, all you need to do is hold out your arm in unbendable-arm position and you can block any punch or kick. The caveat is that you have to have the proper angle. With enough experience, you can feel these angles instantaneously. Practice this until you are confident that your unbendable arm alone could protect you when you need it to.

What I like to do is have my partner punch me in the face using a hooking, or haymaker, style of punch. This is how many inexperienced people punch, and so I like to use this for clear demonstrations. I will stand there and wait for the punch to come in, and then I will raise both of my arms up in the air and say, "I don't want to fight!" In this position, I have successfully blocked the blow using unbendable arm. To the casual observer, it does not look as though I have used martial arts at all. Next, I will drop the hand that I blocked with into my opponent's arm, causing his weight to shift to that side. Then I can step in, and then use my other, outstretched arm to come crashing down behind my partner, throwing him or her to the ground.

This whole sequence looks like I'm bringing my arms up and then down again. Actually I am both blocking and throwing my partner. People watching only saw me raise my arms in defense, and then see what looks like my attacker tripping. This is very useful for disguising our arts, especially from bystanders. We do not want to look like the bad guy in an altercation; we want to appear like the victim.

Yes, one could accomplish the same thing by taking a fighting stance, plowing the attacker in the face, and sending him or her crashing down to the floor. This, however, could make you look like the attacker. Witnesses may see the encounter thusly: "That guy over there (they point at you) took a martial arts stance, then punched the other guy in the face and his face exploded."

I prefer to look like the good guy (which I am). I prefer to do the impossible. But we must plan for this in advance and make our arts look innocent to the uninitiated. Unbendable arm can easily dupe the uninitiated into thinking the block was merely an accident.

When I was still a junior instructor, I once sparred with a novice who had the habit of keeping her guard exceptionally low. To illustrate how open she was to attack, I would tap her on the forehead. Oddly, she didn't think this was a problem. So the next time I did it, I used unbendable arm; I wanted my hand to come in front of her eyes so that she could see that I could strike her face at will. She didn't see my hand and ran straight into it, and her nose broke as a result. What is worse is that once it healed, we did the exact same thing, and I broke her nose a second time. I was amazed at how little effort and how little power I placed in this position, and yet it was enough to snap her nose. I felt like I was lightly touching her, not striking. When you use your entire body to facilitate unbendable arm, it becomes a formidable weapon that can be used for striking or blocking. Now when I do this, I make sure to target my opponent's forehead so I don't break any noses.

Breaking Your Opponent's Physical Structure

Like I've said before, blocking an attack is easy. I can teach an old woman how to block a punch, but blocking the punch alone will not stop the aggression. If you block an attack without breaking your partner's balance, then he or she can simply hit you again with the other hand, or the same hand, or even a foot.

Many mainstream dojo will have you block an opponent and not unbalance or disrupt him or her in any way. The result now becomes a contest of who is faster at delivering the second technique. You can counter, or your opponent can counter. This situation is not ideal, because even the best-case scenario gives you only a fifty-fifty chance of success. This type of blocking is often seen in kung fu movies where there are series of attacks and blocks, the fights taking a long time to find a resolution. I admit I love a good kung fu movie, but this style of blocking is very dangerous in real situations. You may block ten attacks, only to be hit by the eleventh. Instead, work to unbalance your opponent with your block, because once unbalanced, your opponent has little hope of landing a good blow.

A good block should also unbalance your opponent the same moment the attack is thwarted. In overt ways, this can be a push, and ideally your push will spin your opponent to face the other direction. At this juncture, counterattacks to the back of your opponent's head, groin, or kidneys are easy.

Four Easy Ways to Break Your Opponent's Balance

First, face your opponent with your left leg forward (or right leg forward if you are left-handed). Stand a distance away so that your opponent must step in to hit you. Close-quarters fighting is a different skill set, and will be discussed later. Typically if you are close enough to strike one another, there is no such thing as blocking an attack. If you feel as though your opponent wishes to do you harm, strike him or her the very moment you feel that intention. Waiting for an attack at close quarters will inevitably mean that you will be late and subsequently be struck by the attack.

This is why for basic practice, we have our opponent step in and punch. This means your opponent has to cross the distance to you so that you can employ strategies other than counterattacking the moment you sense an aggression.

From a Low Punch

Your partner steps forward and punches to the stomach. Block using *gedan barai* (downward-sweeping block), and make sure to not only block the blow, but to lead your opponent off-line. Strike your opponent near the crook of the elbow, and while blocking, do not move your body, just the blocking arm. If your stance is solid, your opponent will be slightly off-line. From this position, your opponent cannot deliver full-power blows. If you find you are shifting your weight or moving backward, this means you are not confident that your block will work. Moving backward will tell your opponent that you are afraid and will actually bestow more power to him or her. Stand your ground! Train yourself to not move when being attacked. Especially in the beginning of your training, you do not want the habit of moving when attacked. Advanced training can have you move off-line, back, or even toward an attack, but when you first start, make sure you don't have to move at all. This will give you all the confidence you need to know that your blocks are sound and that you can break your opponent's balance any time you choose.

We start out with a low punch at first because it is the safest. A hard body shot can make a novice double over for a few minutes, but there is unlikely to be any permanent injury. Get proficient by having people punch you to the stomach before you insist on blocking attacks to the head or groin area. Bad experiences with these target areas may give you a premature flinch when someone comes to punch or kick you. We want to develop the immovable mind.

The wrong way

The correct way

Middle-Area Punch

Once you have a strong understanding of how to unbalance your opponent from a low-line attack, graduate to a middle-area attack (solar plexus). You partner steps in and punches to your chest. Parry the block with a soft palm block with your left hand. Block uchi uke with your right hand as you take a step forward. Do not push with your arms, but rather use your legs to affect your opponent's balance. Think of this block as though you have a sword and shield. You parry the blow with your sword, and then use your shield to push your opponent back and away from you. Make sure to keep your opponent in range of your fists so that you can deal with a counterattack. Pushing alone may resolve one attack, but you will not be in a position to deliver any counterattack.

High Punch

I would suggest only practicing high-line punch defenses when you are confident that you are not moving from low- or middle-area attacks. Novices often develop a flinch reflex from practicing punch defenses to the face too soon.

Have your partner step in and punch to your face. Use a soft palm block to deflect the attack without moving your body; punch upward like an uppercut with your other hand; then step in and do a high rising block, making sure again to use your legs and not your arms. This will uproot your opponent and put his or her weapons (hands and feet) pointing in the opposite direction. Using this style of block will let you completely eliminate the threat, not just eliminate the one attack. This is exactly what the art of kushin tells us.

This can be performed either on the inside (uchi uke) or the outside (soto uke). If you choose the inside, I would recommend striking underneath your opponent's jaw and pushing him or her backward in the process. You can almost ignore the attacking arm for this type of block. For soto uke, you will not be able to reach your opponent's face because his or her arm will be in the way; however, push through the arm to the face, forcing your opponent to move backward and consequently break his or her balance.

The wrong way. This blocks the attack, but doesn't prevent further attacks.

The correct way. This blocks the attack and makes your opponent off-balance and unable to attack right away.

Front Kick

Being kicked can be alarming and unnerving to the novice. But always keep in mind that in order for your opponent to kick you, he or she must be on one foot and by definition has then already lost balance. We only have to deflect the opponent's power a small bit to affect his or her posture and position. Imagine someone with a bow and arrow, and as the archer fires, you poke the hand holding the arrow. A small poke will make that arrow deviate a significant amount downrange, and the archer will miss the target. This is the same principle we will use with kicks.

Your partner should kick to your solar plexus. Use gedan barai on the inside or outside of his or her shin. Be warned, this is a painful technique and can rupture blood vessels in the calf very easily. I would advise to do this slowly so no permanent injury occurs. When blocking low, do not move your body; simply move your arm in a downward swing. Catch your opponent on the calf and send a shock wave through it. If done well, your opponent will not be able to place weight on that foot for a few minutes. Be mindful not to overdo it; after all, your opponent gets to practice this next. This block will also cause your opponent to lose balance (he or she is on one leg, after all) and will fall in whichever direction you lead him or her in.

These are only four basic examples of how to break your partner's balance while blocking. This should therefore be seen as only the tip of the iceberg of understanding. All of your blocks should be capable of taking away your opponent's ability to fight. Experiment with your blocks to find how to rob your opponent's balance every time, and the fight is halfway over.

When we break our opponent's balance, we usually want to do it in such a way that he or she does not realize that his or her position has been compromised. Sometimes too hard of a push will send your opponent farther away from you. In this situation, you cannot do a counterattack. A master will be able to block a punch; and you will *think* that you can punch again, but your weight will be on your heels and your punch will be no more useful than a slap with a wet blanket. Or you may be completely out of range and not know it. Your punch may land, but it may feel like a light spring breeze to a master.

Other Impossible Blocks

All the blocks mentioned above are very standardized blocks, and after you have spent some time in martial arts, these secrets will be revealed to you. So these techniques are not truly impossible. However, they are often misunderstood and misused, and that is why I felt it was necessary that they receive a solid explanation. True impossible blocks look like they should not work at all. They look fake when you see them done by masters, and you really need to experience these things if you want to become a true believer. After my sensei repeatedly demonstrated these arts, I was completely blown away. I felt as though I had wasted a lifetime worrying about being hit, when in fact, there was never any reason to worry about being hit at all.

Impossible Marionette Block

To demonstrate how easy it is to absorb a punch with minimal effort using my hands, I will bring my hands up and down as though they have strings attached to the backs of them, like a marionette. Then I will stand in one place and ask someone to repeatedly punch me in the chest. Using this puppeteer technique, I can lay my forearms upon my opponent's punching arms and take away his or her power with barely a touch. You don't need to smack the person hard. You don't need to jump out of the way. Simply touching is enough. We want to relax and melt into our opponent as if he or she were not even there. We accept the attack, but we do not panic; we simply touch our opponent and remove the power from the strike. This can be practiced with punches to the face too; however, mistakes mean you will get struck in the head. Primary practice should always be to the body when first learning this technique, to avoid injury.

The psychological effect that this block has on your opponent is enormous. This block looks lame, and one wouldn't think that it has any hope of working. When it does work, it makes your opponent question his or her technique and ability to beat you. This often causes your opponent to tense up and try harder, which actually makes punches easier to block; subsequent punches become even more futile. This robs your opponent of mental power, as well as physical power. You have clearly demonstrated that his or her punches have zero effect.

This block is mostly used to prove you can destroy your opponent's confidence by doing almost nothing. What this block does not do is it does not break your opponent's balance. This type of block is used for demoralization purposes, not for setting your opponent up for a throw or counterattack.

Breath Block

As mentioned earlier, it is possible to block by using your breath. In this method, as you are punched to the face, rapidly inhale through your nose. Use the power of your breath to move your entire head in the appropriate direction. If the punch is coming straight in toward your face, first move back several inches and then roll your face around the incoming fist to the outside of the attack. Sadly, the only way I have found to practice this is to actually get punched in the face. However, to minimize the damage, ask your partner to punch you in the forehead so you don't break anything. Follow the direction of the punch, that is backward, and then roll your head so that it is on the outside of his or her arm at the end of the punch. Use your rapid inhalation to facilitate this movement. Just like we move the hand first in other blocks, you inhale first with this sort of block. If your partner is punching with the right hand, your head should be on his or her right. When employed correctly, you only need correct timing to pull this off.

This technique is not my go-to block, but consider for a moment if your hands were restrained, stuck in your pockets, or even bound. If you have no hands to block with, what are you going to use? Use the breath block.

One-Finger Block

The one-finger block is very much like ryu sui, a soft block. Ask your partner to punch you in the solar plexus. As your partner extends to strike you, reach out toward his or her arm as if you were going to swiftly point to the shoulder. In the beginning, I would suggest using an open hand to point rather than a single finger. If you apply this incorrectly, you may inadvertently break a finger. Point with your open hand to the shoulder of your opponent's punching arm, and then point to your own center. The movement is basically a "come here" sort of gesture. You brush your opponent's arm gently on the top, but make no effort to stop the attack from happening. In fact, encourage the attack to happen. This is a confusing sensation, and the punch will have less power. The punch may still hit you, but the power will be dramatically reduced. By practicing correct posture, you can safely absorb the power of the punch anyway.

The one-finger block is mostly a parlor trick that I use to demonstrate how easy it is to block. Mastery of such a block can build your confidence, knowing you can block anything with just one finger. I would advise, however, not to practice this too early in your martial arts training. Perhaps try this after four or more years of experience so that you do not accidentally break a finger.

Help-Your-Opponent-Punch-You Block

To demonstrate how easy it is to block, I will sometimes ask a black belt to try to punch me to the chest. I will then grab my opponent's punching arm with two hands (one arm near his or her upper arm, one near my opponent's wrist as if holding a sword). While the punch is still in motion, I will force the punch into my stomach, solar plexus, or sternum. By helping your opponent to attack you, all of the power will be transmuted and be completely ineffective. You are controlling the vibration, and so no vibration will come to you. Both of your hands should come down on the arm as your opponent punches. This action mimics the Japanese style of sword stroke called shomen uchi (downward cut). You can choose to arrest the punch early so it does not hit you, but I like to force my opponent's fist into my chest to emphasize that I have stolen its power.

Stealing your opponents' power often makes them feel as if they have no hope of defeating you, and the chances that they give up trying increase. A gun is not as useful if there are no bullets. But stealing power is even worse than being out of ammunition. It is like disassembling the gun too. Create a sense of hopelessness in your opponent, and he or she will then be more likely to begin to think about exit strategies rather than continue in futile effort.

Swinging-Arm Block

With the swinging-arm block, start by having your arms by your sides, and have your left foot slightly forward. Swing your left arm upward so that it crosses your centerline. When you swing your arm up, make sure to have the palm facing down. You do not need to make a fist; rather, "dead arm" it so your arm does not go higher than chest height. Swing your hips slightly to encourage your arm to swing upward. This should look like a rather lame dance move. Then ask your partner to punch you straight to the chest or kick you to the chest. Use the swinging-arm block to deflect the blow. Your arm should contact on the side of his or her arm or leg.

Sometimes when I perform this block, I will move my back leg so that it looks like I'm standing on a tightrope the moment I contact the leg or the arm. This block is very useful if you happen to have your hands in your pockets and are unable to free them the moment you are attacked. You don't need to take your hands out of your pockets, and you don't need to swing your wrist up. You can use the power of your swinging elbow and the movement of your feet to effectively block without your hands. When employed in this manner, this technique looks like a chicken wing.

Belly Block

The belly block works rather well if you in fact have a nice beer belly; however, it can still be performed if you don't have one. I once knew a very fat instructor who would employ the belly block shamelessly. If you punched at him, he would move in and belly smash you. If you kicked him, he would move in and belly smash you. The result was that you could never quite reach his head because his belly stuck out so far. He consistently knocked me down to the ground using this technique. I wouldn't recommend adding pounds just to try this out, but if this is your body type, you may want to try this exercise and add it to your arts.

The belly block can be used in one of two methods. The first is like the story above: simply move in and push with your belly. The other method requires a bit more discipline and timing. Ask your partner to strike you to the chest. As the punch comes out, make your chest and belly bow outward toward your opponent, and as it comes in, have your whole body recoil in a concave manner, as if your body were a glove catching a ball. If you time this block correctly, your opponent thinks he or she is going to strike something, when in fact you remove the target in an odd and surprising manner. The first time my karate sensei did this to me, I hit absolutely nothing. This should be used as a surprise technique only, as your opponent can pick up on the trick soon afterward.

Thrusting Chest Block

The thrusting chest block is similar to the belly block, but it does not have a one-two action in its movement. It is sometimes possible to absorb a punch or a kick by moving violently into it. Start with your hands at your side and face your opponent. Have your opponent punch or kick you in the chest. As the technique is underway, slide in with your front foot. As you do this, bring both hands upon your hips in fists as if you were elbowing someone behind you (a type of karate ready position). At this moment, thrust your entire chest out to meet the punch. If your timing is correct, you can cut off your opponent's strike and render it useless. To the attacker, it feels as though there is not enough weight behind the punch, and he or she will feel his or her shoulder come up. Your attacker's arm will simply become a flattened accordion. Your opponent's power is driven back through his or her shoulder and out behind him or her, rather than through you.

Keep in mind that a punch to the face will still hit you, and this is not an ideal block should someone be punching you in the head. I prefer a variation of this technique, which has you keeping your arms up to protect your head, while leaving your chest open to invite your opponent to strike you there.

Impossible Hook Block

There is a type of hook block I've seen my sensei perform from a seated position. He will raise one hand up, like one would do when asking a question in class, and then he will bring his open hand down several inches, like a hook block. That is, he bends his hand at the wrist in the direction of the thumb and pinky finger, pointing downward to the ground with all of his fingers. At the same time, he bows slightly. The movement looks as though you have a puppet in one hand and you and the puppet bow at the exact same time. The block is performed very close to the body and it doesn't look like it would work at all, but the result is that your entire body weight is placed upon your hand the moment you go to block. This is a short and very hard block, which can be quite painful to your opponent.

You could use this block if your hands were oddly occupied or if you were very late in seeing an attack. Because the movement for this block is small, a woman could do this with a purse slung by her elbow. If done right, the purse won't move. If you are sitting down and you are attacked, you can use this block without getting out of your chair, and with minimal movement so you don't accidentally smash yourself on foreign objects, like a table or a bar.

Impossible Thigh Block

I once kicked an Okinawa master in the thigh with a shin kick. I had to stop immediately because my shin felt like it had split in two! I put my foot back down on the ground and my teacher explained exactly what he did, but at that time I didn't hear a word because I thought he had broken my leg. As it turned out, it was just severe pain, but once that subsided, I was able to ask him what he had done.

It is possible to absorb a full-power shin kick to your outer thigh by correctly placing your weight on that supporting leg. If you are standing with your left foot forward, square to your opponent who is kicking you in the left leg, and then shift your weight into the attack. If your left leg doesn't have enough weight on it, you will take the power of the kick in a bad way. The idea is to form a solid structure so your opponent feels like he or she is kicking an oak tree. You must have confidence in this so that it can work. By backing away from the kick, you will receive the power and possibly an injury.

Use this block if you are unable to move away from a fast kicker, or unable to move forward due to obstacles or other people. Decide you are going to take the blow, and decide that your thigh will crush your opponent's shin. It should feel like a shoulder tackle, but done with the thigh instead of the shoulder.

Impossible Punch Block

The punch block is a punch executed to strike your opponent's arm or leg directly, or to strike near the arm or leg and use it like a wedge to block an attack. As your opponent kicks or punches, you can punch his or her attack. Be warned, this is not a soft technique and often results in painful bruises or worse. I would recommend punching your opponent's shoulder for contact practice.

The X block is another example of a punch block and best performed on front kicks. Often misunderstood, the X block is typically performed incorrectly. Most people block with both hands at the same time in an X position. This may block an attack, but does nothing to your opponent, and now you have tied up two hands on one of your opponent's limbs, leaving you in a vulnerable position. The X block is a downward block followed by a straight punch. The end result is that it looks like an X block, but really, it is block and punch. Against a kick, this has devastating effects, as your opponent will be struck twice in the exact same place.

All of these impossible blocks are performed in a nonchalant manner. You shouldn't have to exert excessive force to produce spectacular results. If you are grunting or forcing a block, you are using far too much energy, and you are not placing your body weight in the correct position. You need to have your weight cascade through your opponent. In this manner, you can cause a lot of damage, as well as unbalance your partner.

The standard repertoire of high, mid, and low blocks are only stepping-stones to the powerful blocks that we can achieve with a mastery mind-set. As you can see, there are a multitude of other blocks and blocking principles that you can employ in unique ways to produce spectacular results. It takes practice to refine these impossible blocks, but with confidence, you will surprise yourself with their effectiveness.

Relaxed Power

Understanding how to relax your body is the key to successfully delivering powerful punches, kicks, blocks, throws, and grapples. To the uninitiated, relaxed power is an oxymoron and seems impossible. If you slap someone with arms that are like wet noodles, you will not have much of an effect. This is not the type of relaxation I am talking about. For example, if you tense up your hands by splaying your fingers wide and then shake your wrists, your fingers will not move much. If you relax your fingers and shake your wrists, your fingers will move rapidly. Relaxation means that we should not be overly tense in the execution of a technique prior to actual contact. For a punch, we must have the same light and fast feeling while the punch is midswing as when we just shook our wrists. This will allow us to react quickly. Tensing up and forcing a punch out will slow it down considerably.

Relaxation in martial arts doesn't come from lying on a hammock in the sun sipping mai tais, nor in feeling like a pile of Jell-O in bed after a hard workout. It comes from a calmness of mind that makes your body relaxed, but ready. It is a state of mind where our breathing is deep but does not overwhelm us. Don't scrunch your face up in pain or concentration, but instead, make your body limber and able to move without hesitation. Once mastered, your techniques should look nonchalant and easy, but will hold massive amounts of power.

To study relaxed power, we must critically look at how we hold our bodies in our daily lives, especially in regard to our posture. If you sit at a desk for a living, you may very well get a lot of headaches if you unconsciously raise your shoulders to your ears. Tension doesn't have to show that dramatically, but if there is tension in your shoulders, you will be more prone to headaches. Pay attention to all parts of your body. Are you clenching your fists for no reason? Are you gritting your teeth? When you feel these things happen throughout the day, make a conscious effort to let things go. Once you can let these subtle tensions release, you will notice that the power of your punches will triple or even quadruple in strength.

If you are truly centered, you are already relaxed. You cannot tell yourself you are centered when you scrunch your face up and raise your shoulders to your ears. Developing this relaxed state in daily life has many side benefits outside the realm of martial arts. For one thing, it promotes better circulation and stronger health, because we alleviate anxiety that manifests in our bodies. By being centered, we will become more aware of our surroundings and our interactions with people. When we are relaxed and calm, we always make the best decisions in our life. If we are filled with anxiety, worry, fear, tension, or anger, then we can make horrible life choices that have long-lasting effects. Studying relaxed power, then, has huge benefits to our lives. The challenge is demonstrating that one is relaxed. For example, someone might ask how you're doing, and you'll simply say "fine" back. We may not be fine, but we may say we are, for whatever reason.

Do you know if you are relaxed or not? Are you tense in the shoulders? Do you hunch over your desk or grip the steering wheel of your car harder than you need to? What about when you practice martial arts? Are you using relaxed power, or are you tensing up more than you need to?

Relaxed Striking

Relaxed power is useful in developing solid throwing arts, grappling arts, and weapon arts, which will be discussed in a later chapter; however, the easiest and most dramatic way to apply relaxed power in martial arts is through striking.

To understand relaxed striking, we will examine the punch. A normal karate punch travels from point A to point B in a straight line without taking detours. We can create more power by relaxing particularly before and during the execution of the punch. Only at the end of the punch do we create a focused effort by utilizing the correct muscles (the pectoral muscles and the latissimus dorsi).

The magnitude of power generated by a relaxed state moving to a focused state is infinitely greater than the magnitude of power generated from a tense state to a focused state. This means we should start our punches from a relaxed state, then launch our punch and focus upon impact. If we start our punch by squeezing our muscles prematurely, this will slow down our punch and will not create sufficient shock in our opponent. Tensing up in the beginning of our punch ruins our power development. Oddly, we might feel stronger if we tense up in the beginning of our punch, but tensing up prematurely has the exact opposite effect.

What we are seeking to do is create a massive difference between being relaxed and being focused. This relaxed state in comparison to the focused state is the key to developing impossible power. The difference between being tense before a punch and being tenser at the end of the punch is finite in nature, and does not build impossible power.

Even if you have Popeye forearms and can hit well enough not using relaxed power, you will not have those guns forever. Over the decades, your muscles will wither away, and you will be robbed of strength and speed. But through the same amount of years, we gain awareness, wisdom, and timing. The root of true power is the mind, not just the body alone. That is why it is imperative to learn how to relax prior to striking.

It can sometimes be difficult to know if you are relaxed or not. And so here are a few tricks. If you are standing or sitting, ask yourself to relax your shoulders. Often there will be a half inch of letting go. This means you were tensing up your shoulders needlessly and probably didn't know it. Now, bring your shoulders up to your ears, and then gently lower your shoulders naturally. Repeat this as necessary.

Your leg muscles and core are working to stabilize your body so you do not fall over; relaxing the legs while standing is challenging for this reason. However, you can minimize how much leg power you are using by trying the following technique. Stand with your feet shoulder-width apart. Come up on your toes and then lower your heels until they just touch the floor. Do not put excessive weight on your heels. Feel your feet melt into the floor, as if they were balls of clay that were thrown to the ground.

If you are having difficulty understanding relaxed power or if you are not seeing any changes in your punching performance, I suggest tiring yourself out before your next practice. Give yourself a workout so that you want to collapse and do nothing. At this point, do some more push-ups, jumping jacks, or whatever to reach complete and total exhaustion. You should feel weak and useless; this is the point. Make sure you feel good and weak; if you don't, lift more weights or do more push-ups until you can barely move. At this point, get up and practice punching. Use a partner, and punch him or her in the solar plexus (your partner should know how to absorb the power). Because you have nothing left to fight with, the only thing you have is your structure and the power of relaxation. Take a good stance and punch. Often you will notice that your power is oddly increased, even though your muscles are exhausted. This is relaxed power in action. Your body is using only the muscles necessary to achieve the punch; it is ignoring commands to other extraneous muscle sets. Listen to your body, and it will teach you which muscles to use and which to ignore.

To have relaxed power in a punch, start with zero power. That is, you are relaxed and not moving your hand to punch. You are not tensing your body or coiling to strike; you are simply at rest. In this position, your speed and your power are zero. When we punch, we do not want to think of our fist as having to accelerate like a car. We want our fist to be instantly traveling one hundred miles per hour when we decide to strike, without it needing to have distance and time to speed up.

Initiate your punch while relaxed and maintain that mind-set while moving your hand to the opponent. Then, focus on the impact to create an infinite increase of power. The difference between the relaxed state before the punch and the focused-muscle tension upon contact will exponentially increase your punching-power output. There are always muscles at work (we have to use our muscles to stand, for example), and so this starting relaxed number isn't exactly zero; however, in your mind it can be. In your mind, you start with zero and explode to a one or more upon impact. The shock created inside your opponent can have devastating results.

Sometimes I punch with an open fist to ensure that my arm is relaxed. Other times I form my fist as it contacts my opponent. This increases the shock wave inside of him or her. Pay special attention not to push your opponent. I want my opponent to drop, not move away from me. If you are seeing your opponent move away from you a lot, this means your punch or kick is too much of a push and requires more shock wave to the strike.

Experiment with punching with your arms at your sides, so that the hand comes upward in an arc toward the heart. This type of punch can be difficult to see, and as a result, difficult to block. If you do this in a relaxed manner, you won't trigger your opponent's defenses, and the attack will go through. Be warned, though: producing shock through to the heart can have traumatic effects. I once punched a senior black belt in this manner, and he had to remove himself from class for a good forty-five minutes. It looked to me as though he were slipping into shock, and I made sure to pay close attention to him so that his condition did not deteriorate. Do not underestimate vibrations to internal organs, as these forces can have devastating effects on some people. Always punch each other with minimal use of force, and dial up your training only if your partner is capable of receiving more. Never punch harder than your training partner can handle. Be safe, so that you can practice more.

An easy way for beginners to learn how to strike well is by practicing a slap. Have a training partner hold out a focus mitt at head level. Then slap the pad without any instruction. Most beginners will slap lightly, and the pad will barely move. To begin your relaxed power slap, raise both hands with your palms facing outward. This position should look like you are being held up at gunpoint. With your weight slightly forward, slap the focus mitt using the heel of your hand. Your hand will naturally orient itself to the mitt on contact. A good slap should be able to knock an opponent unconscious, especially if the jaw is struck. Use your entire body and shift your weight into the direction of the strike slightly. You should be able to notice a great amount of power with this slap if you use your whole body to do it at the precise moment of contact. Hopefully you will notice an amazing difference between these strikes—the one where you just use your hand and the other where you employ your whole body in a relaxed manner.

My discovery of relaxed power came from aikido, which uses relaxation as one of its principles. In aikido, if you are using strength on any technique, you are doing it incorrectly. There was one time a student of mine was being stubborn and would not fall for his partner. I came over and did a light throw. He fell and hit his head and received a concussion. It didn't feel to me like I threw him hard, but for him, it was devastating. I used this idea in my karate training and began to see amazing results with my striking arts. In fact, I accidentally knocked a few of my students unconscious by punching more relaxed (they were unconscious only for a few seconds).

We should strive to make our punches, kicks, throws, and grapples utilize relaxed power, which will not only be more powerful, but also more efficient. Relaxed throws do not look like martial arts, and do not trigger a fight response from your opponent. The result is that your opponent is thrown before knowing there is a problem. Relaxed punches sometimes seem so slow or useless that people don't bother to block them. Then you send your opponent to the floor, with the power reverberating through your fist. The concept of relaxed technique is so critical and so essential to mastery that it should be embedded into everything that you do. Practice relaxing while not in the dojo. Make sure your shoulders are relaxed when you are on the computer, and make sure your face isn't scrunched up when you drive. *Relaxed power is one of the biggest secrets in martial arts* and should not be taken idly. Relaxation might just be the piece of the puzzle that has been missing for you.

The Devastating Punch

Somewhere along the line, I became obsessed with possessing a devastating punch. I became transfixed with the idea of being able to stop a fight instantly with one, solid, overwhelmingly powerful hit. I pursued this right from the beginning of my training, but I got frustrated when none of my teachers could explain to me exactly how to do it. At that point, I had met people who could put me down with one hit, but they couldn't explain how they accomplished it. They may have been gifted martial artists, but they lacked the teaching ability to hand over that knowledge to someone else. One teacher I practiced with in my early years of study could wind me through a 150-pound heavy bag that I held for him while he hit it. When I would ask him how I could develop this sort of power, he kept telling me, "Just punch!" This advice did little to further my understanding of how to accomplish my goal, and so I was forced to look elsewhere for answers.

On the path to understanding the devastating punch, I was pulled by many forces. Many teachers insisted that their way was the right way. For example, I was told to twist my hips to generate power on a punch, and I obediently complied, not knowing what else to do. However, their way did not work for me, and I did not see the results that I wanted to see. It was only after personal experimentation that I began to realize that power did not come from the hips at all. Power came from where I placed my weight and had nothing to do with the twisting of my hips.

Using the twisting of the hips might work for some people, but typically moving one's hips in sync to adequately connect with your opponent becomes difficult. If your opponent moves even slightly, then your punch won't connect as well as it would have otherwise. How often are you fighting an opponent who isn't moving? Twisting the hips also requires chambering your hips for subsequent punches. That is, you have to cock your hips back in order to strike again, like a single-action revolver. This can be trained to be done quickly when you are young, but when you get older, this speed will fade dramatically and cannot be counted on. If you do not twist your hips, there is no need to chamber your hips, which makes subsequent strikes faster.

Avoid twisting the hips for most punching and kicking styles, as it adds little to power generation and can actually hold you back from creating real power. Now, this is a harsh criticism of many styles that use this technique, but I myself used it for many years. I have since abandoned this practice after meeting my Okinawa teachers, who do not use hips at all in their techniques. It was explained to me by my teachers that twisting the hips was created as a method to avoid hurting your opponent. It was likely designed for tournaments, so that fighting could be practiced safely with no grievous injuries. I do not know if this is true or not; I just know the results I found once I abandoned the hip-power theory: my punching power increased fivefold after only three months of adopting the new system, or more accurately, the old way of doing karate.

Transferring power through the fist, elbow, foot, or whatever is a skill that can be taught to anyone wishing to know its secrets. Transferring power operates much the same way that dissipating power does. We must create a shock wave that penetrates through our opponent's center. Striking off-center can cause power loss since your opponent will spin more rather than take the brunt of your attack. Just as we used the image of the pebble being dropped into the pond for the dissipation of power, we can use the same image for creating this shock in others.

Placement of Weight

An important concept to understand about how to do the impossible while punching (or kicking, for that matter) is where to place your weight. If your weight is on your heels when you stand, and you push someone, you are likely to move backward. In this sort of collision, both parties can move. Moving backward while striking means that at least 50 percent of your power is going the wrong way. To compensate for this power loss, I practiced on the balls of my feet for years, thinking this to be the best way to be forward. While this can be true, this can lead to chronic injuries in the knees due to the carrying angle of your leg. I would not recommend placing your weight on the balls of your feet. Nor would I recommend bouncing up and down, ever. Having your heels off the ground will produce exceptionally weak punches and kicks and makes you horribly vulnerable to leg sweeps and other throws. Bouncing up and down is a clear sign people have absolutely no idea how to generate power. This type of practice is often used in sparring so that participants do not injure one another, and for that point it can be valuable, but for real martial arts it should be completely avoided.

So where should we place our weight? Place your weight in the center of your foot. Your feet should feel like a slab of clay that is suddenly dropped to the floor. The clay splatters down, does not bounce, and uses all of the available surface area. When you punch someone using this method of standing, the power goes through your opponent, and you do not move back.

Next is where we place our punch's focal point. A devastating punch's focal point needs to be inside our opponent, not on the surface. Punching to the surface of an opponent will only cause minor bruising at best, and will not disrupt internal organs or break bones. You must be close enough to have your focal point inside of your opponent. It is not that our hands are inside our opponent; our center of gravity is in our opponent. To understand where your center of gravity is, try standing tall, and pay attention to the area near your navel. If you bend over to tie your shoes, this point then moves and becomes the center of the donut shape your body makes. This center then is no longer inside of your body, but outside of it. By having our weight leaning forward, our center of gravity can go inside another person's space. Many martial artists stand too far away, and consequently put their punch's focal point on the outside of their opponent. To find a better distance, place your fist on your opponent's chest at a point where your elbow is still slightly bent; this gives you a lot more room to punch your target.

Once your focal point is inside your opponent, all you have to do is match a body part to that point. If your weight is back, behind you, or to one side, you will not maximize your power. Likewise, if you twist away from the focal point by moving your hips, you will also miss the focal point. Instead of rotating your hips to produce power, feel power develop by stretching your connective tissue. That is, rotate your torso by using your back muscles and keep your hips locked so they do not move at all. See the "Projecting Power" chapter for more information on these concepts.

Developing Devastation

The punch I just described is the signature punch of naifanchi (shurite) and sanchin (nahate) karate. Tomarite and other styles utilize different body mechanics for generating power. I understand shurite and nahate styles the best; my bias should be clear. I don't have as much experience in kung fu as I do in karate, but the kung fu masters that I've met had no problem generating power in their strikes. They just had a different way of getting to the same place. Many of the kung fu teachers that I met described their power, or chi, as cyclical in nature. Karate imagery is typically linear in nature, that is, power is traveling from point A to point B; however, karate came from kung fu, so there are some similarities. Generally speaking, I prefer a more linear approach to power development, where the connection from the ground out through your fist forms one line.

After my experiences with different art styles, I find that martial arts systems are mostly a matter of personal choice. I prefer the Japanese aesthetic; some people prefer the Chinese aesthetic. It makes no difference really, as good martial arts are good martial arts. Likewise, you might be trained by the best in the world in a particular style, but if your heart and mind are not into it, you will not magically become awesome. Getting better is the responsibility of the student, so if you want a better punch, then always leverage the wisdom of others who can demonstrate that ability. Mastery comes from pursuing the mastery mind-set, not from simply being around masters.

For practice, punch to the body rather than the head. This will do two things. One, it will teach you how to take punches to the body, and secondly, it will keep your brain intact. Understand that the power you are developing can easily be used on the head should you choose to, but in class, no one wants shattered teeth, a broken nose, or an exploded eye orbit. Bruises to the body heal nicely and go unseen. Most people have jobs in real life, and so not many of us want to go to work with black eyes. We all know punches to the face work, so there is no need to take full-power punches to the face. Take them to the body and learn how to absorb power. You may still punch to the face, of course; just get out of the way, block it, or otherwise deal with it in such a way that the vibration isn't rattling your skull. I've seen my sensei roll his head while getting struck in the face, and it looked almost comical, but he took no damage to his face at all. I don't recommend this practice for the novice or even intermediate student.

Beginners should first learn to punch one another straight into the solar plexus. If one shuts off his or her solar plexus correctly, all of the power of the punch will be absorbed. Dial up this power on a case-by-case basis. If your training partner can only take a 2 percent punch, do not take it any further. Hurting people needlessly is useless for training and mean-spirited. Build up your confidence slowly. You do not have to learn everything in one day; learn the basic tools and work to improve upon them.

Once you're comfortable with the power level, focus on punching to your opponent's center. A strike to the center of the body creates more devastating results. Punches that are off-center tend to spin or rotate your opponent, and as a result, do not cause as much shock to penetrate through. By practicing punching straight to the center, we can develop two things. First, we are developing a strong focal point. Second, as the receiver, we are practicing how to absorb this type of punch. It is easier to absorb power from something you know the direction of. Changing directions for beginners is not recommended. We do not want to jump to page twenty when we are still on page one.

Create a Shock Wave

If you tap on the side of a glass of water, you will see waves in the water. We want to develop a strike that can create this shock wave inside of our opponent. If you focus on merely hitting the target, your muscles will contract too soon, and then your shock wave starts outside of the target. This would be like putting your mouth close to the cup of water and shouting. The shout has energy to it and may cause a shock wave in the water. But the same wave is easier to make by simply tapping the glass.

The same thing happens in a punch if you prematurely create a shock wave before hitting the target. Your biggest wave of energy will only hit the surface of the target and not penetrate through. If you focus inside of the target, the largest wave will be created inside the body cavity, and therefore have a larger effect on internal organs. If no shock wave is created at all, you will simply push the target with your fist. While this may still hurt or cause surface damage, it is insufficient to stop an aggressive opponent.

Imagine a large wave on a beach during a storm hitting a brick wall at low tide. The wave is your energy; the brick wall is your opponent's outer body. This wave crests, crashes onto the beach, and then travels slowly to the wall and then stops. This is exactly how we do not want to punch. Imagine the same beach and same violent storm at high tide. The wall is submerged, and the water has already reached onto the mainland. The large storm wave then crashes over the barricade. The shock wave begins once it has already passed the wall and not before it. This way, the shock wave causes more damage and more erosion because the wall is now meaningless. Images like this can help you use the power of your imagination to unlock the limitless power you have within you.

To begin practicing your devastating punch, lock your torso so that your entire upper body moves as one. This is a naifanchi-style punch, an easily demonstrated technique that possesses amazing power. Use your back so your upper body swings like a tank turret and your legs become like the treads of the tank. Only move the turret. Create the shock wave by feeling shock within yourself. If you rapidly twitch the muscles in your entire upper body, especially your pectoral muscles and your latisimus muscles, you will begin to see what I mean by shock. This explosive contraction can be used to create a rippling effect inside our opponent. This muscle twitch needs to occur only upon impact. This is not a sustained squeezing of the muscles, but a rapid squeeze and release. This can even be done by squeezing the hand into a fist when contact to the target is made.

Remember: impact, then shock; not shock, then impact. The fist will contact your opponent, and the tissue will move back. At that moment, create the shock wave so it can travel inside of your opponent. I used to punch "through" my opponent, but this image leads people to push their opponent with their fist, which creates a weaker punch. Instead, create a shock wave inside of your opponent; do not push him or her with your fist.

To create the shock wave, you must first believe you can do it. You must first have the confidence that can support such a concept, or you will be doomed to fail repeatedly. Do not allow past or current results dictate what will happen in the future. Learning this punching technique can take a lot of discipline and practice, so do not allow the potential of hurt wrists or bloody knuckles to prevent you from trying this out. Focus on the image of creating this shock wave. This is an absolutely essential step in developing internal power, and it should not be neglected. "Just punch," like my earlier teacher told me, will produce the same results you are getting now.

A good punch will take someone out for at least twenty minutes. He or she may retain consciousness, but will have lost the ability to fight for that duration. You will know what I mean if you have ever been punched in this fashion. Failure to instill this effect means that you are not generating a proper shock wave.

Practice this by using phone books wrapped in duct tape. One partner carefully holds the edges of the book firmly against his or her solar plexus. The other partner now punches the book, using the naifanchi-style punch. This type of practice gives you an excellent way of experiencing this punch so that no one will receive significant injury. If necessary, use two or three phone books. Avoid using pads on your hands or as body armor, as foam has an absorption property to it that weakens this shock wave to a certain extent. Only by punching flesh can you understand how to better punch flesh. Foam hand protection numbs this sensation and makes it difficult to discern between a good punch and a better punch, which can thus produce some sloppy habits. You need to feel the vibration to generate this feeling more consistently. You also need to receive these waves to understand their power. Just intellectualizing this practice will not help you develop internal power. You must go into the pool in order to swim. Be warned, though, that you should dial this up slowly and with people who can take punches. Do not practice this on people with broken ribs, heart conditions, or breathing ailments.

Creating shock waves with techniques other than punches is very possible, though I find punching to be the easiest way to imagine and create this shock. If your knuckles are not capable of this type of impact, I suggest developing a palm strike. There are several ways to make a wave with a palm strike, but an efficient way is to use the flexing of the wrist to help create shock. If you raise your arm up, with your elbow down and your wrist bent toward the ground so that your thumb almost touches your wrist, you can then strike downward with surprising power. A good target would be the nose in real life, but for now, strike to the chest. Use the heel of your hand and flex the wrist back upon impact. Send the wave through.

Punch Bone on Bone

Punching "bone on bone" means that we recognize and harmonize with our skeletal structure when we hit. Recognizing our skeletal structure means that we can clearly see the path that impact reverberations can travel through. There should be a connection from your fist, through the bones in your hand, through the bones in your arm, through the bones in your chest, to the bones in your hips, to the bones in your legs, to the bones in your feet. This circuit is the grounding power to control vibrations you give to others. Imagine you have a spear, and you stick the butt of the spear into the ground; the tip of the spear, you point at a charging enemy. Your enemy runs into your spear and impales himself or herself. This power did not come from you; it came from the ground and didn't have anywhere to go but into your opponent. The only direction of power, then, is through the tip of the spear; this is how you should punch. If this circuit is not complete, or even if there is a weak link within it, you will bounce off the target. Your punch may still do some damage, but it will not be your maximum damage. I have one student in class who has hands that are as heavy as sledgehammers. The only thing currently holding him back from having a Godzilla power punch is that he disconnects his lower body when striking, thus eliminating a great deal of his power.

Pay attention to when your partner punches you and watch to see if he or she bounces off or not upon impact. This error can be fixed by seating the shoulders downward and squeezing the latissimus dorsi and pectorals major lightly. Do not engage the deltoid muscle, as this will not help your straight punch. Sometimes you will notice that your shoulder goes backward when punching. This may not be as dramatic as bouncing off the target, but some of your power is nevertheless going the wrong way. When you punch, you should complete the circuit from your foot to your fist. Remember the imagery of the spearman; your fist is the spear tip that stabs your opponent. If there is a loose link in this chain, your power will leak off in that area. If your elbow is weak, some power will backfire out of your elbow. If your hips are loose, your pelvis may rattle or move on the moment of impact, meaning that there is energy loss at your hips.

I often use an analogy of a lat pull-down machine you see at a gym. Stand in horse stance, pretend to use a lat pull-down machine, and engage your latissimus dorsi muscles. Then angle your arms down so that your fist is pointing at your opponent. Get in nice and close, and rotate your torso and lock your arms in their current position. This is essentially an unbendable arm position with both arms, just at another angle. By punching this way, you will not use the muscles in your arms; you will use the bone-on-bone connection necessary to make extreme power possible.

Punch Using Connective Tissue

One method of punching utilizes the connective tissue surrounding our muscles, rather than isolating chunks of muscle. To see what I mean by this, stand with your feet apart and then reach up high with your right arm without moving your hips. Now bring your arm down in a slapping sort of motion, swinging so that your right arm moves in front of you and then past your left side. The result is that you are stretching your back muscles from the tips of your right hand's fingers to the tips of the toes on your left foot. This sort of connection uses your entire body to effect a strike. Even if you weigh only a hundred pounds, punching correctly allows you to place that hundred-pound weight on your fist to create a devastating strike.

If you isolate muscles, such as the deltoid or bicep, you will disconnect the main line of the connective tissue, making your punch weaker. If your shoulders are up, power will go back out through your shoulders. If your bicep is engaged, your punch may have a spring effect to it and bounce off the target. When beginning to develop your devastating punch, it may be easier to punch with your elbow pointing downward. If your elbow flares to the side when punching, the power can go back out through your elbow and not enter the target at all. This isn't the only way to punch, but it can sometimes be easier to see the bone-on-bone connection.

Another exercise to see this in action is to stand in front of a partner with your feet shoulder-width apart. Punch at your partner so your fist lands at its maximum range just barely on the surface of your partner's uniform. Once you are satisfied that you are out of range, stretch your shoulders so that they go upward toward your ears, and then lower your shoulders all the way down. At the downmost extension of your shoulders, feel your shoulder blades pull apart, causing your upper back to be more rounded in appearance. Punch your partner again, and you will witness that you suddenly gain three inches to your punch by using the stretch of your back connective tissue.

Draw a line from the left hip to the right hand. Stretch using your back connective tissue; do not twist your hips.

Punching Styles

Many different styles of punching exist, but I will only detail the four that I employ because these I have found to be the most effective, not only for me but for the majority of people I teach. Though I believe a mental image of power generation is more important than this style or that style, it is still necessary to have a basic building block to work on. After you understand one or more methods of punching, you can let go of some of the rigid structures and make them your own. But only do this once you have a devastating punch.

There are three main branches of karate, named after Okinawa towns that were within walking distance of each other. Out of these three branches came a large number of styles that have one root, two roots, or roots in all three of these main branches. Nahate styles are characterized by short stances, powerful punches, and a slow, plodding, tanklike quality. Sanchin kata exemplifies this quality. Shurite styles are characterized by horse stance, faster footwork, and a rotation of the torso to generate power from a punch. The main kata that shows these traits is naifanchi. Tomarite was thought to be extinct, but there are a few people left who do indeed practice it. Tomarite is characterized by the kata sesan, and power is generated by sesan dachi. I have practiced extensively in shurite and nahate systems, but I only have a little bit of experience in tomarite.

I look at these three core styles in the following way:

- shurite: cavalry
- nahate: shield wall
- tomarite: spearman

This analogy is something I made up entirely, but it gives one the impression of the focus of each of these branches (keeping in mind I only have a light understanding of tomarite). Please also understand this is an oversimplification. All of the branches of karate share many basic fundamentals with one another, and so generalizations like this one can be misleading. For example, each branch of karate practices blocking, both soft (ryu sui) and hard (ra-ka). Other art forms may have similar ideas to these mentioned above, but I feel less qualified to talk about kung fu and jujitsu than I do about karate and aikido.

Shurite

I think of shurite as "cavalry" because of the horse stance. This stance is often misinterpreted as meaning you are fighting with your back against the wall. This is not so. Horse stance is most useful when your opponent is at a 45-degree angle to you. If you stand in horse stance with someone directly in front of you, with your legs spread wide-open, it doesn't take a genius to figure out he or she can kick you in the groin easily. If you use horse stance more like a front stance, you will see more options for your arts and more uses for this stance. A reverse punch from naifanchi dachi (horse stance) uses the torsion of the torso—not the hips—to generate power. By locking in the physical structure of your upper body, you can create devastating power by using your back muscles instead of your hips. It is my belief that this torso rotation was misinterpreted many decades ago as being a hip rotation.

Nahate

I think of nahate as a shield wall, or phalanx. The Japanese didn't employ shields like the Europeans did, but nahate stances have this tanklike quality to them. It's slower than shurite, but with the iron-shirt idea, it is well armored. You don't have to be fast in this stance, because this stance is ideal for absorbing power. You can stand there and allow your opponent to come to you. Nahate-style fighting is best suited for larger people or older practitioners of the arts. Its power is not based on speed and agility, but rather a calmness and smoothness of action. The nahate punch rolls the body weight forward, like a bowling ball. This forward rolling should be almost imperceptible. This doesn't mean nahate practitioners are always slow; it means that nahate facilitates grounded posture that is ideal for absorbing and transferring power.

Tomarite

I know very little tomarite, but the punch from tomarite is one of the most devastating things I have ever had the simultaneous pleasure and misfortune of experiencing. When I first met one of my Okinawa teachers, he had to have a translator with him to communicate more effectively with me. He raised both of his arms up like a marionette and danced a bit from foot to foot. His hands were open and not in fists. The translator said, "This does not look like martial arts, but it is." Then I was struck. I felt my chest cave in, and I was hurled back many feet. I don't bruise easily and I get punched by everyone, but I had a bruise from this punch that went straight through to my back. You read that correctly: I had a bruise on my chest and my back. For a good thirty minutes, I also had trouble breathing. Had he hit me with full power, I'm sure it would have broken my sternum and spine.

At any rate, the tomarite punch reminds me of a spearman who plants his spear in the ground and sets it to impale his opponent. There is a lunging motion in the tomarite style that is like reaching out with a spear. The body is canted forward slightly, instead of directly upright. When lunging toward your opponent, the front foot sneaks forward without moving the chest until the front foot has gained distance. Then the whole body springs forward, creating this devastating punch.

Ikkyo

An ikkyo punch is an odd style of punch found in aikido. When I first tried aikido, I laughed at this punch, but that was because it was being performed by people who had no idea how to employ it. The ikkyo punch has a natural upward swinging arc of the arm, basically making it an uppercut. Its original intent was for a tanto (dagger) to be thrust upward under a plate of armor through to the vitals. You can practice the same idea with a punch and have the reverberations echo through to the heart—no dagger needed. To do so, stand with your hands in fists and your arms relaxed by your side, then swing your arm upward toward your partner's solar plexus. This punch is easy to disguise so that your opponent cannot see it coming. Starting with your arms at your sides is part of the deception of this technique.

Other Punches

There are other styles of punching in a variety of different arts. One such punch I have come to nickname the "monkey punch." This was first shown to me by one of my Japanese instructors, and it looked so comical I laughed when I first saw it. I stopped laughing once I was knocked to the floor by it. The monkey punch uses the whole body in its execution, and is best described as a hammer-type motion. Imagine you're holding your right arm up in a fist so that your knuckles are pointing to the ceiling and your elbow is pointing to the floor. Your bicep should form a 90-degree angle. From here, drop your arm and put your weight into your target as if you were holding a hammer. Strike with the index- and middle-finger knuckles.

I sometimes walk around like a monkey during class and hit advanced students to demonstrate the fallacy of needing specific forms to generate power. People often get a good laugh at it, but eyes bulge from heads when I knock people down with it!

You may find that one style of punch works best for you, or perhaps it's best for you to combine theories from several punching styles. Remember, all of these things were made up by people like you and me. There's nothing wrong with experimenting as long as you are moving forward.

Punching Strategies for Advanced Practitioners

Advanced practitioners can begin to experiment using different directions for creating shock within our opponents. Power should still be transmitted to our opponent's center, but how we get to that point may be nonlinear in nature. This means that the direction of either our punches or ourselves may be at angles off the opponent's center.

For example, punching downward through the bladder and into the pelvis will shoot your opponent's hips backward, which makes his or her face come forward. In addition to hurting, this could disrupt the bladder, so do this with caution. I recommend going to the bathroom prior to trying this, because sometimes people will let out a squirt of urine. When the face comes forward, quickly follow with another punch to where the face will be. If done right, your opponent will plant his or her face directly into your fist.

The first time I was significantly punched in the bladder, I wished I had gone to the bathroom first. While I wouldn't say that I wet myself, some urine indeed came out. I am fortunate to have caught the sensation in time to stop it. I have been told by several karate masters not to punch to the bladder, as it is possible to "pop" it. I have never seen this happen, but I trust that this could be a potentially bad injury to have. Strikes to the bladder should not be done full-force in class for this reason. Use caution.

Another example is to punch high on the sternum using an upward angle, which will make your opponent break backward, opening up his or her solar plexus. This makes it easy to perform subsequent blows that can disrupt breathing. Take care when punching to the sternum, as this bone can easily break in lightly built people. I once punched a fifteen-year-old lightly, or what I thought was lightly, in the sternum and broke it in two. He disappeared for a long time, but returned with his father, who explained the accidental injury to me. He also said that they would no longer be taking classes in our dojo. I apologized for this accident, but it taught me a serious lesson about how we need to carefully reflect on the power of our devastating punches so that we don't create serious injury when it isn't necessary.

Upward angles can also be used through the stomach, the vibrations of your punch echoing upward into the heart. Take special precaution not to hit the xiphoid process, which can snap inward and break with this angle.

Punches to the side of the body should be aimed also at the heart. Always strike through to the centerline of the body for maximum power transfer to the target. Use precaution here not to hit the floating ribs (which break easily) and to not aim for the liver (right side of the body) or for the spleen (left side of the body). In a life-or-death situation, feel free to strike to these areas, as they are quite vulnerable; however, disrupting these organs, especially the spleen, can have serious consequences, including death.

One of the black belts in my first karate dojo was kicked in the spleen. He complained about the pain, and everyone thought he had broken ribs. He went to one hospital but it was crowded, so he went to a different hospital, hoping to get swifter attention. A doctor came out, saw what was happening to him, and immediately prepped him for surgery. As it turns out, his spleen was enlarged and swollen from the impact, and about thirty minutes from rupturing, which would have killed him. If it were not for the doctor and his quick diagnosis, this man would have died.

I should not have to say this, but I will say it anyway. Full-power punches, or any strike for that matter, to the groin, spine, neck, or face should be avoided during practice. Punch to the body, legs, or arms if you want to hit hard.

I recommend not using pads when first trying out these techniques. After all, you will not be wearing pads or armor on the street. Also, this allows your partner to give you more useful feedback. Don't start with 100 percent power. Dial it up, and talk to your partner to see how you're progressing. As previously mentioned, you should get a phone book and wrap it in duct tape securely. Now punch each other through the phone book held against your chest. Use multiple phone books if necessary. This type of contact training will develop your bone alignment and allow you to punch harder without injuring your partner. It will also give you a more realistic feel for what it's like to strike a person, rather than a foam pad. Foam pads absorb too much vibration, so they can be very deceptive for immediate feedback; phone books provide excellent vibration that can be felt by both the puncher and the one being punched.

After you have mastered a basic straight punch, try to do punches from odd angles that produce the same amount of power you could with a straight punch. This kind of training is also important for the person taking the hit, because it will teach how to absorb power in any situation.

If you superimpose a cross on your opponent's chest, with the center of the cross on the solar plexus, and then imagine an "X" on the same spot, you will see that there are eight directions to the center point, similar to the points of a compass. Try punching along these eight lines toward the center. That is, there are three downward strikes, three upward strikes, and two strikes to the sides. All of these terminate to the center of the body. Practice from a standing position first, and send vibration with your punch to the center of your opponent. You will know when you have the right vibration because most people can only tolerate being struck like this once.

Eight directions to the heart

You should try this while your opponent is lying flat on his or her back to simulate a grappling situation. Be mindful that using power absorption while on the ground is slightly different, so go more lightly for this practice. While on the ground and on my back I find that if I place my feet upon the ground, I can send the power from blows out through my feet. Likewise in this position I can also strike as though I were standing. If you have practiced any sort of grappling, you know that punching sometimes can be difficult to get a good straight shot in. After you master this exercise, it won't matter what sort of available target you have; you'll be able to send in a devastating punch no matter what your opponent is doing, provided you have one hand free to do it.

Challenge yourself to attain the devastating impossible punch. If you cannot knock someone silly with a single punch, you need more practice. When I punch people through phone books, one time is often enough for people to see how the power transfers through, and they back away, not wanting to be struck a second time. For safety reasons, I now punch using only 10 percent power. The power you can gain through these techniques may be uncharted territory for you, so proceed with caution!

Finger Strikes and Other Odd Strikes

The other day I saw a video of a man who could crack coconuts by using nothing more than his index finger. My first thought was, *Wow, that's cool! I want to do that.* Then they showed a close-up of his index finger … It must have been broken a thousand times from this activity and put back together with bubble gum and a prayer. While I admire his persistence and his skill, I don't think I would want that finger to be my finger.

Many strikes in the martial arts utilize odd areas of the hand; I largely ignore all of these now. I find that my punch is so completely devastating that jamming my fingers into someone's eyes is silly, not to mention less effective at stopping a fight. However, there are some odd strikes that can become interesting challenges for the experienced martial artist to master, so I recommend pursuing these strikes if they interest you. Discovering uses for arts is a process that can enhance all of your skills, because you're exercising your mind, not just your body. However, make sure you've mastered your devastating punch first.

That being said, I don't think of finger strikes the same way I think of punches. A punch is a fast, blunt instrument that causes massive trauma. A finger strike, in my opinion, should be much slower and deliberate. It is more important to have accuracy when using finger strikes than it is to have power.

One of my teachers had been a bouncer for many years, and was once attacked as he was leaving his place of work. He reached into the attacker's eye orbit, pulled out his eye, and held it there by the optic nerve. The attacker had a friend, and my teacher asked the other man to cross the street or he would yank the man's eye out from his head. The other man obeyed and crossed the street. My teacher then asked for the man's hand, and he put the eye in the man's hand and left.

This type of eye gouge is not as fast as a punch, but one would admit it could have just as devastating consequences if applied correctly. Some people justify these knuckle or finger techniques by saying that these arts can be used if you break your hand and you can no longer make a fist. These people obviously have never broken their hand before. I have broken my hands on many occasions, and I can tell you right now that broken, splintered bone rubbing against splintered bone is exceptionally painful. Striking with any part of that hand when there is a broken bone is not feasible. I once had my thumb broken all the way back during a sparring match. For the remainder of the tournament, that whole arm was useless. Any sort of vibration to that arm made me want to vomit. If your hand is broken, switch to elbows if you have to strike with that arm; stay away from finger and thumb jabs with that hand.

Similarly, one of my teachers said that if you have enough time to strike a person using precise pressure points, you probably outclass the other and should not be fighting. Another teacher said that striking pressure points is for bonus points only. For me, striking of pressure points is largely academic and more or less a "dojo" art. A dojo art is something you only do in the dojo and would never actually use in a life-or-death situation. If you are scared for your life, you are likely not thinking about striking nerve points so much as you are concerned with taking your opponent's head off at the shoulders.

For myself personally, I want to continue being able to write my name, and some of the practices for these arts can end up destroying joints. If you do them right, your joints will be fine, but often in practice mistakes are made, so take special precautions regarding finger strikes. However, if practicing one-off strikes gives you joy or enthusiasm, do not let my words stop you from their pursuits. Practice what interests you; that way you will be sure to keep practicing.

Punching Paradigm

I often have students punch me in the solar plexus during training. This type of practice is not only for the student, but for me as well. Using power-absorption techniques described previously, I can diffuse power that is coming in to me, but what I'm really doing is measuring several things about where the student's punching paradigm is at.

A paradigm is a series of habits that we learned from somewhere or someone that creates an entire mode for how we think. When it comes to punching, we are all socialized not to strike one another; our culture has a paradigm of nonviolence. This can be a huge hurdle for many aspiring martial artists, creating a paradigm that will impede progress in developing a powerful punch. One may think that this occurs mostly in women, as boys tend to grow up hitting one another. After all my years training, I have seen that we shouldn't generalize who has a nonviolent paradigm based on gender at all. I've had women smack me harder out of the gate than some male black belts! And I've had rugby players hit me like fairy princesses.

I once had a bodybuilder come into my dojo who was perhaps six foot six and weighed about three hundred pounds. I was excited to work with him because his muscles were so massive; I wanted to be hit by someone that big in a controlled environment. When he punched me, I had to continually ask him to not hold back. After several such requests, he stood there stunned for a moment, and I asked him what was wrong. "That's all I got, Sensei," he replied. Looking at this man, you would assume he could punch through a one-inch plate of solid steel, but he simply could not generate enough power to do much of anything to me.

To be able to hit hard, we must let go of the paradigm that it is wrong to hit others. We must be comfortable with striking one another, as odd as that sounds. In the dojo, we should make this practice as safe as possible so we can continue to punch each other. Injuring each other does little to help learn martial arts, as an injury can easily take you out of the dojo for several months. We strive to produce arts that are real, yet safe to practice.

There are other paradigms that we must confront while punching. Another is self-doubt, believing that you are not good enough or not skilled enough to make a punch happen. Time might fix this paradigm, as enough training under the belt makes this go away on its own. However, if you constantly belittle yourself, you will never develop a devastating punch. I have met people who have studied martial arts for thirty years, but still have a weak punch. Don't be those guys.

What paradigms are holding you back?

Some arts use odd ways (in my opinion) of generating power. One style I witnessed had its students shake their hips like hula dancers. I'm not joking. With each punch, they would hula dance. Maybe they were onto something; maybe they weren't. For each punch, they would hula dance three times or so. That is, they shook their hips back and forth three times and then punched. I unfortunately did not have the opportunity to test out firsthand if this style could produce power or not. You can talk all you want about power, but if you cannot demonstrate it, the point is moot. Likewise I can't outright dismiss this technique, as I did not feel it.

We may believe we have the correct image in our minds about how to do something, but if our results are inferior, it is likely that a paradigm is holding us back. You may think your posture has to be a certain way, or that your feet have to be in a certain place. But largely, these things are constructs that end up getting in the way of true progress. Often we cling to false ideals of what a technique should look like because we were taught a specific way.

For example, a man once came to my dojo to practice. He had been studying karate as long as, if not longer than, me. When I punched him, he was unable to block, and when he punched me, I could block all of his attacks. He became frustrated and said, "Well, these blocks work fine on my students, so I'm just going to continue to block that way."

I pointed out that his way did not work, but he refused to hear it. He got frustrated and left the dojo, never to return.

I think it is a shame that he was unable to let go of his paradigms for something of greater value. Always take financial advice from a person wealthier than you. Likewise, always take martial arts advice from someone who can perform a specific skill better than you can. We do not have to guard our arts with our lives, as once may have been the case. There was no TV or YouTube hundreds of years ago, and for a period in Japan, there were no firearms. During this time, martial arts were kept secret because someone could have employed your arts to defeat you. Historically, keeping your arts secret made sense, but in today's world, you do not need to know someone's arts in order to defeat him or her.

If we want to destroy another person, we need only get into our SUV, wait for the appropriate time, and drive over him or her. We can also just shoot someone. We do not need martial arts to defeat other people, and so we do not need to harbor secrets or preserve our arts. This is a fallacy that will hold you back from gaining true power from all of your arts. It should not be our goal to destroy others with our arts, because clearly there are easier ways to get this job done. Destroying others is also obviously illegal, and this book was not intended for criminals but for those who wish to further their understanding of true mastery. Reflecting on your paradigms about violence will, therefore, become an essential stepping-stone toward cultivating the mastery mind-set.

Teacher's Paradigm

It is important to note that there is often a problem that teachers of martial arts develop over their years of practice. Many practitioners' arts change once they become more experienced; this is where people become teachers and stop learning. I call this the "teacher's paradigm."

123

Many of these people have this problem and do not even realize or acknowledge it as a paradigm. If you stand in a corner during class barking orders without actually participating in class, you are showing the first symptom of the teacher's paradigm. If you practice a striking art, then you should be actively engaged in class by punching others and being punched. If you do not allow people to punch you, how can they believe in the absorption of power? If you do not punch people, how can they take your word for it that you have a devastating punch? If you do not kick others, how will they know what a devastating kick really is? We can't just talk about martial arts; we must practice them. Talking more than actually doing is the second symptom of having the teacher's paradigm. You can chat after class over a beer if you want, but class time should be reserved for practice, not chitchat. We must actively demonstrate and show our arts to our students so that they may absorb all of our knowledge.

If you are in a throwing style of art, such as aikido, judo, or jujitsu, you should be wary of a teacher who is never thrown by his or her students. As a teacher, you need to be thrown by your students to judge whether or not they are on the right track. With a teacher's paradigm, you may believe that you are unable to be thrown. This is nonsense. You are not invulnerable, and pretending that you are invulnerable is the ultimate sign of vulnerability. You do not have to do a million throws with your students, but you do need to be thrown by them from time to time. Only in this way can you see their arts firsthand.

There should be no such thing as hiding your techniques from others. As discussed earlier, if someone wants to kill you, there are easier ways to do it than spending ten years with you to learn your secrets. If you are hiding knowledge from your students on purpose, this is a third symptom of a teacher's paradigm. If you want your arts to get better, and the arts of your students to get better, let this go. Get in there, show them what you have, and do not hide behind the teacher's façade. People will eventually see through this and leave you.

Sometimes a teacher's paradigm may make you afraid of feeling weak in front of other practitioners. Know, however, that this paradigm will keep you where you are and will not push you to new levels of understanding of mastery.

I sometimes see some black belts take a lot of notes when I teach, not practicing anything during class or a seminar. They may get up and do a few punches, but they won't actively engage with the other participants. Martial arts are a participation activity. Get involved. Get punched, and do some punching! If you are older, you may not want to do a million repetitions and this is understandable, but at least get a few licks in.

Recognize what paradigms control you. Critically analyze your thoughts, and you will already be well on your way toward your goal. Neglect reflection, persist in doing what you have always done, and you will be doomed to the exact results that you are seeing now. If you have been training twenty years and do not have absolutely spectacular results, don't you think you owe yourself the opportunity of growth and change? Why bang your head against the wall thinking that somehow this method will one day work? If it doesn't work now, it will not work in the future.

Training Mind-Set

A training mind-set is a number of practices that are used in the dojo that are supposed to help us in real situations, but many times they hinder us in real situations. For example, thinking that you need punching bags or focus mitts for practice is a true sign that you are stuck in a training mind-set. This stuff is for beginners and should be used sparingly by serious martial artists. Lose the sparring armor too; you will not be carrying a breastplate around with you every day. Learn to absorb power, and you will not need breastplates. If you want to get better at striking humans, you have to strike people. If you want to get better at absorbing power, you need to be struck by others. Focus mitts, punching bags, and armor will not make your strikes better than they already are. You have to step out of this training mind-set in order to progress in the development of your arts.

Speaking of body armor, I've never worn a cup either, over the entire course of my career. This is a personal preference, and I am often looked at as crazy. If you are wondering—yes, I've been struck so hard in the groin that it made my head spin. I still see it as part of my training; because I don't wear a cup in daily life, so I don't wear one on the mat either. Fortunately for me, when I work out, my testicles ascend into my body cavity. When I'm on the mat, at least, strikes to the groin have less effect on me. I wish I could do this on command, but over the years, this just sort of developed on its own. I wish I could teach others how to do this as well; maybe it's the next impossible technique I should work on.

It's for this reason too that I don't wear hand protection. This is my biggest criticism of Mixed Martial Arts matches. Having hand protection ruins the bone-on-bone style of punch that lets you project reverberations through your opponent. With this handicap, your punches are severely reduced in power. You must learn to feel this vibration if you are pursuing a mastery level of punch. Without this direct sensation, you are blind to the energy you are creating—or more appropriately, failing to create. You can still punch hard with gloves on—make no mistake—but you will be unable to feel subtle differences in transference of power.

Punching bags are useful for getting a good workout, but they will make your punches worse and should be avoided. This is because bags do not behave the way people do. Meat, bone, and internal organs have different vibrations than a punching bag. If you want to get better at fixing cars, you fix cars. If you want to get better at punching people, you punch people. It really is that simple. I've met many kickboxers who are fantastic at kicking focus mitts and pads, and yet when it comes time to do the real thing, their techniques are terrible. They are so used to how impact is treated through pads that they are unable to translate their skills to the human body. Also, using pads reinforces the paradigm of nonviolence. By constantly hitting one another, we can break down this crippling barrier to our training.

The same sort of misconception can be seen in pistol training. Many people bring their pistol to a range, take it out of the case, load it up, shoot, and then check their targets. This is for marksmanship only; this will not teach you how to fight with a pistol. Combat pistol shooting is completely different than range shooting. Range shooting is for safety, so no one gets killed and the owner of the range has less liability. If you stand in one place and aim while someone is shooting you, you are likely to die. Hitting a stationary target is very easy. Also, if you do not practice how to draw and shoot your pistol, you will be clumsy with it in a real-world engagement and may even inadvertently shoot yourself in the process. Use calm, focused techniques of drawing and shooting your pistol. Pistol practice is like martial arts practice in many ways.

Most pistol fights happen at very close quarters and in low-light conditions, like a rowdy bar. If you have not trained in the point style of shooting (i.e., not looking down the sights), you are at a serious disadvantage if your opponent has, just like if you are used to throwing punches to focus mitts held to the side of your opponent. Likewise, if you have never pulled the trigger on your pistol at night, you will be blinded by the flash and deafened by the bang, as you might be stunned into nonresponsiveness by a surprise attack on the street. You have to train these things in order to know what to expect, so don't rely on the ideal circumstances of stationary targets holding pads to win fights.

What sorts of things do you do in your arts that are for safety only? If you have only punched the air or have been pulling all of your punches, what makes you think that your punch will work? Likewise, if you have never received punches yourself, then how would you know how you would react by being struck with tremendous force? You may even have yourself convinced that what you are doing is combat-effective. Have you ever seen those Michelin-man bodysuits worn in those stereotypical self-defense classes for women? How many people are attacked by men in Michelin-man outfits? This may be a useful exercise to do once, but for daily practice, these sorts of illusions must be examined and eliminated from our practice.

I've met some people who refuse to punch me in the chest because they claim that their arts may kill me in one hit. I call BS on this one. If the masters I've met can strike me without killing me, but still take me out of a fight, then so can anyone else who understands this skill. These people only fear that they are unable to do it. I've had individuals come into my dojo who had years of training in another style, but weren't interested in what I had to offer; they just wanted to sell me on their own style.

I'm a good sport, so I listen to what they have to say (it was after class and wasn't that disruptive). One person wanted to show me this devastating palm strike that he developed that can disrupt the opponent's breathing. "Give it a go," I said, and I just stood there and made no attempt to block his attack. He did a palm strike to the side of my ribs, aiming at my diaphragm. I moved my torso about a half inch to cover that spot, and I absorbed the power. He blinked at me, clearly expecting a different result. He tried three more times, and each time he had more anxiety than the time before.

He then stopped, squinted, and said, "That's odd. It usually works on my students." Yes, I've heard that before many times. It is easy to beat up others who don't know what they are doing. It is easy to smack down your students because you taught them all the good and bad habits you have. When you experiment with such techniques, make sure you try them on others who are your same skill level, or your results may be very misleading.

People of your own skill level will let you know if you are on the right track or not. They may not even need to tell you; you will be able to see the results firsthand. By closely practicing with people of the same mind-set, you will both become better, not only with the arts but with teaching as well. Solve problems together. It is important to have feedback for the arts that we practice so that we can inch our way forward toward mastery. If you isolate yourself from this feedback, you are doing yourself a great disservice; you should consider changing this habit and the paradigms about your arts that are holding you back.

Projecting Power

One of the fundamentals for projecting power into something or someone is the placement of your center of gravity. When I teach, I ask my students where their weight is. Often they do not know, or if they have to guess, they say that their weight is at their own center. Guessing isn't good enough. Knowing where to place your weight is essential for developing your impossible punch, impossible block, and impossible throw. We punch using body weight rather than muscle alone, we block with our body structure and not only our arms, and we throw using our center of gravity and projecting power by subtle shifts in body weight.

If you do not know where your weight is being placed, how do you expect to maximize your power? By working out in the gym to get bodybuilder biceps? Try maintaining those into your fifties, sixties, or seventies, and let me know when you discover the frustration that comes with knowing that sometimes big muscles actually get in the way of you performing these impossible techniques. Regardless of your art or style, using your body weight, rather than pure muscle, to project power will ensure that your arts are their most efficient and powerful, and allow you to maintain that power throughout your years as muscle strength deteriorates.

Finding your body's center can be accomplished by comparing our arts to meditation techniques. One of the many centers in meditation is located two inches below your navel; this center is the most useful for martial arts because it can be both a physical and mental center. If you draw a stick figure and then draw a circle around that stick figure, the center of that circle should be in the abdomen area of the drawing. This point represents the center of your body and your center of gravity.

This center need not be in a fixed position, however; it can move. If you put your weight on your heels, your center rocks backward. This posture isn't ideal for humans, as we are forward-facing animals. That is, our eyes, nose, mouth, and ears are oriented forward. Our feet carry us forward, and our hands are oriented forward. Having your weight behind you does little to aid in any martial art practice.

By shifting your weight slightly forward to the point just before you have to take a step, your center moves in front of you. This is one of the keys for projecting power. If you can feel your body weight ever so slightly forward, you can then imagine moving this point inside of your intended target. When we punch, elbow, palm strike, or whatever, we can draw on the power of this centerpoint to focus our body weight and cause it to seemingly create an explosion inside of our opponent. At this focal point, we cause the most amount of trauma, and if aimed correctly, you can even disrupt internal organs. A light tap can compress the heart and cause increased blood flow to the brain. This surge will cause immediate dizziness and loss of balance.

Be careful not to practice such things on people with heart conditions. I found this out the hard way when one of my students fell to the floor and begged me to get her nitroglycerin. I didn't think to ask if she had a heart condition, because at the time, I had yet to realize the power that these punches can have. I once punched a man who had arrhythmia. Again, he did not tell me. When I punched him, his heart stopped, but only for a few seconds. If you have a heart condition, you should not engage in this practice. I hope this is obvious. And never forget to ask people if they have a heart condition before trying reverberating strikes to the heart. Once you learn how to create shock in the body and receive feedback from training partners to discuss your progress, this knowledge can be easily applied to real targets, such as the eyes, maxilla, jaw, temple, throat, ears, or groin. Practice-striking these areas should be "mimed." Save the full-power blows for the body.

Make sure your punch's power goes into a target, instead of bouncing off of it. If you are experiencing a backward movement of either your shoulder or your body when you strike, some of your power is going out your backside. To avoid this, squeeze your latimus dorsii and your pectoral muscles as your punch connects with the target. This will lock your body in position at the moment of the impact and decrease the bounce-off effect. Avoid the temptation to flex your deltoid, which will only block the movement of your body weight into your target. We want a truly explosive collision, where all the power goes to the target and not back toward you. Think of what happens to the cue ball in billiards during the initial break; when done well, it stays put, transferring the power of your hit into the other balls, which explode in every direction. Your fist is the cue ball—your opponent's insides are the others.

Another way to test where your weight is can be done by practicing a downward block. Have your partner perform a midlevel punch. Now, using only the hinging motion of your arm, strike your opponent in the arm in a downward motion, and concentrate specifically on the placement of your body weight synchronizing with the impact of your block. If your weight is in the correct spot, your partner will be off-balance and unable to take a second blow. Sometimes the momentum of your partner's punch will continue, but since your body weight is being projected through your arm and into his or hers, your partner will take a few staggering steps off-line. If your weight is not in the correct spot, then your partner will be able to counterattack with the other arm. You must create a shock wave through your opponent's arm with your body weight. To do this, do not move your body, and especially not your hips. Moving your hips to generate power will not only slow you down, but will bleed out part of your power in the wrong direction from the strike.

Pushing vs. Projecting

There is a time and a place for pushing, but if you wish to develop a powerful punch or kick, pushing is the worst way to go about it. When you push with a punch or a kick, it merely makes your opponent move away from you and does little to damage him or her. This may have some advantages in certain situations, but if you really need to strike someone, he or she will receive very little power from a pushing technique. Many people develop a pushing punch or a pushing kick through incorrect practice, and they may not even know they are doing it. They may think because their opponent moves back when they hit him or her that they have power. If a bullet flies through a person, it does not transfer all of its energy to that person; therefore, it loses damage potential. The bullet that goes through a person may still be lethal, of course, but there is a chance that it won't be. Hollow-point bullets are made to stop inside of a person instead of flying through the target. Hollow-point bullets therefore transfer all of their energy to the person they are hitting, and therefore do much more severe, and more likely fatal, damage. We want our punches to be like hollow-point bullets.

Hollow-point bullets fired through ballistic gelatin (to simulate human flesh) show a larger cavity than normal bullets. This is because the bullet expands upon impact and creates more shock energy in the gelatin. This is the visualization we want to have for our strikes.

The hardest punches I've received by masters made me collapse downward, not backward. Any backward movement I experienced was me trying to get out of range so I wouldn't be hit again. As mentioned earlier, to practice this safely, use a phone book that is duct-taped and place that over your opponent's solar plexus. Strike the phone book with the intention of projecting your power into your opponent's body. Don't worry so much about the phone book. A good punch should be able to go through the phone book and affect your opponent so well that he or she should not want another. If your opponent moves backward, you have a push punch. If your opponent is still standing and not complaining about pain, you have a weak punch, but you are on the right track. Do not use hand protection, as this interferes with creating shock. Once you are capable of absorbing power, I would recommend leaving the phone book aside so you can fine-tune each other's punch by direct contact.

When you practice with your opponent in class, make sure to communicate with one another if a punch was good or not. You will know a good punch when it hits you. Be honest with each other, and above all, be honest with yourself. Some people are very good at hiding pain and may not say anything, so make sure you communicate to see if you are on the right track or not. Strike and let your power echo through your opponent. Once you have developed a good punch, try starting with your fist closer to your opponent. This is like a one-inch punch, but without the push.

Projecting Power in Close Quarters

In class, we often practice one step away from our opponent. The reason for this is that at this distance, an attack becomes recognizable and easier to predict. This is useful for novices to practice blocking, counterattacking, kicking, evading, or doing takedowns and throws. However, this distance is not realistic in most fights, and projecting the power that we are used to in the dojo becomes difficult when in close.

In a real fight, you will be face-to-face with your opponent, each of you in striking range. It is difficult to react quickly in this position, whether it is to attack or block. By law, we must wait until we feel threatened before we act, but an opponent entering conversation distance with an aggressive attitude constitutes an attack. My advice at this range is that as soon as you feel an attack coming, immediately strike and do not worry about his or her punch. Don't hesitate. Overwhelm your opponent with sheer brute force.

In close-quarters fighting, there is no "block and punch." It's just punch. Do not worry about your opponent's attack. Overwhelm him or her with your attack, and keep your weight forward so that your opponent cannot push you backward. You want your opponent to feel suddenly on his or her heels. When our opponent feels this retreating sensation, he or she will continue to retreat when you forcibly move in to attack. Should your opponent try to strike you at this moment, his or her punches will be weak because your opponent's weight is behind him or her. You can steamroll an attacker who is retreating because moving forward is faster and easier than moving backward.

If you are in a clinch with an opponent and cannot seem to get a hand free to punch, roll your shoulder backward in a circle. This will give you an inch or two of space, and that should be enough to crush through his or her defenses. Simply bringing the arm back at close quarters can be easily blocked if you are already in a clinch. If your opponent is trying to arrest your arms, a head butt is a good choice, but aim for the nose, not the forehead. I prefer to smash downward upon his or her arms using my own arm like gedan barai (downward block) and resume my regular regime of punching. If you need to, you can rotate your hips as you block to ensure that you are free from his or her grasp.

Elbows too are a good choice when in bad-breath distance with an opponent. If your wrists are held by your attacker, you can still strike with your elbows. The key is to keep your weight forward and to keep pressing your attack. Do not stand still and trade blows. You could lose this way. Force your opponent to go on the defensive by continuously pushing him or her backward. Once your opponent is on the defensive, you control the fight.

When I find myself in a clinch, I push my opponent, not with my hands, but instead with the power that comes from my legs. That is, I touch the person with my hands, but I do not push with my hands; I push using the strength in my legs. My legs are stronger than most people's arms. I can squat a lot more weight than I can bench-press. So I lock my arms using the unbendable-arm technique, and push with my lower body. It is easy to stop someone from pushing you if he or she is using the upper body. But by using the lower body, you maximize your potential and take control of the encounter. We can create and project an impressive amount of power in this situation when we utilize this technique.

To practice this, hold your partner in a standard judo hold. That is, one hand on the lapel and one hand under the elbow. Your partner should hold you in the mirrored position. From here, do not force movement with your hands or upper body. Lock your arms and upper body in place, and then use your legs to push your opponent forward. You may need to set your center lower by bending your knees and flattening out the small of your back. This causes your pelvis to rotate forward and puts your weight in front of you, making it easier to push with your legs. Take turns pushing each other around the dojo to practice this technique. You'll not only get a good sense of how to place your weight, but you'll also get a great workout.

Once my opponent is on his or her heels, I can strike. Push, strike, push, strike, and push, strike. Don't just stand in one spot; your opponent can hit you there. If your opponent is occupied with regaining balance, he or she is not kicking your ass. Likewise, if your opponent is busy defending, he or she is not kicking your ass. This buys you a lot of time, and will break your opponent psychologically. It's even better if you can spin him or her around to face the opposite direction. To spin your opponent, catch one of his or her arms, cross his or her own body with the arm, and then push through that arm and shoulder, and the result is that your opponent will turn slightly. With subsequent pushes, your opponent can be completely turned around, exposing his or her back to you. Now you can hit freely, and he or she cannot block.

Having the sensation that you are plowing forward will boost your morale and weaken your opponent's. Be an unstoppable tank that keeps rolling forward. Continuously force your opponent backward. Should he or she kick you, push, and his kicks against you will do nothing. Keep pressing forward and don't give an inch backward. Sooner or later, your opponent will realize that he or she is losing and will try to disengage.

To practice this mind-set, sit seiza (kneeling) and look straight forward. Have your training partner approach you while standing from the front and push you on the shoulders with constant pressure in an attempt to knock you over. While you continue to look forward, lightly touch your opponent under the arms and send his or her power through your body and into the floor. You should be able to hold this position indefinitely.

For advanced practice, do the above, but have three people in a line push on you. That is, each opponent is pushing one another in a line in front of you. Ground out the power of this push and remain seated and looking forward. This is the exact feeling we want to create while standing. Once you've mastered the manipulation of your body weight through this and the above methods, you will be able to create shockingly powerful techniques at a range where most people's strikes are nothing but wimpy shoves and pokes.

The Devastating Kick

My sensei one day asked me to shin kick him in the knee. At this point, I had about eighteen years of experience in karate, so I looked at him like he was insane. I have seriously injured people with my kicks in the past, and doing this exercise seemed like a really bad idea. After all, he was in his sixties. "Kick me," he shouted, so I kicked him with about 25 percent power. He didn't move. "*Kick me*," he insisted. So, using full power, I shin kicked him again to the knee with no effect. I then hammered my shin to his knee repeatedly until he casually raised a hand for me to stop.

Then it was his turn.

He lifted his leg off the ground in a scooping motion, the exact way I was told never to kick by my other teachers. When his shin reached thigh level, he turned it in 90 degrees, but in such a way that I didn't even think to block or move. It looked so pathetic, and for a split second, I thought the old man had lost it. Tap. I was on the mat, clutching my thigh in agony. I had never, ever been kicked that hard in my life, and I've done stupid things like walk straight into kicks to the face and groin. This was off that scale.

As I was on the ground, he looked over at me and said, "Get up. I'll teach you how to kick!"

While I personally view kicks as being a secondary means of striking, they do have uses. You may be puzzled as to why I believe kicks are secondary over hand techniques. Here are a few reasons why: you have to be on one foot to kick, you cannot move while kicking, kicking can be difficult on some terrain like ice or gravel, kicking can expose your groin to attack, and, most importantly, kicking is generally slower than hand movement and more difficult to change your mind about midway through execution. Good luck trying to kick anyone running away from you. Also, an interesting side note: in some states, kicks are legally considered lethal use of force and a purposeful escalation of a confrontation.

In the state of Washington, if someone punches you, and you kick your attacker, then you have escalated the fight and you may be charged with assault, even though you did not strike first. If your opponent kicks you first, then you are allowed to kick in defense. This is a strange law, but it is a law nonetheless. If you use kicks as your primary defense, you may find yourself in a legal battle should you actually need to employ your arts.

I like legs for attacking legs and the groin. It is very difficult to block low kicks and sweeps. Feet should primarily be used for locomotion and disruption of balance in your opponent, not for striking. Your arms are free (that is, they don't have to move you around like legs) and can move quickly and change direction. Hand speed does not change much over time, while kicking speed drastically gets worse as you age, making kicks less useful later on.

Most striking arts learn sparring-style kicks, which are used to gather points in tournaments instead of actually hurting anyone. Kicking with the top of the foot is one example why. A shin kick to the head is a devastating kick if you have the flexibility. But if you use the top of the foot and actually catch someone hard in the skull, you are more likely to break your foot than break your opponent. The top of the foot is a target, not a striking point. Using the top of the foot gives you reach for getting points in tournaments, but that's the only benefit it will give you. I've had people break the tops of their feet on my elbows during sparring. If you have good physical structure, you don't need to move much, and all you need to do is plant your elbow into the top of their foot. It will break just fine, while you might end up with a bruise. The times I have done this, it wasn't even intentional; I was just covering up my floating ribs. Groin kicks should use the heel of the foot, the shin, or the knee, never the top of the foot, because one mistake can mean your foot is broken and out of action.

The Impossible Lame Kick

I lovingly refer to the devastating round kick that my master dropped me with earlier as the "impossible lame kick." This is because it looks like nothing at all—just a lame twitch of the leg. Practice it by standing in front of your partner, with both people having their right legs back. Raise your right leg straight up so that your toes point to the ceiling without increasing your height (don't rise up on your supporting leg). Your shin should be close enough to your opponent's thigh that it brushes up against it. Once your shin is near the top of the thigh, rotate it over and into your opponent's thigh. Use the blade of your shin and bite deep. Make sure your support leg is solid and grounded. This kick should look like you are raising your leg up and slightly angling it in on impact. It may seem odd that you're targeting the thigh with your shin, but this target is the best way to safely practice this kick. When done well, the result will basically be the worst charley horse the person has ever experienced.

Most people can only take one of these kicks, so you will know when you do it right when your partner either falls down or backs away. Don't take my word for it; try it out. This kick is exceptionally easy to land because it doesn't look like it would do anything. In fact, I once showed this to an incredulous student. He fell down and immediately went into shock. He turned pale like a white sheet, slumped to the floor, and had to prop himself up against the wall. Doesn't sound so lame now, right?

If your partner can take more than one shot, you need to work on weight distribution to the target. To develop this sense of where your weight is going, do not use pads at first. Have your partner take a front stance, while you lightly place your knee to his or her thigh. Imagine your power going through both legs, but don't put much effort into it. If done correctly, the strike will place your entire body weight into your knee at the moment of contact. All you need is a tap. Don't try to force this exercise, or you will have poor results. Relax and feel your weight going forward, as if taking a step. Have the knee contact your partner's thigh at a 90-degree angle. If you do this right, you only need to do it once, and your partner will not be able to take more.

Most striking martial artists have a bit of resistance to being struck to the outer thigh, and so a better target would be the inner thigh, but the issue of safety comes up. The inner thigh is very sensitive and has large blood vessels in it. The potential for severe injury here is not worth the risk during class, so ease up on the power when kicking to this area.

After my student from earlier recovered from shock, he expressed just how amazed he was that something so little could have such a profound effect on his mind and body. This is precisely how we want to develop our arts: minimal effort with maximum results. Use your body weight and place it in the correct position, and you will be stunned with the conclusion.

Kicking Risks

As a general rule, I agree with my first karate sensei, who said, "If you want to win a fight, keep both feet on the ground." At first I didn't understand what he meant by this. I was fifteen at the time, and he would consistently knock the wind out of me through a heavy bag with his front kick. That seemed like a fight-stopping technique to me. Much later, I realized that his kicks only worked because of the ideal circumstances in the dojo. In reality, kicking in a fight only works if you have a tremendous window of opportunity. Opening an engagement with a kick will often leave you vulnerable, and in my opinion, kicking is less useful in real situations than one may think. Typically when we are scared, our feet do not behave the way we want them to, making movement sluggish and unresponsive. Kicking in moments like this makes us even weaker and more vulnerable.

I have eliminated many high kicks from my repertoire, my targets with kicks now being mostly legs and the groin. I prefer legs as weapons to use against the legs while an opponent is standing. Low kicks are difficult to block and can often be disguised as merely stepping forward. Or if your opponent is down, kicks to the head or neck are possible, albeit likely to give you grief in a court of law. High kicks become increasingly more difficult with age, and they do not buy you much in the way of effective technique. Legs are better tools against legs, and more often than not should be used for throwing or unbalancing your opponent.

This doesn't mean kicks shouldn't be practiced; it means they should take a secondary role in a striking style of self-defense. You may find, though, that your body is well suited to developing kicking arts, and if so, I encourage you to pursue that goal. If you do, remember that your kicks, just like your punches, must have your weight inside of your target. Match your shin, knee, ball of the foot, or heel to that location, and enjoy the results.

I once witnessed a bar fight where a karate practitioner and a big man squared off and fought. The karate guy was smaller, so he backed up and would only come in to kick the man in the shin and then back away. Each time the bigger man attempted to come closer, the smaller man kicked him in the shin. This went on for some time until the bigger man collapsed from the sheer amount of pain that limb had received. No punches landed, and no other techniques were done. To some, inflicting so much pain to a particular part of the body may seem like a brutal method of self-defense, but I disagree. No one was seriously injured, and everyone got to keep their body parts, especially their faces.

Striking while Grappling

Grappling is a monster of a topic that could easily be the subject of an entire book. However, many of the techniques that I've discussed have practical and impressive applications when utilized on the ground. Because of this, I will mention grappling insofar as how it pertains to striking and absorbing power. When utilized, our devastating punches and kicks will make the flailing or biting attacker feel as if you just dropped an anvil on him or her.

I have a friend who is a jujitsu practitioner. He is exceptional at grappling, and I must admit I have a very hard time tapping him out if playing by the rules. However, if I get one hand free, he's dead. Grappling is very much like sparring in my opinion. It is an exercise and shouldn't be thought of as real fighting. It teaches you many important skills, the most important one being to remain completely relaxed and calm, but it also ignores some real-world dangers, such as knives, guns, can openers, glass, multiple opponents, or whatever. You don't want to go into a grapple in an alley that is filled with used needles. You may win the fight only to contract some terrible disease.

At any rate, it is very possible to learn how to absorb and generate power from the ground. One of the biggest shames of most modern dojo is that neither of these skills is practiced. As a karate person, you should be able to punch from any position without any decrease in power. If you practice grappling arts like jujitsu, then you should still be proficient in absorbing power, because you never know how hard your opponent can punch even though you've got him or her in a compromising position.

For punching, lie upon your back and have your opponent in the guard position; try to ground your power by touching a foot to the ground. Rotate your torso to punch and strike with the same side. If you are in the mount, this is perhaps the easiest way to strike, but a good jujitsu person will try to pull you close or otherwise render your strikes useless. But we only really need one. If you can't get a shot in to the head, hit the arms and cripple them. Keep hitting the same spot until the bone breaks. If you cannot get a hand free to strike, go to fingertips and shoot for the eyes and throat. When you have your opponent in a side hold, it is fairly easy to get in elbow and knee strikes to your opponent's head and ribs. If enough force is placed upon even an arm, this can cause your opponent to vomit. Sloppy or weak strikes will likely not buy you much. Feel where your weight is, and strike the focal point for maximum effectiveness.

Punching on the ground takes practice to become good at it. This is why back fists, hook punches, and crescent kicks suddenly become very useful on the ground. Sometimes I will have students hold kick pads on their chests and then lie on their backs. I will then strike the pad in unusual directions, including from my back. We should get used to being able to project power from whatever position we may find ourselves in. If you are a little wary of this, place a kick pad directly on the floor and practice falling on the pad with your elbow. Also, kneel on the pad with one knee and then strike the pad with downward punches. When you are lying on your back, roll over to one side and hit the pad with a hook punch or back fist.

Hook kicks may seem useless in stand-up fighting; I believe that hook kicks (crescent kicks) were actually designed for grappling situations and not for stand-up fighting at all. Practice these by lying upon your back. Have your opponent be in your guard (between your legs), and then scoot your hips to one side and crescent kick your opponent in the head. Obviously use caution when doing this, and do not use any power to avoid injury to your opponent. If you want to practice contact with your crescent kicks, I would advise striking your opponent in the back or other fleshy area.

As for absorbing power from the ground, attacks to the chest behave the same way as when you are standing, so it is relatively easy to absorb blows to the body, though this may require you to shift more than you would while standing. Touching your opponent's arm or leg when he or she strikes will take some of the sting out of the blow as well. Absorbing blows to the head requires the use of your arms and a soft touch so that you may diffuse the power of your opponent's blows.

If you are untrained in grappling, I suggest learning a little bit of it. You don't have to be a master grappler; you just have to know what someone may try to do to you while on the ground. Know the basic grappling positions and how someone may try to attack you with them.

If your opponent is a better grappler than you are, you must conserve your energy and play defensively. If you are overly aggressive, your opponent will break you fast. Do not overextend, and use relaxed postures. Being on your back if you are not as good is safer because you can relax more. Look for that one opening, and blast. If the only target you have is your opponent's thigh, crush that thigh!

A fun drill you can do, especially if you have mats, is to roll back and do hammer fists to the ground, as if you were practicing hard falls. After you are good and warmed up, have your partner lie down and hold a pad over his or her chest. Practice dropping your weight from a standing position and punch directly down. The primary power from this style of punch comes from rapidly dropping your weight. If you have a big enough pad, you can drop your knee at the same time. You can practice the same method by striking with your elbows, which is always a favorite. By preparing yourself for these sorts of situations, you'll be able to maximize the use of your arts in any position, even if someone stronger may have taken you to the ground. This is a scary place to be for those who practice striking arts, but hold on to the visualization and structure you use for your devastating punch, and you'll find you can cause as much pain while on your back as you can while on your feet.

Using Deception to Create Power

I once squared off with an Okinawa master who told me he was going to punch me in the head and that I should block it. The instruction was simple; I was warmed up and ready to defend myself. I watched him carefully and was poised to block his attack. He then punched me in the head, politely pulling the strike so I wouldn't die. I didn't even flinch, because I didn't even see it coming. I only felt his knuckles on my forehead. I looked at him and smiled, and he smiled back because he knew that I understood the lesson.

What had happened was that he rapidly moved his feet so that they changed positions. His left foot had been forward, and he quickly switched his position so that his right foot was forward. He did this without any part of his upper body moving. The movement produced a quizzical response from me, rather than a defensive one. Replaying that moment in my mind, I thought, *What the heck is he doing?* I didn't have time to think, *OMG, I have to block!* He used deception to disguise that he was about to strike me.

Blocking is easy; even novices can protect their heads in crude ways that still work. But if your opponent does not see a strike coming, there is no such thing as a block or bracing for impact. One cannot steel his or her muscles against a blow if he or she has no idea it is underway. So one of the skills a martial artist should learn is how to deceive our opponent so that he or she does not see or feel our attacks, or counterattacks, coming. Deception seems to amplify the energy output of your attacks, because the opponent has no way of absorbing power that he or she isn't expecting. By "deception" I do not mean lying, stealing, or other nefarious activities. I mean sleight of hand, and creating false openings

146

so that your opponent is not aware of where your attack will come. It is by using *damashi,* or cheating, that we can set people up so they do not see us about to strike them.

For example, if you are accustomed to bringing your arm way back on your hip for punching during practice, you may very well do this in a fight. By moving your shoulder, you signal your intent to your opponent, who can now instinctively know where the attack is coming from. This is precisely the type of thing we need to avoid in our practice. We want to develop the element of surprise so that our techniques penetrate much more deeply than an attacker is prepared for. If done well, your attacks will seem to land with impossible speed and precision. However, this is really just catching your opponent off guard.

Unnecessary movements, such as raising the shoulders, preparatory foot movement prior to taking a step, and improper chambering of techniques, must be eliminated. In general, the top of the head should stay at the same level throughout most movements (though there are exceptions, where an up or down movement is *intentional*). These extra movements slow you down, waste energy, and demonstrate sloppy technique. If these mistakes are made in a fight, it will telegraph your intentions to your opponent. This is why many fighting styles have forms, or kata. With diligent practice and attention to specific details, we can hammer these principles and make them part of our subconscious. Fixing these errors in kata and in general practice can directly improve your fighting ability.

If you mindlessly perform your kata because you think you have to, you will miss 99 percent of the lessons learned in these forms. Kata should be about fighting. If you practice forms with long stances but you fight in short stances, your kata is not doing you any good. Original karate had very short stances in the kata, and this is how martial artists fought. Long stances are great for athletics, but almost useless for fighting. Kata should be about subtle shifting of weight, how to deceive your opponent, and how to create power and absorb power. If your kata is just a set of blocks, punches, and kicks, then these forms have no soul.

Study the subtleties of your kata so you can learn how to induce all sorts of deception to confuse or mislead your opponent. Many arts already have strategies for doing just this, but often these things are deleted for the sake of running "fair-fight" tournaments. When martial arts are used for real, there is no such thing as a fair fight. Use what you have to (legally) so you can get home for dinner.

Some deceptive strategies can be quite simple, such as leaning in toward your opponent with the left side of your face, making your opponent believe that strikes to this side could be done easily. We are luring him or her into a trap. Once you know where your opponent is going to strike, you can then know how you should respond and even preplan it. My karate sensei would often feign like he did not hear you, placing his face in closer to you. It looked like you could hit him in the face easily, but since he knew what the target was, he could beat you there. The same holds true with Japanese swordsmanship. My aikido sensei would often hold his sword low, making me think that I could strike him in the head with my sword. But since he was ready for my attack and he knew the target, he could adequately prepare countermeasures.

By creating these deliberate openings, we can make our opponent attack almost anywhere. For example, if we cover up our head and leave our body open, our opponent may naturally believe that he or she will be able to strike us in the chest. By using this strategy, we are leading our opponent's mind and energy. With our hands pointing upward, we can still use powerful elbows and monkey punches (described in an earlier chapter). Having your hands up high does not take away your weapons—it makes other weapons more readily available.

Soft blocking is another strategy we can employ to lure our opponents into coming closer to us. If we block hard, we stop our opponent short, meaning that for a counterattack, we must then step in or shuffle closer in order to hit because we have arrested our opponent's motion. The time it takes to move in is sufficient for your opponent to recover from a hard block.

Soft blocks encourage your opponent to overreach; in this way, a counterattack is much easier because you need not move at all. I prefer to stand my ground and let my opponent attack me; as soon as he or she steps close enough, I can lay the smack down. I don't have to extend my reach; my opponent is overextending to reach me. I do not have to waste energy chasing him or her, because my opponent is freely wasting energy to get to me.

You can practice another type of deception using blocks that do not even touch your partner. Imagine you are standing toe-to-toe with your opponent. He or she steps in and punches you to the face with the right hand, right foot forward. "Block" this attack by extending your right arm on the outside and parallel with your opponent's punching arm very briefly, then bring your arm back to you with your fist pointing toward the ceiling. At this moment, twist your body off-line of the attack. The punch will miss by an inch, and you will not even have touched your opponent's arm. In this moment of confusion, you can easily provide a counterattack.

No-touch blocks typically look like regular blocks that have full commitment up until just before contact would be made, but in that split second, you choose not to contact and move slightly off-line. People will expect to be hit by your block, and therefore brace for sudden contact because they can see your movement. By not hitting them at this moment, you take away their attack's energy, creating an opening for you to do something else. Your opponent will often feel a stuttering sensation from falling slightly forward. This allows you to take control of the situation in a number of ways. You can move away, move in, counterattack, or even throw your opponent. Since your opponent is off-balance, he or she has done most of the work for you. This type of strategy is often employed in the arts of aikido and jujitsu.

Damashi is a strong fighting tactic to ensure that if you must fight, then it's you that has the edge. Boxing matches are fifty-fifty. Fighting fifty-fifty sounds fair, but this means you have a 50 percent chance of losing. Those are terrible odds! Tip things into your favor by employing these techniques that hide your devastating punches, kicks, and throws in such a way that it seems like you are performing the physically impossible. Fair fights are encouraged in tournaments, but in the real world, we do not want to fight fairly. We want to ensure success, and a big part of that is stacking the odds in our favor.

Relaxed Power in Throwing Arts

Entire volumes of books have been written on how to perform throwing arts. In fact, it would probably be possible to write one book for each throw and all of its variations. My goal is not to inundate the reader with a million arts; my goal is to outline a few that are common to many art styles, so that mastery can be attained by using the principles of internal power. When we learn how to use relaxed power while throwing, we suddenly take our arts to a higher level.

I joined an aikido dojo after having practiced kung fu and karate for five or six years. I wanted to believe in aikido and its emphasis on internal energy to further my understanding of all the arts. Internal power seemed like the key ingredient I had been missing in my training, as I had largely been practicing with an outside-in approach. In one class, our sensei was talking about a technique called *kokyunage*, which translates roughly to a "breath and rhythm throw." To me this technique looked like the person being thrown was faking it. It was so implausible that I raised my hand and called my sensei out on it.

My sensei asked me to come up to the front and attack him. "How?" I asked.

He merely shrugged and said, "Whatever; it doesn't matter."

So I squared up with him and took my best shot with a lunge punch. My teacher evaded the attack, jumped behind me, and then the next thing I saw was my outstretched fist pointing downward at my feet. I remember thinking, *That's impossible!* Then I flipped upside down and landed on the back of my neck. I was winded, twitching, and for a moment wondering if I had hit my head and suffered brain damage. I couldn't move. I then saw my sensei's face lean over me as he asked,

"Are you okay?" For the remainder of the class, I said nothing; I had become a believer in aikido arts.

This made me realize that there are throws that look fake, and yet are very real. Likewise, there are throws that look real, and yet are fake. This oxymoron baffled me from an outside-in approach to training, and so I began to develop an inside-out perspective to comprehend what my sensei was trying to impart to me.

When you attempt to throw someone while tense, your partner will mirror you and tense up as well. This is a very natural reaction when people meet resistance. Imagine you push on a door that seems stuck—what do you do? Push harder. The solution, however, may actually be to pull the door open.

Relaxation is the key piece of the puzzle to develop sensitivity to which action should be applied in any situation. Relaxation allows for a better sense of awareness regarding your and your opponent's balance. Relaxation can confuse your opponent, so that he or she misinterprets your intention, allowing you to execute a throw with ease.

Throwing while tense will create a battle of strength, which will work fine if you are stronger than your opponent; however, if you are not stronger, this will quickly become a losing proposition for you. Likewise, if you create a push-pull dynamic, your partner can sense your changing force and easily compensate, potentially throwing you in the process. We need to disguise our entry, as well as where our shifting weight is, to calmly execute the throw without alerting our partner to this imminent danger. Failure to do so will alert your opponent and create a strength-on-strength tug-of-war.

Developing relaxed power while throwing is one of the most dramatic ways to make the impossible possible. A small woman may throw a large man if she has the will and the relaxed technique to do it. If you go to throw an opponent who becomes stubborn and aware of your intentions and tries to stop you, you may experience a difficult time. If you simply add more power to this situation, you may be met with the same results—a stalemate. You may have had the experience of trying to throw someone who just did not go down to the mat. Ask yourself: were you going the correct direction? If you try to throw your opponent one way and he or she does not fall, it is likely because the transition of weight and intention are in a completely different direction than you are trying to send him or her. This may not be obvious at first, and you may dismiss this as the person simply being stronger than you are. My aikido sensei is five foot four and weighs 135 pounds. I am six foot and weigh 200 pounds. My aikido sensei has absolutely no problem throwing me with any technique he wants to throw me in. I am much stronger than my aikido sensei, and yet he can throw me at will. He does not use force, as I can easily defeat him in a contest of strength. He uses leverage, subtle shifts in weight, relaxed technique, and a bit of cunning.

I once went to lift my aikido sensei up underneath his arms. I could tell I caught him off guard, and I certainly had enough power to lift him straight into the air. I caught him smiling at me, as if to say, "Nice try, boy." He shifted his hips perhaps a quarter inch to one side and touched my left forearm with his own. The result was that I simply had no power or leverage to pick him up. He changed the angle of my approach so expertly that I had no time to compensate for it. He then grabbed me by the head and threw me to the ground.

To your opponent, a good throw should feel as if he or she weren't ready. The best sign that your throwing arts are working is if your partner gets up off the ground and says, "Okay, now I'm ready." This is the exact feeling we want our opponent to have. We want surprise, but a surprise that comes from entering personal space so gently that he or she does not realize the actual danger until it is too late. We must *lead* our opponent to unbalance, rather than pull or push him or her into unbalance. After we have taken our opponent's balance in a subtle manner, we can throw him or her many different ways.

To make these concepts easier to understand, I find it useful to group these arts into either core throws or extremity throws.

Core Throws

Core throws utilize the weight of your own body against your opponent. These arts typically require moving in close, unbalancing the opponent, and then using your mass to easily down your opponent. These throws are characteristic of judo and jujitsu, which have huge assortments of techniques that use this principle. Because it can take a lifetime to understand the intricacies of all of these arts, I won't do them a disservice by briefly glossing over all of them; I will simply mention the two that I sincerely believe all martial artists should be able to do: *osoto gari* and *sayunage*. These arts are simple and easily mastered, and many would-be opponents know how to do these arts, so it behooves us to be prepared for them. Even if you do not practice a throwing art, having a few basic throws is a good thing to include in your repertoire. Often you will find that these two body positions happen by accident during fighting. When one of them does, you should be able to continue striking, or simply throw your opponent down to the ground.

Osoto Gari

Osoto gari is seen in sanchin kata from nahate styles of karate, and is an outer reaping of the opponent's legs. It is also typically found in judo or jujitsu. This is a fast, and often hard, technique that can be quite devastating, as your opponent can land in very uncompromising positions. The name *osoto gari* actually comes from jujitsu; our Okinawa karate teachers never named it themselves—it just happened to be identical to the jujitsu form. Similarly, the name *sayunage*, a core throw from naifanchi kata, which is from shurite-style karate, comes from aikido. Our Okinawa teachers did not call it this, and I never thought to ask them about the name because I already knew the art from aikido. We find, however, that most students prefer to remember arts by name, and so we named it after the identical throw found in aikido. To me, good martial arts are good martial arts, regardless of history or style. If you find something that works for you, adopt it as your own.

An easy way to perform osoto gari is to hug your opponent, move his or her center in the direction you want him or her to fall, and sweep out your opponent's legs with the back of your own. In judo practice, you may grab hold of the collar with one hand, and underneath the elbow with the other hand. Attackers on the street won't likely be wearing a uniform, but the throw always works the same way: subtly lead your partner off the centerline in a way that eliminates the sensation of pushing or pulling. Then take out the support leg with your leg. If you do this well, you don't even need to sweep the leg at all! This may seem impossible, but if your weight positioning is correct and if you lead your opponent with relaxed technique, you won't need to kick out his or her support leg. Your opponent will simply fall due to loss of balance.

Osoto gari is one throw that every martial artist should know. It is just as important as knowing how to punch, block, and kick. Any simple clinch can be swiftly resolved with this art. Also, knowing this technique may protect you from an opponent who also knows how to do this.

Sayunage

The other essential core throw, sayunage, is characterized by stepping behind your opponent and transferring your weight onto him or her so that the opponent basically trips backward over your front leg. To perform this technique, enter in behind your opponent on the same side as his or her leading leg. Often this technique will be performed as you deflect a punch or other strike while entering. Then, place your inner thigh against his or her leading leg, and then with both arms, move your weight over to your opponent. This will cause him or her to fall over your leg. When done in a subtle way, your opponent will fall without realizing why he or she is falling. If you tense up, your opponent will too, and then this art will turn into physical struggle, thereby making it useless.

Exercises with Sayunage

Standing

Before jumping into using throws from a dynamic attack it is sometimes useful to break things down so you can isolate key portions of a technique. Sayunage requires a very subtle changing of weight, and this lesson can be overlooked or missed entirely if you just jump in at full speed. Ask your training partner to stand in a fighting stance with his or her arms at the sides. Move close to your partner and put your front leg so that it is behind him or her. Stand in a horse stance and perform the holding-ball exercise. Turn your torso to face your partner and push, making sure to use your back muscles and not your arms. If you use your arm power, your partner can resist you easily and will not fall. If you use the correct placement of weight and torso rotation, your partner will fall.

Low Punch or Front Kick

Have your partner step in with a punch or front kick to your stomach. Step forward and deflect the attack with your leading hand lightly; you should be entering to the outside of the attack. Place your foot behind your partner, and imagine holding a large sack of potatoes and then tossing this sack onto your partner. The result should be that he or she falls.

High Punch

It may be difficult to get your leading hand over your partner's outstretching punch if it is coming at your face, so go underneath it instead. Deflect the attack upward as you step in and behind your partner. Shift your weight onto your front leg and allow your partner to trip on your leg.

Double punches seen in kata, such as naifanchi, typically sayunage throws rather than two punches. You can certainly interpret a double punch as two punches or even a block and punch, but you'll miss out on a valuable technique. Kata often have many motions that appear like strikes, but are actually throws.

Core throws have the advantage of working the majority of the time because our entire body weight is employed during the execution of the throw. Even a sloppy core throw will usually down an average opponent. The disadvantage of core throws is that you have to get super close to your opponent to use them, which is fine if the opponent is unarmed, but potentially deadly if he or she has a knife or pistol. You don't need to learn all the variations of core throws if you do not study a throwing art; osoto gari and sayunage are enough—they are simple, easy, and devastating throws.

Extremity Throws

Extremity throws utilize joint manipulation, and therefore typically work better when our opponents' arms are outstretched. Extremity throws are ideal if your opponent has a weapon such as a knife, gun, or any other sort of improvised weapon, such as a wrench or broken bottle. With an extremity throw, you can not only disarm your opponent, but you can throw him or her down to the ground in the exact same motion.

If our opponent guards his or her hand or arm from this manipulation by bringing the arms in close to the body, these arts become more difficult to employ. However, typical use of weapons requires your opponent to stretch out with the arm in order to stab, slash, or bludgeon you. This stretching places him or her in a position of vulnerability that we can exploit with impossible extremity throws.

Kote Oroshi

Naifanchi kata demonstrates *kote oroshi* (called *kote gaeshi* by other styles), another art similar to and therefore named after one found in aikido. To visualize how this wrist throw works, look at your left palm, and place your right palm on the back of your left hand. Then grab the base of your left thumb with your other hand. Your right thumb should be between your left pinky and left ring finger in the metacarpal region of the hand. Now, stretch the hand to its limit by moving both wrists downward toward your waist. You should feel a stretch through your left wrist all the way to your elbow. When done on a partner, kote oroshi produces a stunning amount of pain, and the only escape from that pain is to either sacrifice the arm or fall down. Most people fall down rather than break their arm.

In practice, kote oroshi works well if a partner lunges at you with a punch or stab. Move off-line, and then catch his extended hand with whichever hand you have closer to the partner. For example, if he or she punches with the right hand, move off-line and catch with your left hand to apply kote oroshi with the help of your right hand, which will follow your partner's fingers to the floor. This technique is difficult if the partner is in the motion of retracting his or her hand backward. Abandon this art if it fails at this point, because the partner will be in an excellent position to counterattack, with you unable to block because both your hands will be occupied holding his or hers. Rather than stubbornly force the throw, step in and perform a core throw, as the energy has gone from extension to retraction. Follow the energy, and you will have a more powerful throw; work against the energy, and the throw will be laborious.

If your shoulders are tense and rising upward toward your ears, you will have a difficult time throwing kote oroshi. Relax your shoulders. Additionally, if you are reaching out toward your partner, you are reaching your arms into "his" or "her" world. Bring your partner's hand into "your" world, which is closer to your center, and you will see a dramatic improvement in this throw. Thus, you must stretch out your partner's arm and bring it closer to your center so that you can place your entire body weight (via your hands) to bear on his or her wrist. It is very difficult to resist this much power with only the wrist.

Ikkyo

Ikkyo is a dynamic and complex art that can be performed in a variety of ways. At its core, you are grabbing your opponent's wrist or hand and crossing his or her body with it while swinging your opponent down to the ground. This technique uses the bone-on-bone chain discussed with punching, but uses it against our opponent to connect his or her entire structure to produce a stunning, face-first fall. When I was first thrown ikkyo, it spun me around in the opposite direction of my teacher, and my face smashed against my knee. My teeth actually penetrated skin, and for a moment, I wondered if I broke a tooth. While I was busy pondering this, I was laid out face-first upon the ground and pinned there before I could react. The speed at which I was taken off-balance and rendered useless on the floor shocked me. I had thought I could have counterattacked during the throw, but not only was I not able to counterattack; I was not able to do much of anything useful.

Ikkyo is an extremity throw used in aikido, but it is also seen in nahate style's sanchin kata. This art takes your opponent's arm upward toward his or her face, turning the body away from you because of the natural connections in the arm. From here, you can send your opponent down to the ground with ease. There are dozens of ways of getting to this position, but an easy one to do immediately is this: grasp your opponent's right hand with your right hand, but with your thumb facing downward, not extended like you're shaking hands. Squeeze the metacarpal area with your hand and then bring your opponent's arm up by bringing your elbow down. From this position, squeeze your fingers in a fist, starting with your pinky finger, and bring your arm down by your side. Do not push toward your opponent; simply drop your arm.

Aim your opponent's fingers in the direction of his or her forehead. This straight-down feeling should be like you are cutting your opponent in half with an invisible laser. Use this, or whatever imagery you want, to lend power to this technique. This pain comes on suddenly, so be careful not to injure your opponent. Most people will twist away from this pain, and will then be facing the mat. If the opponent twists the other way, he or she will essentially throw himself or herself by going directly into the pain. At this point, you can send your opponent to the mat by pointing his or her fingers downward and applying pressure to the elbow.

Failing to have this laser-beam type of feeling that cuts our opponent in half usually results in moving the hand away from your opponent and in front of him or her. This will merely twist your opponent's body and encourage him or her to keep twisting. An experienced martial artist will then rotate and do a spinning back fist or spinning elbow with his or her free hand. With both of your hands occupied on your opponent's one arm, this leaves you in a horrible position. That is why it is imperative to squeeze your fingers that are holding your opponent's hand, so that it takes the slack out of his or her muscles and stretches them correctly. Your intent must go through your opponent and not around him or her. Going around your opponent means you are avoiding his or her center, and your opponent will be less affected by this technique. When done well though, ikkyo creates sudden, shocking pain and a downward momentum that your opponent will not have expected.

Kote oroshi and ikkyo are opposite arts; one art throws to the outside of the body, and the other throws in the inside. This opposite effect is one of the primary reasons why these two extremity throws are so essential. If your opponent were to grab you one way, you could easily slip into kote oroshi. If your opponent grabs the opposite way, you could throw ikkyo instead. By knowing both of these arts, we can be prepared for either attack.

Just as jujitsu has an impressive array of core throws, aikido has an impressive array of extremity throws. This is because historically aikido dealt more with armed opponents, and extremity throws work well against those who have objects in their hands.

However, extremity throws require more finesse to apply than core throws, and the application of your weight can have subtle yet drastic changes to the throw. Your body weight needs to be in the correct spot at the correct time; otherwise you will meet with failure. If your weight is slightly back or the angle is slightly off, the technique may not work; a slight degree in the right direction with the correct placement of weight, however, and the throw becomes devastating. You must diligently practice these arts to see and experience where the correct angles are. Explanations and pictures do not do these arts justice; you have to feel them to know exactly what is happening.

This is why it is important to throw as many people as we can. It's amazing how different body types behave in different manners. Throwing a skinny person is different from throwing a fat person, just as throwing a short person is very different from throwing a tall person. Once you can sense someone's weight, it doesn't matter what your opponent's build is, because you've got him or her. However, you cannot simply intellectualize this practice; you need to get on the mat and throw everyone. Likewise, you need to be thrown a lot. Being thrown also teaches you how to throw. If you discover that the pain makes you behave in a certain manner and someone is manhandling you in a different direction than you would naturally fall, then you can see his or her error. You can learn from his or her error and apply it to improving your arts.

Relaxed Power while Grappling or Restraining an Opponent

Many real fights often get taken down to the ground and rapidly devolve into a grappling situation. I am told this was not always true in the fifties and sixties because society was brought up on boxing, which made it more acceptable to go toe-to-toe with an opponent. Today, many people are familiar with Mixed Martial Arts, and there are a great many armchair martial artists who may know vaguely how to tie someone up by bringing him or her to the ground like in MMA matches. No matter what your style is, you should be familiar with the basics of grappling, as this is a very real possibility. Learning how to conserve your energy and save your strength while in a grapple may save your life. This is why at least a rudimentary understanding of grappling is important for the mastery mind-set. If you are a karate practitioner but only study karate techniques, then are you truly focused on mastery?

Any martial artist can benefit from grappling training. We do not want to waste energy when we pin an opponent; we want our opponent to waste his or hers. Whether this is a choke hold, wrist pin, arm bar, leg hold, or simply sitting on our opponent, we must relax. We want to conserve our energy while he or she wastes energy with futile attempts at escape. Even if you do not manage a perfect choke or masterful restraint, sometimes it is simply enough to hold the person still. This lets you catch your breath, while he or she can only squirm.

I once grappled with a friend of mine who is an exceptional grappler. The grapple lasted about twenty-five minutes to a standstill, but I had to give up—I was exhausted. He could have outlasted me through endurance and forced me to tap out once the last of my strength had left. You may assume that he was in better shape than me, but this was not the case. He had a more relaxed mind, and he allowed me to be like a crashing wave on the beach; all he had to do was wait out the storm.

To practice relaxing while grappling, one may simply just do more grappling practice. However, for those who do not practice grappling arts, I would suggest the following exercise. Have your opponent start with his or her back on the ground, with you in his or her guard. That is, you will be between his or her legs, and for the purpose of this exercise, start in seiza (kneeling position). Your opponent will then attempt to pull you closer and try to choke you in any way he or she can (if you wear a stiff uniform, this is a good starting point). You will resist the attempts by placing both hands on his or her chest and practicing unbendable arm. You will relax your body and your mind by looking up and over your opponent. Do not shrink your mind by narrowing your field of view. For those who lack experience with grappling, the most important thing you can do is calm your mind through steady, relaxed breaths. Do not go on the offensive, as you will waste your energy. Wait it out.

As soon as your opponent gets tired and gives up, it can then become time to act. For those in striking arts, this is when we strike—when our opponent has wasted all of his or her energy trying to take us down. For grappling specialists, this is the moment that we put on that inescapable pin.

Another easy grappling strategy may be to simply lay your chest on your opponent's chest and become deadweight. Even if you only weigh a hundred pounds, your opponent's breathing will be more difficult, and if he or she panics, he or she may become exhausted quickly. When doing this, protect your head and try to keep your opponent's arms trapped by your elbows and knees. A good grappler might be able to get out of this quickly, so do not act aggressively until you have a straight shot where you can employ a good strike.

Many grapplers are used to dojo rules: no eye gouging, no groin crushing, and no small-joint manipulations. This is obviously to play it safe during practice, but real grapples can become as messy as it gets. Don't hesitate to get nasty if need be. If you find a finger, break it and rub the two ends of bone together. Dig your fingers into eyes, or even bite if you have to. I once ended a grapple with a simple pinch to my opponent's inner thigh. Simply catch a tiny piece of flesh in a tender spot and give it a good squeeze. If you grab too much flesh, this will not work; it will be a dull pain. We want a sharp, severe pain. My opponent leaped to his feet and jumped back and away.

Another time I was sparring with a second-degree black belt in jujitsu. She was not used to sparring, so she tried to take me down to a grapple. I punched her in the face three times, then lifted her entire body in the air over my head and slammed her into the mat. She's a good sport and a gifted martial artist, but this was too much for her and she tapped out. She then said that what I did was illegal. I looked at her quizzically and replied, "Not in my dojo!"

If you do study grappling, understand that grappling is like sparring in many ways; it is the "sport" incarnation of your art. While a great exercise, it is only a piece of the puzzle. Whether you are a grappler or not, relaxed power is still your best friend on the ground and sometimes the only way to ensure victory.

Weapon Arts

When I first started training in martial arts, I thought weapon practice was stupid. After all, I am never going to carry a spear, sword, *nunchaku*, *sai*, or *tonfa* in daily life. I suppose that one could argue that you could grab a chair leg or pool cue and really get mediaeval on someone, but introducing weapons to a fight will only escalate the situation. Moreover, it will be looked on poorly by law enforcement and courts, potentially turning you into the bad guy. In many places, martial arts weapons are illegal to even walk around with. I remember standing in my kung fu studio holding a Chinese broadsword and thinking, "I don't even know how to punch. Why am I bothering using this thing that I will never carry and never use?"

There is some truth to this, and certainly for your first ten years of training, I would not recommend weapon arts too much, as the time it takes to get better at these skills does not necessarily give you more of an advantage in anything directly applicable to modern self-defense. Once you have the ability to competently actuate unarmed defenses, armed arts begin to have an appeal. Armed arts may not be about realism, but they do offer things that are valuable to our practice. First of all, weapons are cool, and if you are having fun training with something, you may be more likely to practice. Also, if you get bored with your daily training routine, you can change it up by picking up some weapons and practice weapon arts.

I practice swordsmanship and *jo* (short staff), mostly because these are the arts of aikido that I studied when I was a live-in student. Today, I look at the subtle things that weapons training can do for us. The most valuable benefit is that weapons will magnify your bad technique and really show you what you need to work on, for example, whether you are relaxed or tense in your techniques. If you hold a sword with stiff hands, then the sword will rise and fall with your breath, which your opponent could use to anticipate your timing. Additionally, this type of grip will often indicate that you're overcompensating during your swing, making your blade bounce at the end of the strike. This means, should you cut something, your sword will stick in your target and not slice through it. If you are making your breathing obvious to your opponent, he or she can sense your timing and therefore exploit it. This sort of thing can also be happening from an unarmed fighting stance, but you may never know it because of the safety of dojo practice. Training with weapons can therefore be a useful exercise to enhance your other techniques, even if the only benefit is to focus your mind toward increasing control over the subconscious movements of your body.

Target practice with weapons that far outstrip your physical reach will improve the accuracy of your hands and feet when used unarmed. When I first heard about "aiming" punches, I thought my sensei was mad. You aim guns, not fists! Then he proceeded to dodge my punches by subtly shifting his body so my fists glanced off of him harmlessly. He didn't have to block because my fists were off-target. Training with weapons allows you the opportunity to see these things much more clearly because the misses will be obvious; therefore, you can easily set goals to hone elements of your unarmed techniques. Sometimes you may have a habit in your unarmed arts that is not obvious until you hold a weapon.

Weapons are fantasies to the extreme. Swords are obsolete now, and if I ever had to use one on a battlefield, we would have to have some serious problems in the world—maybe an industrial collapse that prevents us from making firearms, or some kind of zombie apocalypse or something. This is not very likely. However, understanding the sword is imperative to aikido, because all of the arts of aikido can be done with, or without, a sword. The movements of aikido were designed so that you only have to learn one set of arts, arts that have application whether you have a sword or not. Likewise, the arts of the tonfa for karate are similar to the blocks and strikes in unarmed arts, and so training in tonfa has immediate benefits to our unarmed training.

By practicing with swords, your aikido throws will be better. This is because the sword cuts well when the cutting lines you make with it are straight. If your hands are stiff when you cut, the lines you make in the air with the sword will waver, and thus the sword will be forced to cut through more material. With live blade cutting (*tameshigiri*), this type of poor sword swing will result either in your sword sticking in the target or knocking the target off the stand altogether. For aikido throwing arts, if you cut down in a similar fashion while unarmed, your throws may not work at all. The straight cut, then, is useful in developing a clear sense for the motion of throwing opponents down. In fact, there are several arts in aikido that treat your opponent's own arm as if it were a sword, the throws being initiated by you swinging his or her arm in very sword-like motions. Sometimes these throws end in simple falls, others with you tying your opponent's arms up like a pretzel, but no matter the outcome, the same control that you must demonstrate here, you can learn by honing your skill with a sword.

Weapon training is another way to practice relaxed power. You should be able to take a wooden sword and cut through another wooden sword with ease. If you are not able to do this, I would argue that you do not understand relaxed power as it relates to an extension of your body. My aikido sensei would often make people's *bokken* (wooden swords) explode during class to prove that it was indeed possible.

To do this, you need a relaxed, yet firm, grip. Too tight of a grip, and your sword will "bounce off" the other sword; too loose, and you will drop the weapon. Your body weight must be a part of the strike, and your weight must match the focal point in the same way we punch or kick. You must also understand the natural swing of your own arm. That may seem like a stupid bit of advice, but when most people swing a stick or sword, they have an upward movement with their weapon at the end of the swing. This upward feeling will take away 90 percent of your swing's power. Your feeling must be down and *through*. Remember that this shouldn't be a push. Pushing through with your stick on your opponent's stick will have no power to break the other's weapon. Pushing will probably make you inadvertently strike your opponent's hands.

The skill required to break a wooden sword by using a wooden sword can be translated over to unarmed practice. Training with wooden swords in this fashion will help improve all of your blocks. This type of force teaches you how to create vibration and shock in something else. You can try this out by having your opponent stick out one of his or her arms in a fist, palm up. Practice striking downward upon the arm using a downward-sweeping block (gedan barai). At the point of impact, do not push your opponent. Your hand should remain at the point of impact, and your opponent's arm should be the one that moves away. Squeeze your hand lightly at the point of impact to create that shock wave to send through your opponent's outstretched arm. Remember to dial up the intensity to an appropriate level for your opponent. Don't just smash him or her using 100 percent power.

I have stopped destroying other people's bokken in this fashion, as I am usually the one who has to pay the bill. I taught a seminar once where I demonstrated this, and after impact, I saw the student wince. I took another look at his bokken and realized that it was a really nice one. He had paid $80 for it, and he had it for only a week or so. After that, I refrained from demonstrating this anymore simply because it was rude. Yet it is completely possible once you've mastered the technique. Because the same feeling can shatter arms just as easily as wooden swords, there is an incentive to rack up a little bit of a bill to experience it firsthand. Just be sure to get all the splinters off the mat!

If I were armed with a sword and had to fight an unarmed opponent, I would win, unless of course he or she were a faster runner than I am. I have seen BS arts where people catch the sword with their bare hands midswing. This may be possible under controlled situations, but one twist of the sword and the person loses body parts.

A friend of mine practices European sword arts with live blades and real armor. One day he was fencing with another practitioner, and he decided not to wear his leg armor, as they were just practicing. He parried a thrust that was redirected *through* his calf. The other man pulled his sword free, and my friend did not feel the pain so he thought it must have been a scratch. Minutes later, his boot filled with blood, and he had to be taken to the hospital. He was really intrigued by his first real sword wound because it caused very little pain, and yet he could have bled to death.

It is really easy to hurt each other with these things, and it would be very difficult to disarm someone who was hell-bent on killing you. A simple poke with a three-foot razor blade can be the end of your life. Practicing with a live blade gives you a new perspective on many arts.

Karate kobudo has many weapons: bo, sai, tonfa, kama, and nunchaku, to name a few. The two that I find most useful are the nunchaku and the tonfa. Weapons like nunchaku are excellent at building hand-eye coordination, but be warned: everyone who practices with this weapon will hit himself or herself in the head painfully. I've seen fourth-degree black belts whack themselves in the face with nunchaku, and they had over twenty-five years of experience.

Tonfa are useful in teaching beginners how to block. The blocks employed with this weapon are identical to the standard blocks in karate practice. Downward block, rising block, uchi uke, and soto uke are all the same. By using simple drills with tonfa, you can practice basic blocking procedures that are very clear about the direction of an attack. They can spice up a class and make a lot of exciting noise, but I would not carry any of these weapons around with me.

Sai and kama are fun, but have even fewer real-world applications. A dagger or an axe is a much more potent weapon than the kama or sai could ever hope to be. The sai is blunt and heavy; a dagger is light and swift. The sai was supposedly carried in threes, one to throw and two for use in melee combat. People will make the argument that the sai could be used to catch and deflect weapons, but since you will not be carrying a sai, let alone two of them, this is a moot point. One can easily carry a knife daily. Also, for anyone remotely trained in sword, to catch a swordsman's blade with a sai would be an amazing feat. I've only seen this in demonstrations, where the swordsman had to go deliberately slow so that the practitioner with the sai could catch the sword. If you had to face someone with a sword and the sai was all you had, you would use it. But if you had a sword, you would use that because it is simply a better weapon.

The kama, if used to chop like an axe, would surely break, and so a simple hatchet would outperform a kama. The kama is great at cutting grass. I would choose a three-inch knife over a kama any day.

The bo staff is too big in my opinion, and the jo is much faster and can be employed with one hand if need be. If you have an injured hand, you will not be able to effectively swing a bo one-handed. You can choke up your grip on a jo and effectively strike one-handed. Also, when I go hiking, I sometimes bring a jo because it just looks like a walking stick to the uninitiated. This is the only martial arts weapon I ever carry.

Perhaps the single most important weapon technique you can practice is the swordsmanship strike called *shomen uchi*. Shomen uchi is a downward strike, where you raise the sword above your head and then drop it straight down. It seems so simple and basic because it is, yet the combination of coordination, weight placement, and intent make it invaluable in focusing your mind in ways that can positively impact all of your arts.

When I first learned this art, my aikido sensei would make me swing the sword at least one thousand times per session. I thought the old man was crazy, and each time I asked him about sword technique, we would just end up doing more of this downward strike. We rarely practiced blocks with the sword, and this puzzled me. Isn't blocking more important? It was only years later that I realized just how significant this practice was. The Japanese swordsmanship mind-set should be only to cut down your opponent. There is no such thing as a block if your mind is fierce enough; you will force your opponent to stop attacking and go on the defensive. If your opponent rushes in, you strike downward. If your opponent cuts diagonally toward you with a sword, you cut downward. If your opponent tries to cut your leg, you cut downward. If your opponent tries to cut your head, you cut downward. This single-mindedness means that your brain is not cluttered with technique or strategy. Your strategy is to murder your opponent from head to toe.

When I would face my teacher, he would employ this method and simply strike at my head with his wooden (and sometimes real) swords. He would always stop before he killed me, but his strike was so swift and so filled with intent that I was simply unable to reach him with any attack I threw at him.

It is this single-mindedness that should be the core of our mastery mind-set. We have a job to do, and we do it. There are no arguments in our minds. There are no questions in our minds. There is only the purpose of surviving by overwhelming your opponent with this force of will. This is the true reason for practicing weapon arts. Sure, we can learn how to employ improvised weapons in a real situation perhaps, but this is a secondary reason for learning how to use weapons. We are using weapons to better understand the power of death. We use it to conquer our own fear of death and to make others fearful of us should we ever need to use any of our arts, not just our weapon arts. Sometimes when your opponent faces enough fear, he or she disengages and the fight can be over before someone dies.

Throws as Defenses against Weapons

Both kote oroshi and ikkyo may be employed to disarm attackers wielding weapons. Be warned, however, this is much easier to do in the dojo than it is to do with a live opponent who wants to kill you. Even though you might disarm your opponent, you will likely be cut, stabbed, or clubbed in the process. I like doing these arts in demonstrations because they are dramatic and interesting; however, these might not be the most realistic defenses against weapons.

My best advice to defeat an armed attacker is to simply get away. There's nothing cowardly about escaping from armed hostility. But if you are cornered and have to fight, arrest the weapon arm with a grab, but do not attempt to take the weapon away. Once you've immobilized your opponent's arm, use your free hand or feet to beat the attacker senseless. This is why I believe it is important to practice punching from a variety of nonoptimal positions. You should be able to punch when you are grappling just as hard as you can punch while standing.

There is one advantage you have against an armed opponent: his or her mind will tend to be fixated on using that weapon. I've found that people with a knife will focus only on using it, and won't kick or punch with their other hand. Impede the use of the weapon, but not so much that your opponent wishes to switch hands with it. Your opponent must feel as if he or she has a fighting chance with whatever hand he or she initially had the weapon in. Use this fixation to beat him or her senseless, almost ignoring the weapon. You may still get stabbed, shot, cut, or clubbed, but you have a greater chance of surviving than if attempting a foolish takeaway.

I often illustrate how deadly knives are by practicing an exercise in class. I give one student a wooden dagger and tell him or her to attack another student anywhere but the face and groin. The defending student is instructed to take the knife away from his or her opponent. In about two minutes, the person with the knife will have stabbed or slashed his or her unarmed opponent twenty to fifty times, regardless of martial arts background. Even if you know how to disarm knives from opponents, doing this in real time is a very different exercise.

There are some who believe that by practicing defenses against knives, swords, or pistols that they will become invulnerable to attacks with these weapons. This is a foolish delusion. A knife wielded by a novice can kill an experienced martial artist easily. If a murder weapon, such as a knife, enters a fight, your first defense is to flee. I don't care how much experience you have and how weak your opponent is. One mistake can cost you a finger, eye, spleen, or your life. Do not look at knives as cutlery; knives are murder weapons. If you cannot get away, your objective is to seize the weapon arm and crush the person wielding it. Do not attempt to disarm the opponent. Hold his or her weapon arm so you don't get stabbed and then wreak havoc on your opponent's vitals, starting with the face and throat. Only attempt a disarming technique when your opponent is subdued or incredibly distracted. All other attempts at disarming will likely result in catastrophe.

As an aside, do not carry knives as self-defense weapons. Knives are often looked at with more suspicion than guns are in a court of law. In Washington State, you may get a permit to carry a concealed pistol, but this does not cover carrying a concealed knife. Knives in urban areas are often restricted to less than three-inch blade length. Also, stabbing someone is a serious offense, even if you were in the right to do so in defense; the gruesome nature of stabbing makes it very challenging to prove that you were right. Leave the knives at home. Learn how to make greater use of your body for self-defense.

Falling

The art of falling is a martial arts skill that, while incredibly useful and arguably the most important aspect of self-defense, is likely the least romantic. When compared to devastating punches and power-absorption techniques, practicing falling seems very lame. However, consider this: how embarrassing would it be to become a master of martial arts, only to fall accidentally one day and become horribly crippled or die? I feel compelled to write about falling arts because I have had a number of extraordinary experiences with them that have changed my life.

The first time was when I had helped organize a self-defense seminar to be taught by my aikido sensei. For the first two hours of the program, we did nothing but falling. This is not what I expected at all. He later explained that if you are going to die accidentally, it is going to either be in a car or by falling down. So knowing how to avoid death from a simple fall is an awesome skill to have. It might not be sexy, but living is much more sexy than cracking your head open.

Think of how many times you have fallen in your life. Is this number greater than the number of times you have gotten into real fights? Have you ever tripped on ice? Have you ever walked down a flight of stairs, only to miss a step and fall face-first into the floor? Have you ever been walking outside and tripped over a fallen branch? Have you ever slipped on a freshly waxed floor? Have you ever fallen while skiing, snowboarding, or skating? Falling down happens more times than we may remember, but as we get older, falling down can have very serious medical complications or even cause death. Practicing the art of self-defense, then, must include arts for falling.

We used to do aikido demonstrations during a local street fair. One year, the fair committee forgot to bring us mats, but we did the demonstration anyway ... on the concrete. When we found out, all we students could do was stare at the ground, our eyes bulging. Our sensei came over to us and said in the most ominous tone I've ever heard him use, "Don't worry about the ground; worry about me."

We did the demonstration, but I was still worried about the ground. This state of worry only makes falling safely more challenging. If you are in distress about falling and you fear injury, your movements may be stiffer and less supple in nature, resulting in harder falls and more damage. My hesitancy to fall likely made my sensei feel the need to throw slightly harder; after all, we were at a demonstration, and his reputation was on the line. Because I was so tense, I ended up chipping my right elbow on the concrete. This was an experience that I would not want to repeat, and yet I did anyway the following year in the same demonstration. Yes, I chipped both elbows, and for the next three years, I had a bone chip floating in my elbows; I could not rest my elbows upon chairs for this entire time, nor could I practice elbow strikes. But the third year I had learned my lesson on falling, and I did not use my arm as much to stop the fall. I was also more relaxed, and my worry about falling had diminished to the point where it no longer bothered me. This taught me that the biggest factor in falling is your mental attitude toward it. Fear it, and it will hurt. Accept it and roll with it.

For many people, taking hard falls (flipping in midair and landing on your side) without injury is a challenging skill to learn. To do a hard fall on concrete, do not slap the ground. Touch the ground lightly with your arm that is closest to the ground, and make sure that your body lands in unison on the ground. When you are in the dojo, this can be described as hearing one sound when you fall. *Womp.* If you hear several sounds while you fall, it means that you are impacting the ground with different parts of your body. That could be your knee, hip, ribs, elbow, or whatever. In the dojo with mats this won't matter at all, but on concrete, this means the force of your falling body will hit at a single point first and probably cause injury. We must displace the energy by having a large portion of our body contact the ground simultaneously so that damage is spread over a larger area rather than a single point. Hearing multiple sounds when you fall is a bad habit that should polish out with practice; it will get you seriously injured if you have to fall on concrete.

Ideally your fall should make absolutely no sound when you hit the ground. This sounds impossible, but it isn't. One need not be only a hundred pounds to accomplish this task; one must only study falling to understand its mysteries. Think of this like walking silently. You can stomp your feet and make noise, or you can place your weight down softly and make no noise. The same holds true about falling, and I would argue that walking in its strictest sense is merely falling and catching your balance. It is for this reason that to get better at falling silently, you must also master silent footsteps.

To land without noise, one must remain relaxed and calm, and take control of the body when falling. If you resist the ground by bracing for impact, you will make a tremendous *thud* sound. You must accept that you are falling and take control of the momentum to slow it down or speed it up as necessary.

Another key component to falling well is to tuck your chin. Failure to tuck your chin can result in your head hitting the ground. This is probably the worst thing that could happen while falling. I once did a demonstration where my partner punched me in the chest; I jumped behind him to drop his shoulders to the mat. I missed his shoulders, so I grabbed his face instead. This caused him to rotate in midair, and he landed on his shoulders, almost on his neck. His head then snapped back and hit the ground. He was only unconscious for a second or two, and he popped right back up. But he was done for the day and sat out for the rest of the demonstration. Fortunately for him, the injury wasn't too bad because we had mats that time, but had he tucked his chin a bit, I believe this would not have happened.

I got to practice a real-world application of these two falling concepts, being relaxed and tucking the chin, when I had a painting job during my time as a live-in student. I was on a ladder two stories up when I suddenly lost balance. I fell two stories, ironically being able to not only remove my leg from between the rungs but also place my paint bucket on a ledge moments before tumbling back headfirst! I relaxed into the fall and landed in the grass, my head remaining safe thanks to my body's muscle memory of doing it a thousand times during class. (Tucking the chin means to tilt your chin toward your chest; this protects the back of your head and your neck from any whiplash that may occur from a fall.) I immediately got up and checked my legs and body to see if they were broken. I was fine! Then a smile grew ear-to-ear, and I looked around for witnesses. No witnesses. (It would seem that there are only witnesses if you actually get hurt.)

Another type of falling, and one that can make practicing falling arts sexier, is sacrifice falls; however, these tend to be a little bit dangerous to practice. For instance, once a good friend of mine was in class when another student did a bear hug on him. The man doing the bear hug was known for his "iron grip of death," which very few could escape. My friend tried to get out of the grip using our standard techniques, but when these failed, he leaped into the air, taking his bear-hugging attacker with him. He then flipped and did a hard fall on top of the attacker. He got free, but it also broke the man's ribs.

Sacrifice throws are not my favorite method of self-defense because you have to throw yourself down to the ground in order to throw your opponent. If there is only one opponent, a sacrifice throw may make sense, especially if you are falling down anyway. But in a multiple-opponent situation, a sacrifice throw may spell death for you. It is nice, however, to have one or two of these throws up your sleeve for that "just-in-case" moment. Jujitsu has a myriad of one-off versions of sacrifice throws, but I've found I only really need one or two of these. Where these throws really shine is when you are in a situation where you are already losing balance and about to fall. You might as well take your opponent down with you.

A Disclaimer on Fighting

When I was a live-in student, I really wanted to test my martial art skills in the real world. I would prowl around bad neighborhoods, and for a period of a few months, I would even creep through dark parks at three in the morning. I was looking for a fight, waiting for some bad guy. I was hoping for something terrible to happen so I could swoop in there and save the day. But then it occurred to me: *I was the weirdo in the park*. I had this OMG moment, and I walked home in shame. I never found a fight, and I think that this is really the best outcome. Perhaps there is a one-weirdo-in-the-park limit, because I never met another, or maybe some angel was looking out for me; either way, I stopped doing this sort of practice.

Letting go of the need to prove your arts is a reflection of maturity, which helps set you on the road to mastery. Masters do not pick fights. Masters won't provoke others to fight or otherwise engage in hostile actions unless it is absolutely necessary. Many of us join martial arts schools to learn how to fight, but once that skill is learned, we begin to see the harsh ramifications there are to fighting.

Real fighting is dirty, ugly, and unpredictable. Even if you punch the guy and knock him out, his buddies may draw guns and shoot you in the back. A best-case scenario is that you drop the guy, and then the police arrive and you fill out a statement and then go through the legal system. This could end up costing you time and money, but look at the worst-case scenario: the guy gets the better of you and breaks something you love, like your spine. Or you drop him, while his buddies stab your girlfriend. Or maybe you drop him, and weeks later he and his friends find you and tear your car to pieces.

Fighting should be avoided at almost all costs. If your life or someone else's life is in danger, then act accordingly and fight. If a drunken man bumps into you at a bar, then there is no reason to go to guns. You don't really realize the ramifications of these kinds of violent encounters until they happen to you. Even then, they can't be thought of as black-and-white situations.

For example, I was once attacked by a drunken man. He took a swing at me, and I sidestepped it. In that moment, I thought, *He tried to hit me. I should hit him back.* I didn't, though, and he kept swinging. I dodged each swing because he was so inebriated that he couldn't even see straight. I didn't even have to raise my hands to block. He took perhaps twenty swings at me, got really tired, and then cursed like a sailor at me and left.

About ten minutes later, a police car pulled up and asked me if I had seen anyone that matched this guy's description. "Yes," I said, "he tried to punch me twenty times." The officer explained that the man assaulted a couple down the street and had run away. It was then that I felt a tremendous amount of guilt. I had protected myself, and I thought I did not need to strike this person, because after all, he was too drunk to do anything really. But he was too drunk to hit me, not untrained people. People got hurt because I failed to act, and this is something I will never forget. I had thought that this man could not cause anyone any harm, because he did not cause me harm. But I am well trained, and more importantly, well disciplined. My mind did not think of how this person could have affected others; my mind was stuck on my own well-being. In hindsight, I should have detained this person and called the police. Knowing when to fight, then, is not necessarily cut-and-dried.

Even the wisest person cannot see all possible outcomes of how violence will shape and influence the future. One small fight could escalate into more violence and uglier retaliation. Developing the wisdom to see potential consequences to our actions is vital for the larger picture. If someone simply attacks you randomly, then you should defend yourself instinctually and not worry about the bigger picture. Worry about the bigger picture only if violence is looming and hasn't actually happened yet. Learn from my mistake about the drunken-man encounter. This man was clearly dangerous to some people, and I had the ability to do something about it, but I failed to act. I had succeeded in protecting myself, but I failed to protect others. As masters, we can help improve the world through our action, especially if we can accomplish it without hurting people.

Martial artists often fantasize about violence, but the arts play more with violence than actually experiencing it. This is why I don't think style is all that important when it comes to self-defense. Arts have a tendency to devolve once panic, fear, and rage set in. Try not to get your head caught up in a dojo mentality. Many things practiced in the dojo do not translate well when actual violence is occurring. For example, even taking a basic fighting stance may communicate the wrong message. If you take a fighting stance to defend yourself and say something like, "I don't want to fight!" your body language is saying exactly the opposite of what your words are.

In the dojo, even if you are knocked down, thrown, or tapped out in a grapple, the fight will usually stop there. I've had some students get heated and continue fighting after I called to stop, but even then, no serious blows were struck. Emotions may have been hurt, but no one was really physically damaged. No one is going to lay the boots to you in the dojo, even if things did get out of control. We all know that this safety net is there, and it is there with good reason, but knowing it is there affects our behavior and arts. In real situations, you don't have the luxury of a safety net.

We must always remember that our training in the dojo, no matter how sincere our practice, is not real fighting. People who really want to do you harm will not stop if you are knocked down or thrown—they'll trash you as you lie on the ground. People really wishing to kill you will likely use weapons ruthlessly—there won't be clean attacks or fair warning.

If you've practiced for a good length of time, you might think that you're ready for anything, but think about this: when we are in the dojo, we are warmed up, well stretched, and hydrated. This can sometimes give us an illusion of greater ability than what we actually have. If you just got fired from your job, dumped by your girlfriend, or are feeling the buzz of a few drinks, do you think you are at your best to handle a surprise situation?

Also, there are some really bizarre laws governing self-defense. In Washington State, a kick is considered lethal force and an escalating factor in a fight. This means that if someone punches you and you kick him or her in self-defense, you are at fault and potentially going to jail. If someone kicks you, you are allowed to kick him or her in defense, but not before. For skilled martial artists, this doesn't matter, because we can cause as much grievous injury with our hands as we can with our feet, but in the court of law, this doesn't matter.

Also, throwing is considered a softer defense and can be used quite freely. I find this odd, because throwing is perhaps the easiest way to really hurt someone. One leg sweep, and you can trash someone's skull on the ground and possibly kill him or her. But in the court system, you were trying to de-escalate the situation by choosing a throwing defense.

Check your local laws, and make sure you are practicing arts that won't end you up in jail should you use them. Remember too that the fantasized image of martial arts combat is just that: a fantasy. Poor arts will fail you as a fight devolves into a messy, intense tangle of limbs and curses. If you can achieve the arts of the mastery mind-set, that won't matter, because you will remain calm and adapt to any situation that even a skilled professional thug can throw at you. Coming home at the end of the day is, then, the true self-defense, not being able to execute an acrobatic spinning back kick.

Be Wary of the Undefeated Champion

MMA has done a lot for martial arts, but it has also westernized them, making them even more sports-related than they already were. Like it or hate it, it looks like MMA is here to stay. However, I say this to in no way criticize the methods employed by MMA fighters. These guys are tough; they train hard, and they fight hard. I have no intention of going toe-to-toe with any of these people. I have a great deal of respect for the things they have accomplished. The flip side to this is that I believe these people are practicing a "young man's" style of arts.

These arts, while exceptionally useful when we are young, start to go away when we are old. I would not want to fight these people now, but I will say that if I had to duel with any one of the champions, I would make one rule: we would fight when we are seventy years old. If you practice like a twenty-year-old when you are a senior citizen, your body will wear out.

I've met some karate practitioners who were in their early sixties and had been training for over forty years. This is enough time to become a master of the arts, but these people decided to continue practicing like they were young. The result was that they had bad backs, bad knees, and poor health. They could not punch well, kick above the shin, throw, or otherwise do much of anything. They were so stuck in doing things the "old ways" that they forgot to train smarter, not harder. They lost the physicality that once made them great fighters, and with their strength gone, so were their arts. This is why we must practice from an inside-out method. This is why we should pursue internal power. You do not have to be a has-been if you train for sustainable arts that can last a lifetime. You can be the wise old master until the day you die.

I am also wary of those who claim they are undefeated. Anyone who is undefeated has likely only faced opponents that were of lesser skill than himself or herself. Fighting people who are worse than you does nothing to make your arts better. You need to have your ass handed to you by people so skilled that it makes you awestruck. Only then can you truly attain higher levels of mastery, because you can observe more powerful techniques and reflect upon how they can strengthen your own. Being undefeated means that you will perpetually remain at the same skill level. We get better through adversity, not through smooth sailing.

Thoughts on Sparring

I have eliminated almost all sparring from my training. This is because sparring can inadvertently teach us bad habits. Sparring has rules; it creates the model of a fair fight, and insists on the idea that you have to fight instead of de-escalating the situation. Before we spar, we are stretched-out, hydrated, warmed-up, and ready to go. These are a lot of assumptions.

If you have never experienced sparring, then I feel that you should try it. Get a few years of this practice under your belt, because it does add an element of chaos that cannot be practiced other than by picking fights with strangers on the street. But if you are a seasoned veteran, then sparring will only increase your bad habits. When my students get closer to black belt, I shy away from this sort of practice. I believe sparring creates some terrible paradigms that are sometimes so difficult to erase that it is just simply better not to do it in the first place. First of all, in sparring, we are making it a fair fight. In martial arts, there is no such thing as a fair fight. A fifty-fifty fight means that I have a 50 percent chance of losing. Those are terrible odds.

No one is counting points on the street, so why would I count points in the dojo? Point-based sparring teaches people to engage and then disengage. It teaches people to head straight in, bounce on their toes, and pull punches. If you want to lose a fight, bounce on your toes. Doing so makes your punches and kicks weaker, and it also makes you vulnerable to foot sweeps and other throws. It's also easy for your opponent to match your timing, because it becomes obvious with each bounce.

I'm of the mind that if someone wants to strike me, then he or she has to approach me. If someone steps into my striking range, then that's it. I don't have to chase someone around like a fool. Sparring will train you to chase your opponent. In baseball, the hitter doesn't run after the ball. He or she waits for the opportunity and hits the ball out of the park. Sparring movements will train you to waste time and energy.

A sparring punch might miss by a good six inches and still get a point. On the street, all you will have is a missed technique; there will be no reward. Likewise, you won't be wearing hand, foot, groin, head, and chest protection every day, so you need to learn how to fight without these things. Besides, a good punch will blast through martial arts–style armor anyway and do little to stop broken bones; the only thing pads save against is minor abrasion.

Let's take a look at some of the many rules in tournament-style fighting. Think about these for a moment, and then consider the outcome that would follow if you adhered to them while being jumped by goons on the street:

- You *must* fight—back down and you're disqualified.
- You must fight fairly (e.g., always face your opponent).
- You have to fight in a designated area that has boundaries.
- There can be no full-power contact (punches and kicks are usually pulled).
- There can be no groin hits or eye gouges.
- There can be no knee strikes or strikes to the foot.
- There can be no strikes to the neck or throat.
- There can be no striking a downed opponent.
- There can be no weapons or foreign objects.
- There can be no joint breaking or manipulations.
- There can be no biting or scratching.
- There can be no pushing.
- There can be no grabbing and holding on to an opponent while striking.
- There can be no striking your opponent's head into the ground.
- There can be no using the referee as a shield.
- When grappling, there can be no finger or thumb (or toe) manipulations.
- You must wear hand protection (and foot and groin protection, too).
- Some styles even have punches to the face count as illegal contact.

These rules might as well have you put on a Michelin-man suit and use only pillows to contact each other. These rules are created for the safety of all participants, so that there is no liability for the dojo or for the organization running the tournament. Because these rules must include everyone from the novice to the veteran, the young to the old, they are very strict. As a result, sparring does nothing to prepare for real-world situations, because an actual attacker will never follow such rules. If you are conditioned to practice inside this box, you are in for a rude awakening. Criminals do not play by the rules—that's why they're criminals.

Using the full power of your devastating punch while sparring is forbidden because we don't want to kill anyone. By focusing on sparring, you'll inadvertently be negatively impacting your potential to create truly impossible power behind your hits. Still, all striking-style martial artists should at least understand sparring, but in advanced training, I feel that it should be completely abandoned.

Instead, practice primarily one-step sparring: one person is the designated attacker, while the other person is the designated defender. By attacker, I mean the person initiating the conflict; and by defender, I mean the person who is on the receiving end of the attack. This is an important distinction, because in my opinion, there is no such thing as offensive and defensive arts. The defender will be receiving an attack, but his or her defense will become as much an attack as it is a block or evasion.

For beginners, the attacker should have a very clear strike, so that the defender can practice his or her arts in a clear and effective manner to develop muscle memory for each technique. More advanced students can attack randomly or with multiple attacks. In each case, I prefer the scenario to end in a clear resolution. That is, an opponent attacks, and we block, counterattack, and throw or pin. Unresolved practice, such as just dodging the attack, does not conclude the scenario. If you dodge or evade an attack, then you have done nothing to resolve the conflict. You are still fighting, and your opponent can still harm you.

Also, for advanced practitioners, you should punch at full power to the chest. As the attacker, you may punch at full power to other parts of the body; just be ready to pull it to vital areas, such as the face and groin. Advanced people should experience what it is like to have someone really try to take your head off and really try to smash your groin. This is something that sparring does not do. Everyone is pulling their punches and kicks, and there is no real danger of anything.

In one-step sparring, we can create that real sense of danger in a very safe manner. We can practice full contact without crushing faces or popping out eyeballs. It allows us to feel what it's like to both project and to absorb power. With one-step sparring, we can practice a scenario over and over until we get it right. Another advantage is that in one-step sparring, we can discover solutions to attacks by implementing a variety of techniques. Maybe we were either too slow or did not know the correct technique well enough to employ it effectively, but with repetition, we can learn and advance. Regardless, this practice should be performed with all of the fundamental elements I have discussed thus far in the book in mind (relaxed power, proper structure, using deception, and so on).

One-step sparring will give you all of the tools you need for self-defense without training bad habits into your routine, like bouncing on your toes. You will develop the muscle memory to do your arts, as well as confidence. You'll be able to absorb power realistically and move when you want to move, not reactively every time an attack comes your way. This is the way that martial arts have been practiced for centuries. Historically, sparring is something that was added to martial arts much more recently; it was absent from karate until it was changed to a sport after World War II. Don't worry about dropping sparring from your training routine; you will be doing yourself a favor. Besides, if you are truly hitting with relaxed power while sparring, you are going to see a significant rise in injuries to your partners. Be smart, be safe, and practice real arts.

Offensive Arts vs. Defensive Arts

I do not like the distinction that is often made between martial arts as being "offensive arts" or "defensive arts." I believe there are just arts. A parallel might be between handguns. Guns are not inherently evil. Guns can be used to do evil, such as murder or commit other crimes. Guns can also be used for good, such as stopping others who are committing crimes. The gun is neither offensive nor defensive; it's just a gun. Likewise, I see the arts as neither offensive nor defensive in nature. Even aikido arts can be used offensively, and aikido is considered an art of peace.

A good analogy might be to position yourself in a movie about your life, with yourself cast as the hero. I think most people think of themselves as the good guy, and rightly so, as we likely won't be the ones instigating violent confrontation with other people. We won't start fights or goad people into a rage so that they may attack us. Good guys protect others and have sincerely the best interests for everyone. Good guys do not hit first, and good guys are slow to anger.

From this perspective, "defensive arts" means that we are not the instigators of violence, because we aren't looking for a fight. We should be like the chivalrous knights that protect the weak and defend our friends and family. We only use our arts should it be absolutely necessary—when diplomacy and negotiation have failed us. Good guys have honor and integrity and should not make the first move to engage an opponent.

Some styles of arts refer to your opponent as "your partner." This may hold true in the dojo, where we are all friends, but outside of the dojo, an aggressor is not perceived as a partner at all. It is for this reason that I prefer the word *opponent* on purpose. If we are indeed fighting, we have created an opposition, one that for whatever reason cannot be fixed by diplomacy. In this light, I call this imaginary person an opponent and not a partner. Many art styles will dance around the idea of having an opponent and choose instead to call this adversary your partner. Let go of this paradigm.

Our arts should not be strictly defensive in nature. If someone throws a punch, your best solution may actually be to strike first. Beat the opponent to the punch; hit the opponent faster and harder than he or she could ever hope to hit you. The other person technically started it through his or her aggressive intentions, but by taking the initiative, you finished the fight. Is this defensive or offensive?

If you think you have to play a defensive role in a fight, you may miss opportunities. Being defensive may make you wait too long to do something. You may be struck while in an observational mode, unable to move into action fast enough. If your opponent has made up his or her mind to hit you, he or she has moved out of thought and into action. If you remain in a thinking mode, you will always be late. Your timing will be late, and you will likely be struck, or worse, taken to the ground.

Conversely, having a strictly offensive mind-set may make you jump the gun when action is not warranted. If you suddenly hear a sound from behind you and you spin and punch at that sound, you may have just punched your mother. Even if your offensive mind-set doesn't create physical damage, you'll be viewed by others as someone who is constantly on edge, or even a jerk.

We therefore cannot have a defensive mind because it is too slow, nor can we have an offensive mind because we are not the bad guy. We must adopt both strategies, and employ whichever strategy makes sense at the time. If you hear a sound behind you, turn to look; if it is your mother, you don't strike. If it is a bad guy coming to get you, you strike.

Walking around all day while assuming everyone is a potential threat is exhausting. We should pay attention to what is going on, certainly, but at some point we need to let this go. Unless you are a CIA operative in deep cover somewhere overseas, most civilians do not require this level of paranoia.

Develop a neutral mind-set by not becoming defensive and passive, nor offensive and aggressive. If you were sized up by someone with hostile intent, your goal should be to give off an uncertain feeling to him or her. He or she shouldn't see you as being on the defensive, because in my opinion, this is what targets look like. Likewise, you shouldn't be too aggressive, lest you attract aggressive persons looking for a challenge.

Imagine a well-fed tiger that is casually strolling along. It has a full belly and is therefore not desperate for food. If a tasty gazelle were at hand, the tiger wouldn't feel the need to pounce because it's already full and not looking for trouble; it's looking for a nice walk. You need to present this image of the tiger. You're not on the hunt; you're not assessing everything that moves as food or a threat; you're just out for a stroll. The idea is that people should see you as competent, but not hostile. Predators do not want to fight other predators, because they have a chance of losing. Against a tiger with the mastery mind-set, losing should be a sure thing.

Be neutral, and pay particular attention to your eyes. Relax them! Not only will you be able to see more with relaxed eyes; you will have a softer face and will appear less aggressive. If you wear a look of concentration on your face, this can be mistaken as hostility. Also, try to keep your eyes level on the horizon as you walk, and make sure to look people in the eye when you pass them. Keeping the head up will naturally allow you to see more and will also help with tension headaches (looking down fires muscles in your back and neck).

You can take this neutral mind-set with you into your workplace. Try not to personalize the work you do; actively listen to coworkers, and never raise your voice. The tiger can eat all of the coworkers anytime it wants to, so there's no need to roar or bring out the claws. Relax and soften your eyes so that you don't evoke feelings of distrust or aggression.

Emotional Attacks

Think twice before you speak, because your words and influence will plant the seed of either success or failure in the mind of another.—Napoleon Hill

Most martial artists do not include emotional defenses in their training, probably because this is less interesting than the fantasy of beating up a bad guy in a dark alley. However, even a basic attack is usually guided by some preceding emotion. People don't just randomly attack others without some escalation of emotion first. Sometimes fighting has little to do with an actual problem, and more to do with reactions to and emotions about a problem.

For example, let's say Doug and Mary are divorced and have two kids. The court allows Doug visitation rights on Saturdays. Now let's say for some reason, Mary wants to change this to Sundays, and calls up Doug to tell him that she's changing his day with the kids. Doug has his band practice all day Sundays and Mary knows it; he's had band practice on this day since even before he was married. Doug may become furious at this request and yell at Mary; Mary in turn will yell back. When the lawyers get involved, and after a few thousand dollars are spent, some resolutions arise. In this example, the problem is a scheduling conflict. The problem never escalates. The emotions are what caused the escalation. Emotions, therefore, are the core basis of all attacks and indeed all conflict.

Emotional stress may not have to originate from you; it can come from anywhere. If someone is under a lot of stress at home or at work, he or she could have an emotional outburst, and you may be a target of this attack. Understanding emotional attacks means to understand the core basis of all attacks, both physical and emotional. The most difficult part about emotional attacks is that we may not see them coming—and we might not recognize when we are the ones doing the attacks. When someone punches you, it is obvious that an attack is taking place. Likewise, if you are struck, it is usually understood where the pain is coming from and how long that pain will last.

Psychopaths might attack people at what would seem at random and maybe even without emotion. I'm not talking about these sorts of attacks, as these things are largely unavoidable. The true psychopath is a terrifying predator, for sure, but we do not encounter these people often, if at all. Who I'm talking about is you, me, and everyone, because everyone gets angry. Normal people lash out at others when they are angry. Because we live in a world of mostly normal people, understanding how to defend and prevent these emotional attacks then becomes an essential part of our self-defense. Not just from the standpoint of protecting us during the encounter, but rather in fostering good relationships that will keep us healthy in the long term by minimizing stress.

Ask yourself this: when was the last time you were in a real life-or-death fight? Last year? Ten years ago? Never? Now ask yourself: when was the last time someone verbally attacked you, or when was the last time you verbally attacked someone? I'm willing to bet that most of us fight verbally and emotionally much more regularly than we fight physically for our lives. Learning defenses against such attacks may not be romantic, but such attacks are something that will be in your life whether you want them or not.

Emotional attacks are invisible, insidious, and deadly. Emotional attacks may build up unseen over time and cause terrible manifestations in the body, such as chronic pain, cancer, heart disease, or stroke. If you are truly interested in self-defense, as well as committed to improving as a martial artist, you must pay attention to this lesson.

How do you handle stress in your life? Do you find yourself becoming angry easily? How do you live with powerful emotions like fear, worry, and doubt? What steps do you take to protect yourself from the negativity of others?

Some would argue that there is a difference between verbal and emotional attacks. I say that these things are the same because they come from the same place: emotions. Verbal attacks can only harm you if you react to them, and your reaction will always be governed by emotion. People can only upset you with words if you are emotionally involved with those words. If a toddler calls you a "dumb dumbhead," you can smile and shrug it off because you shouldn't be emotionally worked up over the opinion of a three-year-old. If a coworker sarcastically makes light of your mistake by saying something like, "Keep up the great work, genius," you may have an entirely different reaction. We cannot choose the actions of others, but we can choose how we react to anything in our lives.

As martial artists, we should endeavor to never initiate, or fight back, using emotional warfare. Emotional warfare destroys both sides of the conflict, and doesn't win over anyone. It is our duty to look through this emotional fog of war to see the nature of the problem. Battling with emotions is very destructive and gives little benefit to anyone. This doesn't mean that you should back down from any verbal engagement, though. Backing down from emotional confrontations is just another type of emotional warfare, this time waged against you. Turn the other cheek often enough, and soon your belly will be filled with rage or depression. Either one of these things is bad news for your mind, body, and spirit. Use your head, keep calm under all situations, and find tactful ground that benefits all parties involved.

If you are the type of person who gets a hot head quickly, then develop a plan of action prior to reaching this point. Your friends, family, and especially your spouse should know what this action is. Too often our frustration manifests as sudden action that can be misinterpreted by others, even the ones we love, so establishing your "rules of disengagement" is a great tool to maintain healthy relationships. Some people like to talk and resolve things right away, while others like to sit on things and mull them over before talking.

Find out what your partner's style is, and more importantly, what your style is. Know yourself.

Should you find yourself overly angry, openly hostile, or otherwise extremely agitated, step back and consider the source. Problems themselves do not cause these rises in emotion. What causes these burning events in us is far deeper. Only by exploring why something makes you agitated can anything actually be done about it.

When I am ready to leave the house, I get up and go. This action takes me less than thirty seconds. My spouse has to check all of the electrical appliances, check her makeup, kiss the cat fifteen times, check herself in the mirror, maybe go pee twice, and so on. I cannot change her behavior, but I can change how I feel about her behavior. Sometimes I will sit down and just wait for her to be done, or look at my phone or play on the Internet. For me, this alleviates the odd stress I feel when she dawdles.

I once measured my blood pressure when I was annoyed at my spouse—not mad, not enraged, just annoyed. To my surprise, it was insanely high. I was shocked how much of a physical effect this seemingly trivial emotion had upon my body. I did a brief period of meditation, and I found I could lower my blood pressure. This is good news, and something we need to make a habit of.

We all have pet peeves, things that annoy us and create buttons available for people to push. I once trained with a woman who had very bad coordination and a bad attitude. When we would practice throwing arts, she would always lean far to the opposing side of the throw, making me improvise and switch up the technique in order to take her down. As a result, she wouldn't necessarily be prepared to take the fall I would put her in, but her poor balance made my job easy. Afterward she would get up off the ground and curse me for not doing the technique the sensei was working on.

This woman could not best me with technique, so she was trying to antagonize me in the only way she knew how: emotional warfare. Emotional warfare is sadly part of the human experience, which creates a lot of friction in our lives that can simply be avoided. We may not know where an emotional attack is coming from, but we can prepare ourselves internally for such occasions. What is your go-to method of dealing with stress? Do you freak out in retaliation? Or do you stop what you are doing and honestly listen to the other person's problems?

We can all be better listeners. Listening is a skill that we should hone, just like our punches and our kicks. Listening is the foundation for growing communication between two or more people. Rather than simply waiting for your turn to speak, actively listen to others so you can understand their view. Another part of listening well is to not offer advice too quickly; sometimes people just want to be heard and do not want solutions to their problems.

Absorbing Emotional Attacks

No one can upset you without your permission.
—Bob Proctor

Absorbing emotional attacks is a temporary solution to a problem, but is a useful skill for a martial artist to have. This is because we have developed our bodies to be able to destroy people physically, and in a moment of rage, we could kill someone before we even meant to react. So it is imperative that we understand ourselves emotionally and really look inside to what pushes our buttons. This way we will always be in control of our weapons and ourselves. People can only push your buttons if you have buttons to push.

When I was much younger, I had a problem with rage—not surprising since I come from an alcoholic family. At any rate, once I was at a party where I had a fight with my girlfriend. I went upstairs, away from her and the party, to calm down. After some time, I decided I had cooled off and was willing to patch things up. When I went downstairs, I saw a friend of mine slow dancing with her. Then the next thing I remember is a crowd of people around me, and me holding my friend against the wall by his throat. I have no memory of how I crossed that distance nor actually attacking him. He looked scared, and I dropped him, and then I took a look around and instantly felt stupid. This was one among many outbursts I had into my twenties. I've attacked people without realizing I was punching them or kicking them. These outbursts led to many awkward moments, bruised egos, and hurt feelings. Don't let yourself become a victim of emotional attacks, and especially don't let yourself victimize others because of your emotions.

To safely absorb emotional energy, I find the "pebble in a pond" analogy useful. When emotional energy is created by an encounter, focus that wave of energy serenely to your center, like ripples in a pond but coming inward rather than going outward. Have those incoming emotional attacks sent there instead of letting them rise within you to your mind. Imagine those feelings of rage, anger, hatred, or whatever being focused and compressed into your body. When people are angry, we say they are *up*set and we tell them to calm *down*. Down is calming; rising is infuriating. When we are sleeping, we are perhaps the most relaxed and calm that we can be, not surprising because most of us lie down when we sleep. Imagine that you are sleeping peacefully, but you suddenly arise from a loud noise. Your heart rate spikes, you sit up violently from bed, and your mind furiously tries to make sense of the situation.

We want the calmness we have while sleeping to aid us in the dissipation of emotional energy. The next time you feel an emotional attack affecting you, feel the weight of your body move down toward your center, or even better, cascade all the way to the floor. Make sure your hands are open and not in fists. Breathe through your nose and exhale through your mouth. A slow breath will help counteract the harsh emotions you are feeling. This method of self-defense helps you in social situations, such as taking criticism at your job without being defensive, or in potentially hostile situations, like composing yourself while having your seat kicked by some jackass in a movie theater. After committed time with this kind of meditation training, my outbursts all but disappeared before I was thirty.

Absorbing emotional attacks is very useful for short-term dissipation of power, but we must realize that there is still emotional training to do afterward. If we simply absorb every negative emotion created, we will inadvertently be piling up the pain in the corners of our mind, only to explode over something ridiculously stupid in the months or years to come.

There are healthy and unhealthy ways to dissipate this energy in the long term. For example, I knew a guy who would cut himself when he felt feelings of rage. He might also bite his tongue hard enough to cut it. This is not a healthy way to deal with emotional pain long-term. I recommend not going down this road, as self-mutilation can become a distinct psychological problem of its own.

So how does one get rid of emotional attacks for the long term? We communicate. Talk to people whom you have problems with, but the key is to confront them about issues in a safe manner. Do not confront people about emotional issues when you are upset or in a rage. This will do nothing to resolve the situation. Make sure you are calm, and be at ease before you open up a dialog with anyone. Second, make sure you are in safe surroundings and alone with just that other person. Write down on a piece of paper what you wish to say, and either memorize it or read it directly from the paper. Once you say your piece, you do not need to resolve the conflict right then and there (though this sometimes happens), because just making the other person aware of your duress is a sufficient start toward purging yourself of negative feelings. Most normal people probably never meant to hurt you anyway and will take steps to reconcile with you naturally.

I have in the past worked as a bodyguard for close protection services. One of the things I would talk to my clients about is escalation of emotion prior to us going anywhere. Clients tended to feel much freer to escalate things into ugliness when they have muscle to back them up. I let people know that I'm not muscle for hire and that I am there to keep the peace and not start or contribute to violent confrontation. One would think this to be obvious; but nevertheless, clients that initiated confrontations while emotionally volatile will figuratively go to their guns immediately, losing all hope of diplomacy. This showed me that it was always preferable to be there as emotional support to my clients as a voice of calmness and of reason, rather than going in there with my sleeves rolled up and ready to swing.

With the skills of martial arts that I know, I am a very dangerous person. I have to master my own mind so that I do not flip out and crush someone to death. There has been a multitude of times where I considered striking a coworker or boss for one reason or another. I have learned to hold these desires in check, because I really do not want to go to jail.

I was injured on a jobsite once, and my doctor filed a claim without me knowing. This caused my employer's insurance to go up, and I was fired as a consequence when I returned back to work. The boss believed that I had been injured in class and that I was trying to make a false claim. When I confronted him about it, things got very heated, and I must have done something because he backed down and moved away from me very quickly. At that moment, I was about to strike him. He must have felt my rage, and he moved deeper into his office and I could see him suddenly begin to shake with fear. I wanted to pounce on him and rip his face off, but I didn't. At this moment, I managed to snap myself out of it, and I simply stopped arguing and left the office. It took a great deal of mental fortitude to not hit this man.

A few days later, we were able to speak to one another like civilized people. I still lost my job, but I did not want to work with this person any longer. However, I felt that it was polite to end our working relationship with respect, so we made peace with one another. Compare this to the outcome that would have resulted if I laid into him with a few devastating punches: me in jail for assault ... or worse.

Continual communication with the person you are in conflict with will be necessary so that the damage can be repaired, allowing both parties to move on. When I have confronted people like this, I have always had positive results; in fact, in many encounters, the other person admits to me that he or she is surprised that there was an issue in the first place. Often, our negative emotions develop because of misunderstandings or assumptions, not malicious intent. People with malicious intent are not really worth talking to, and if you can, just avoid these people.

Some individuals will erect barriers that you simply can't break down. For your own health, then, it becomes important to simply see these people less often, or for a shorter duration if you are obligated to be around them (such as your family). When you are not with them, purge your mind of thoughts about them, as these negative feelings can have long-lasting effects on the mind, especially if they are replayed over and over. Do not replay past negative experiences in your head. You have already paid the price for these moments; stop losing time, energy, and happiness by reliving them. Fill your mind with joyful thoughts and stop wasting time on conflict reruns and clip shows.

Staying calm in all situations demonstrates true mastery of martial arts. If you can't keep a cool head, you are failing as a martial artist. If you raise your voice many times throughout the day, know that you are raising your blood pressure and therefore your chances at an early death. Dying early is not in our curriculum. Masters do not die young; they persist into old age and gain wisdom through calmness.

Sarcasm and Loudmouths

Sarcasm is the lowest form of humor, as well as an emotional attack that hits below the belt. Masters of martial arts do not use sarcasm, and neither should you. I once had a very labor-intensive job in a warehouse that kept me working sixty hours a week; it was grueling. Despite this, my boss would come up to me and say things like, "Wow, you are doing a terrible job. Ha-ha, just kidding!" How do you think that made me feel? Do you think that motivated me to work harder? Do you think that pushed me to make changes in the job to make things more efficient? I once saw a coworker in this same warehouse destroy thousands of dollars worth of product with a hammer, box it up, and ship it to clients. I laughed so hard when I saw this, I almost peed my pants. Do you think I went to the boss with that information?

Sarcasm is one of the easiest ways to make enemies, especially in the workplace. When you are with friends, you may use sarcasm, but I would say even then, it should be avoided. Sarcasm will only create misunderstandings, because others can't always know when you're joking.

Usurping conversations and talking over people is also an emotional attack. What makes this different from sarcasm is that the people who do it often don't even realize that they are. They must be used to having people tune out and look away or even walk away during a conversation. They probably believe that being a loudmouth is normal, everyday behavior. I have found that some people refuse others a chance to speak; they simply talk over anything anyone else has to say. This is an attack. I find that talking louder does absolutely nothing to remedy the situation. But communicating through your posture can help you. I've turned away from people who are rambling, and continue about my day like they weren't even there. Sometimes I just get up and go someplace else without waiting for an opening to do it. I make the opening. This usually ends conversations fast, as I am no longer present to participate. Do this if you don't mind harming the relationship. Treating loudmouthed coworkers in this fashion, I think, is acceptable—but it it's your boss, probably not acceptable.

Another strategy is to wait it out and listen to what the other person has to say. As martial artists, we should become good listeners. We should hear what people have to say, no matter how boring it is. You don't have to sit there and take a lecture from just anyone. What I'm saying is that you should give every person time to express his or her thoughts. I have found that sometimes this tactic allows people to follow through a stream of consciousness and come to a conclusion because you are offering no resistance. Sometimes a combination of the two strategies also works. Listen for a bit, then turn your back or leave.

You may not agree that avoiding these two kinds of behavior is self-defense, but history has shown us otherwise. We've all heard stories about employees who have reached their breaking point and gone into the workplaces intent on gunning down their coworkers. This doesn't happen every day, but it does happen. If this happened in your workplace, would you be one shot, or one spared? How do you treat your coworkers?

I once worked with a pair of coworkers who were married. The couple divorced in the time that I knew them. The husband was a quiet man, and unassuming; you would miss this man in a crowd of five people. The woman was loud, obnoxious, and boisterous. She lost a lot of weight after the divorce and started dating. My desk was near to hers, so I was privy to how she treated the people who worked under her. She was not a kind woman. Well, after a lot of hurt feelings, her ex-husband shot her to death and then shot himself.

I'm not saying the woman deserved what she got; no one deserves to get killed. No one deserves that type of evil to land on him or her. The man was obviously psychologically disturbed, which doesn't excuse his actions, but I will say that she cultivated the feelings that manifested the crime through her rude comments and noisy demeanor.

You may not be able to protect yourself from crazy people. If someone wants to blow up a railway station and you happen to be there at the moment the bomb goes off, there is not much you can do about that. But we can actively make friends instead of using sarcasm or belligerence to make enemies. It takes the same amount of energy, so why not make friends?

Taking the High Road

Do not argue with an idiot. They drag you down to their level and beat you with experience.— Mark Twain

There is a low road and a high road to all human interaction. We should get into the habit of always taking the high road. That is, we do not have to react to emotional attacks that are directed to us. Taking the high road means not allowing negative comments and attitudes to affect you. The low road means reacting to negativity with more negativity. If someone tells you to "fuck off," you can tell him or her to fuck off right back, sure, but this is the low road. You may have a disagreement with your spouse about something, but endeavor to always find the high road and leave the low road behind.

If we are constantly seeking to better ourselves, people will notice this, either directly or indirectly. This will help you in self-defense in many ways. If you are accused of something that you did not do, your reputation as being a good person who always takes the high road will have people naturally rushing to defend you. If you are known as a womanizer and become accused of harassing a coworker, people will assume you did it, even if you did not.

We all know where the low road leads us. Do not be dragged down to someone else's level by giving in to petty arguments. Stay clear of this poison, as it has no use in our daily lives.

Defensive Strategies in Noncombat Situations

I once worked with a coworker who clearly had no respect for anyone in the office. Granted, this man was gifted and very good at his job, but he was also very defensive and openly hostile if one questioned anything he was working on. I knew I could punch this guy dead in one hit, so his verbal attacks meant nothing to me in terms of physical self-defense; however, this obviously wasn't a viable solution to the problem. But because this man was making my working life less enjoyable, I decided to experiment with body language and postures to see what worked and how I could approach him.

I started out with a head-on approach. That is, I made sure he was standing, and I walked right up to him and asked him some questions. This did not work at all; as he became immediately defensive. I tried to change my physical posture to have a more calming effect, but nothing seemed to work.

To understand what I did next one must understand a concept in karate called *sei chu sen*. This is the vertical centerline that exists in everyone, and can be thought of as the line your spine makes from your head to your pelvis. This centerline is the most vulnerable part of our bodies as on this line is the brain, the throat, the heart, and the genitals. We can manipulate how people feel about us on a subtle level by how we show or hide our sei chu sen, or centerline, to others. This vulnerability can also be used to create a hostile intention because facing your sei chu sen toward your opponent conveys a message that you are confident that he or she cannot harm you.

Previously what I had been doing wrong was allowing my opponent the opportunity to face his sei chu sen towards me, which gave him the illusion that he was in control. In subsequent encounters I used my sei chu sen to attack his sei chu sen. I took a position that seemed as if we were facing each other, but actually my center was facing his center and his center was facing away from mine. In martial arts, I could hit him before he made an effort to hit me. On a subconscious level this creates dominant and submissive roles for those involved.

I found this was easily done when the man was sitting down. I approached his desk in such a way that he had to spin his chair a bit to see me, but he couldn't spin it all the way around to face me entirely. This meant his sei chu sen was not facing mine, putting him in a psychologically weaker position. He actually leaned back and away from me in his chair in a subtle way. I then calmly presented my argument to him, and he became uncharacteristically submissive. The change was so drastic, I nearly gasped. It had worked. And so, whenever I had to deal with this person from then on out, I would use this strategy to ensure his full cooperation.

One day on my commute to work, I had what I thought was a very minor traffic incident. I had to change lanes, and there was a motorcyclist who refused to let me either in front of him or behind him. I had my blinker on for a long time, and then I sped up and changed lanes in front of him. As it turned out, this was a manager at a software company where I worked. We arrived together at the entrance, and I opened the door for him, not expecting what was about to take place. To my surprise, he took off his helmet and raised it to strike me. He then said, "If you fucking cut me off again, I'm going to fucking kill you."

I responded by letting the door go and zipping up my jacket as I squared off with him. I then said, "Are you threatening me?"

This man immediately seemed to realize that he was at work; he backed up and became defensive. He obviously didn't know who I was, or he would never have made the threat. He had a reputation in the office for bullying people, but I wasn't about to be bullied. He backed away from me, and then proceeded to explain how I had cut him off.

I then asked if he had seen my turn signal and if I had allowed him enough time to move in front of or behind me. He actually agreed that I gave him enough time. I finished this encounter by saying that this was not me cutting him off, but was simply a lane change.

For me, the encounter was over, as I did not really fear this man. However, I retold the story to a coworker, and another manger overheard and forced me to go to HR with this story. The man was immediately fired.

This story may be seen as a success because I clearly won. I didn't back down from the attack, and the man got fired for giving a coworker a death threat. However, if this man were crazy, I just gave him a motive for killing me.

If you continually harbor negative thoughts about people, even if you never speak these things, those thoughts are out there in the universe. People may pick up on subconscious clues and resent you for it. We must endeavor to watch what we say and watch what we think. This is martial arts at its highest level.

Meditation

We have all heard that meditation is good for us. We know this in the same way we know that vitamins, fruits, and vegetables are good for us. Yet many times, we neglect meditation arts in our practice. Why is this exactly? Do we think we already know all the secrets of internal power? Do we think that since we already know how to breathe, we don't need to practice it? Is it that we crave action over stillness and calmness? Is internal power really that boring?

You might ask why we need to become mentally stronger if we already possess devastating technique. Have you ever had a real-life fight experience? Have you ever had a *near* fight experience? What happened when you felt that adrenaline rush? Could you communicate easily? Could you walk normally? I personally have noticed that my feet don't work the way they should when I have an adrenaline response. By understanding the inner clockwork of our minds, we can have better control of our bodies. Meditation helps us achieve this.

When we are frightened or surprised, our minds may paralyze our bodies into inaction. Inaction during an emergency can get you killed. I would argue that the best self-defense is to have the mental prowess necessary to be able to see what is happening and react appropriately. For example, one may look outside and witness an earthquake. Should one freeze at this moment and not take proper cover, he or she may be killed by falling debris or collapsing buildings. At this moment, it doesn't matter how strong the body is or how good the punch is; what matters is how strong the mind is. We must therefore exercise the mind to make it stronger.

Many martial artists enjoy the feeling of moving and training their bodies. New physical techniques are fun to learn; moreover, it is very easy to see how to train the body. If you wish to get stronger, you can do push-ups and sit-ups to meet this goal. If you wish to get a stronger punch, kick, or throw, simply practice these arts. But how does one develop mental strength? How do we practice honing our mental prowess?

Thinking is not the same as mental strength. Thinking constantly can also be a burden in an emergency, creating results similar to inaction. Our goal is to clear our minds so we can perceive things clearly and therefore act accordingly. We are not trying to become superhuman nor practice magical hocus-pocus; we are trying to remove unnecessary mental debris to remain calm in all situations. When we are calm and relaxed, we always make the best decisions for ourselves. The result is reactions that might seem impossible to gawkers unused to this kind of mental exercise.

Meditation in the martial arts is mostly concerned with our physical center, which is located two inches below the navel. This is our center of gravity, but it can also be thought of as a mental center. It is clearly not the location of the brain, but it is useful to think of this as the source of all your thoughts. Many meditation styles speak of more than one center, or *chakra,* in the body, but we are less concerned with these as they don't hold the same significance to our style of practice. The center of gravity in the human body is much more useful a tool to understand our own balance, as well as understanding the balance of others. Learning to maintain your balance has enormous health, as well as martial arts, benefits. If you yourself are not balanced, how can you hope to unbalance your opponent?

Some Benefits of Meditation

There have been many benefits claimed to result from meditation. Among them are the following:

- It relaxes the body.
- It relaxes the mind.

- It alters your mood positively.
- It removes stress.
- It creates good posture.
- It creates balance.
- It allows one to perceive things more clearly.
- It cures insomnia.
- It cures headaches.

First of all, one must remove all preconceived notions of what meditation is in order to get closer to its goal. The goal in martial arts–style meditation is to clear the mind and learn how to relax inside our own bodies so that our mind seems to speak with one voice within us. Fear and doubt may inhibit you from proper action when it is the most crucial. People have been known to freeze in the presence of danger. Doing push-ups and sit-ups makes your body stronger. Meditation makes your mind stronger, so you will not freeze in moments when action is needed the most. A practical benefit to this kind of thinking might be seen when you are merging into a highway. If you meander in the acceleration lane and hesitate, you may end up doing more harm to yourself than good, forcing yourself to wait forever or even jeopardizing your safety. Here, focused thought allows you to judge and time your movement precisely, ensuring that you and everyone else speeding by stay safe. Take a deliberate, calming breath before you undertake even everyday actions like this, and you'll discover the worth of meditation.

Meditation shouldn't be thought of as torture. You don't need to sit seiza for hours in order to benefit from it. If you approach training like this with these negative preconceptions, you will not take the time to do it; you will find something else to occupy your mind. So instead, dedicate only five to ten minutes to meditating, so you will be more likely to actually pursue it. This advice is sound for most martial art practices. Find five minutes a day to work on your arts; this will impress into your subconscious mind that you are "always practicing." We brush our teeth, take showers, make meals, and sleep daily, so finding five minutes to practice should be easy. Do not hesitate; just do it.

I find two types of meditation most useful: sitting meditation and breathing meditation. Both of these can be done while sitting seiza, cross-legged, walking, lying down, or even jogging. When new to meditation practice, it's easiest to understand its principles by sitting seiza; this position naturally tends to lend great strength for balance. If one has an injury that prevents him or her from sitting in this position, using a chair is fine. Don't allow a disability to discourage you from practice.

Sitting Meditation

- Sit seiza or cross-legged.
- If you cannot sit seiza or cross-legged, use a chair.
- Lightly close your eyes.
- Relax your hands in your lap.
- Relax your body, but remain upright.
- Breathe normally.
- Imagine waves of energy concentrating into your center, compressing to a single point of energy within yourself.
- Once you can no longer imagine your center getting smaller, expand it outward like a shock wave.
- Repeat this image in your mind.
- Once you have done this image a dozen times or so, let it go and relax.
- Should you find your mind wandering excessively, return to the visualization.

Sitting meditation is good when you do not wish to make noise. You can practice this on an airplane or in your room with your spouse without getting strange looks or disturbing others. Try practicing this mediation at work, on the bus, or even waiting in a movie theater; you will begin to see results in mood and state of calmness.

Breathing Meditation

Breathing meditation tends to be more focused than sitting meditation, and therefore has a greater effect on the individual. Sitting meditation can lead to a meandering mind, and novices may find it difficult to stay on task. With breathing meditation, since you have something to focus on and measure yourself against, it is much easier to have sustained concentration. Breathing meditation is particularly good if you are having a difficult time warming up your body, as this increases blood circulation, or if you have insomnia, as this breathing style is a similar rhythm as while we sleep.

To perform breathing meditation, focus on the following:

- Breathe in through your nose at a slow, steady pace.
- When you come to a full inhale, come back to a neutral position; your spine should be in an upright position.
- Exhale through your mouth using the same deliberate pace.
- When you come to a full exhale, lean forward slightly.
- For the novice, attempt ten minutes of meditation per sitting.
- Try to make your breath even, rather than choppy, especially during the transition from inhaling to exhaling.
- For the novice, try to inhale and exhale for at least ten seconds at a time.

Visualization

Imagine that each breath comes through your nose and into your center, and each exhale comes from your center and out of your mouth. We all know our lungs are not located in our lower abdomen; however, this visualization will allow you to breathe deeper and longer. As you get better at meditation, try to extend the times of both the inhale and exhale; one minute per inhale and one minute per exhale is a good goal and may take several years of practice to achieve. Make sure your transitions of breath are smooth and seamless, rather than explosive or shaky.

Continuously monitor how relaxed your body is, especially your abdomen. Let go of excess tension and be open to receiving positive energy; allow yourself the luxury of forgetting past or current troubles.

The practice of meditation is perhaps the most simple, yet complex, of all techniques we employ. When many people think of meditation, they assume that they need to empty their minds of thoughts. Do not seek to quiet the mind, because this is like sticking your hand in a pool of water to stop the waves. Your brain is an organ, and its function is to think, just as your heart's function is to pump blood. Allow your mind to settle by thinking about whatever it needs to think about. I typically just allow my mind to wander in a gentle relaxed way, not being consumed by anxiety. I direct my thoughts toward relaxing images, rather than stressful thoughts.

You can also try tricking you mind into becoming calm. By concentrating on our breathing, we naturally settle our minds, so there is no such thing as trying to empty your mind. That is like hearing someone say "pink elephants" and then trying not to think of them. Give your mind a task, such as breathing or some sort of visualization. In that way, your mind will have something to do.

Walking Meditation

One can also practice meditation while walking. In this method, start by inhaling for a number of steps, and exhaling for an equal number of steps. Try to have smoothness to your gait, and don't stomp or walk lazily; this will interrupt your breathing. Make sure you look toward the horizon, and relax your body; allow your arms to swing naturally. Try to use your belly to breathe rather than having your chest cavity rise upward. Imagine that your shoulders remain where they are with each breath. Belly breathing is one way to absorb power to your abdomen. The visualization that you are filling your stomach with air acts like a cushion of protection, which in turn will teach us how to properly diffuse energy through our bodies.

Impossible Healing Techniques

It is easy for many people to hold a paradigm that the power to heal oneself and others through touch or willpower is impossible. I disagree with this statement, and I'm going to show you how to make this possible. This is not faith healing, nor is this magic. Before I get into the how, set aside your paradigm for a moment, and simply believe that you have this power already. It doesn't require burning incense or visiting a witch doctor; just harness the positive energy that you already have inside of you. Here's how you do it.

To heal yourself, or others, we must first ask ourselves if we are in the correct vibration or not. We discussed what I mean by vibrations earlier in the book, but if it's easier for you, you can think of them as simply being your emotional state. If you are in a negative vibration, angry or depressed, for example, you will have little energy to give for healing. This energy is already being spent on something else. You must first redirect your vibration away from negative states and find a positive one. If you view yourself as a generally positive person and therefore think that you're always in a state of positive vibration, I advise you to critically examine your posture at this very moment. Are you tense anywhere in your body? Are your shoulders and abdomen slightly tight? Are you furrowing your brow? Are you clenching your teeth? Are you hunched over? Are you constantly shifting around to get comfortable? Are you stretching your neck or other part of your body? Do you have shallow breaths? If you answered yes to any of these questions, your body is telling you that you are not in a positive vibration, even though your mind might be telling you that you are.

If you are sitting down, sit up. If you are standing, stand tall. If you are lying down, let go of your body's tension. Allow your breathing to be smooth and even. Changing the physical is often deceptively difficult. Many of us carry stress and emotions in our posture. If we are angry, we may clench our teeth or tighten our fists subconsciously. If we have anxiety, our shoulders may raise up slightly without us being aware of it. If we are sad, we may slouch or otherwise have poor posture. You may believe you have good posture but then habitually lean on one foot. This poor standing posture tilts one side of your pelvis up, and can create back, hip, and knee problems over time. You may think you are sitting upright, but your weight may be absentmindedly over to one side. You may be hunched over at your desk, or you may cross your legs, which can constrict blood flow. To heal yourself, you must first have good posture to allow your blood to flow freely and your muscles to have sufficient relaxation to release tension.

We can often trick our minds into a different mood if we find our posture out of alignment. If you are feeling sad and you are slouched over, stand up tall and breathe deeply. If you are angry, lie down on your bed, close your eyes, and allow the tension to pass.

The more difficult part is changing how you feel on the inside, as this can be invisible even to ourselves. Most of us have made a lifetime career of disguising our emotions. So perhaps altering our posture may help us change the inside.

How do you feel inside? Are you happy or bored? I say bored because sadness is easy to detect. Often we are bored, but because we don't feel sad, we think we are happy. This isn't true.

If you truly believe you are in a positive vibration or positive emotional state, we may now begin the impossible: healing ourselves or others. If you find that you are in a negative vibration, which sometimes may be difficult to detect, analyze yourself by doing meditation prior to practicing healing arts. Clear your mind of worry, doubt, sadness, and even boredom.

The basic premise for healing is that you will carry a positive vibration to the injured part of the body; remember that you can consider positive vibrations as being genuinely relaxed or benevolent emotions. In order to extend this energy, we must first feel the energy. If the well is dry, you can crank the hand pump all you want, but there will be no water coming from that well.

This type of healing art has a dramatic effect on headaches, stomachaches, food poisoning, and minor sprains. If you simply have sore muscles, go to a massage therapist, as that type of healing works best for simple lactic-acid buildup. Likewise, this healing art won't help you much if you are bleeding and have broken bones. You need to see a doctor! These techniques aren't meant to replace health professionals, but rather ensure that non-life-threatening injuries do not wear down your pursuit of the mastery mind-set, or even just your ability to live a life with minimal pain and illness.

Injuries

A common reaction to injuries is "guarding." This is where the wounded person covers the injury with his or her hands or other body part. This is a natural response to injuries, and we will use this as the first step to help us understand and heal our own injuries. This guide for healing injuries assumes that you have already received any immediate care necessary for survival, or that the injury was never life-threatening to begin with. After you have received the treatment necessary to stabilize yourself or prevent the injury from worsening, you can begin your own treatment to speed your recovery.

Injuries such as sprains, strains, muscle bruises, torn muscles, and tendonitis can all benefit from our involvement in the healing process. Open wounds such as cuts, scrapes, or rashes really require medical attention and time to heal, and self-healing techniques for these ailments are limited. Broken bones, bone spurs, or cartilage damage require a lighter and more careful touch during our healing process.

As a starting point, use the tips of your fingers, or the tip of your thumb, and press lightly to the injured area. Feel a wave of relaxation come over you, and send your energy into the injury. If it hurts too much, don't press so hard. You do not need to poke; a light pressure will suffice. What you are doing is causing neurons to fire in the areas that sense your touch. By having more electrical activity to this area, we are increasing the body's natural healing functions, that is, blood flow, lymphatic drainage, and the electrical impulses that flow through us. Therefore, this simple, focused touching of an injury stimulates and hastens recovery.

Work up and down the injury, moving your fingertips in gentle lines following the injury. That is, if you have tennis elbow, you can press from your fingertips to your shoulder. This entire line can become tense and stressed due to the injury, even though the symptoms may only appear at the elbow itself.

I tend to focus on meridians that I learned with *kiatsu* (healing with ki), which are the same as shiatsu lines. Typically these lines run lengthwise on our limbs and body. There are lines from the shoulder to the fingertips, and there are lines from the hip to the toes, for example. One need not know all of these lines; just work the soft tissue that precedes and follows the injury. That is, if your ankle is sprained, you might work on your calf along the line of the injury to your toe tips. You can reduce swelling of a sprained joint by applying light pressure with your thumb or fingertips to the swelling area. This is not a test of pain tolerance; press as much as you need to feel the pressure, not to blast out the swelling. If the injured area is painful to the touch, simply cup the injury and do not apply direct pressure. By sending positive thought into an injured area, we are commanding our body's electrical impulses to pay special attention to it.

You may find yourself spacing out or having a wandering mind when you do this. That's okay; sustained concentration is a skill that gets better with practice, so reconnect with what you are doing, rather than beating yourself up over it. If you verbally bash yourself, you will enter a negative vibration. Masters of this art can penetrate their positive vibration deeply into an area that is injured, achieving desirable effects. While a negative vibration at its worst can be detrimental to recovery, typically a negative vibration only echoes within you and really goes nowhere. This is usually because we tend to cling onto negative emotions and replay negative events in our minds like movies. Worrying about your injury or doubting you will recover from the injury is also a negative vibration. When we are happy, we are less inclined to do this, as we simply extend positive emotions.

Healing arts can be applied to many types of injuries, provided you have first consulted a doctor to make sure your injury is not serious or life-threatening. Many times wrist injuries, I have found, are simply wrist bones that are out of place. Sometimes with a leg injury, all that is required is simple traction. If you are paying attention to what is going on and really seeing the symptoms, you can trust your intuition to know what to do in many situations regarding the injury of yourself or others.

I was once thrown during a demonstration in a wrist control art, which ended up dislocating one of my finger joints. My partner let me go, my hand shaking because it was so painful. I looked down at my hand, and I saw one of my finger joints pointing 90 degrees the wrong way. Not cool. I simply pulled the joint up and realigned it quickly. It popped back into place before the swelling kicked in. I would not recommend this to others, as a misstep could leave you with a permanent injury. Just know that in a pinch, you can do these things yourself. I've set toes and dislocated shoulders in a similar fashion.

At the time I received this injury, I did not have health insurance, and so a trip to the doctor was out of the question for me. I have since learned to trust my skill and intuition regarding my own injuries. I know my body better than any doctor out there, and so I know when it is safe to do something and when it is not. I do not subscribe to the "doctors know everything" mantra that many people believe. I think massage therapists and physical therapists know more about the body than doctors do, at least when it comes to the kinds of injuries we sustain as martial artists. I trust their advice more than that of a general practitioner when it concerns muscles and connective tissues.

The advantage to trusting yourself with these types of injuries is that you do not have to rely on others. For broken ribs, a doctor can do very little for you other than give you painkillers. All doctors can do for a dislocation is set it back to its original position, so why not do it yourself?

I trust my intuition when it comes to the healing arts. I have sustained many injuries in martial arts, and so I can recognize pain symptoms from injuries. I've had broken bones, sprains, strains, dislocations, blood clots, a bone in my wrist out of alignment, torn muscles, mild concussions, tennis elbow, and more bruises and aches than I can remember. Some techniques will often create injuries, and it is good to know how to correct these things when you see them. I once had a technique done to me in aikido called *sankyo*. Imagine your elbow pointing to the ceiling, while your fingertips are pointing to the floor. Your wrist is then twisted toward you. Sometimes the bones in the wrist can pop out of place during this art. The pain will continue after the technique is applied, and many people will shake their wrists, as if to pop the bones back themselves subconsciously. If you grab their wrist so that both of your thumbs are on the tiny bones in the hand (where the hand bends near the forearm bones) and you use a whiplike motion, you can pop these bones back into place. The area will be a bit sore for a day, but will clear up after that.

If you sit seiza for too long, your hamstring muscles can tighten up in a terribly painful way. When people are experiencing this, they will immediately stop sitting seiza, and they will try to massage their own legs. If you ask them to sit down and stretch out their legs, you can apply traction to their legs by lightly pulling on the ankle, thereby stretching the hamstring. This should make the pain immediately subside.

Headaches

If you have headaches on a frequent basis, then you probably have a problem with being unable to relax completely. Headaches tend to occur at the front of the head in the sinuses, or in the back of the head. To cure a headache to the front of the head, close your eyes and cup your hands over your eyes, so that you form a sort of vacuum seal on your eye orbits. From here, rest the weight of your head into your hands and imagine your eyes relaxing and bulging a bit from your head. We want them to drop slightly. You can perform this at a table or desk with your elbows resting comfortably on the surface.

After about five minutes of this, bring your head up, but keep your eyes closed. Then, take the tips of your thumb and find the sweet spot by the base of your nose near your eyes. Move your thumbs around until you find a spot that feels good. Then relax your head again and let the weight of your head sink into your thumbs. You can work your way around your eyes as you see fit until the headache expires. Many headaches are tension-based, and by relaxing specific muscles in the head, face, and neck, we can remove the headache entirely. Migraine headaches and sinus headaches are a bit more stubborn and require more time to alleviate the pain.

If you are experiencing a headache concentrated in the back of the head, I recommend bringing your head forward toward your chest and stretching the back of your neck. From here, take both hands and make hooks with your fingertips. Place your hook hands on either side of your spine by your neck and press down. Hang your head like you are bowing, and relax all the muscles that support your head. Do this for five minutes or so, and adjust the position as necessary. I sometimes find the base of my skull and rub that area with my fingertips too.

You can also bring your head to one side trying to touch your ear to your shoulder. On the opposite shoulder, the muscle that is stretched from your ear to your shoulder can be worked on in similar fashion using your hook hands. Remember to relax and breathe normally.

For any headache, I also like to run my fingertips through my scalp, moving my head and not my hands. Pulling the hair also helps relieve the tension.

I use a mix of massage and pressure points to relieve most headaches for myself and for others. When doing this on another person, you must have continuous communication with him or her to know where to press and how much. For this reason, this is much easier to do upon yourself because you know where the pain is and how much pressure to apply. For others, you will need your intuition and patience to work with them. The goal is to have your patient relax so that he or she can accept what you are doing. If your efforts make him or her resist you, this will be an exercise in futility. He or she must be calm and relaxed, and so must you. If you are anxious or tense, your patient will mirror this.

Pushing Out Poison

Perhaps the most dramatic of all cures that I have done on myself and others is to push out food poisoning, reducing the overall downtime one has near the toilet. Of all martial arts skills to possess when you are really sick, this skill is a godsend. Who cares how to punch at this moment? Just get me through this one night!

This technique was passed down to my sensei by Koichi Tohei Sensei, who discovered it during World War II when his men ate some bad rice while on campaign. Like most things, I was skeptical of this art, and I wondered why my teacher showed it to me. I was there to learn martial arts, not massage. But at any rate, I listened to him, and I learned in earnest because I trusted that he knew what was best for me. Weeks later, I encountered my first run-in with food poisoning. I woke up in the middle of the night, and my guts were in knots. I had to press on my stomach or else be paralyzed with gut-wrenching pain. Immediately I began doing the art that my sensei showed me. It did not work right away, so I repeated it several times, not knowing what else I should do. After about a half hour of this, the pain suddenly stopped, and I could move again, but I had to make it to the toilet pronto. This, however, is the entire point. When our bodies have taken in poison, the only way to cure it is to get it out!

Since that time, I became a believer in this method, and since then I've used it on myself and on others to cure constipation, food poisoning, stomach flu, and any other digestion issues. With this method, you can bring whatever it is up, or move it down and out. I prefer down and out, as I rank vomiting as the number-one least-pleasant experience in my life.

To perform this technique, start by lying on your back. Use your primary hand and push down your centerline using your fingertips. Relax your hand as much as possible and use your free hand to add more weight if needed. Hold and press each spot along a line for ten to thirty seconds. Move from the top of your stomach to just below your navel, then work in a circle going from the center to your right. Follow the rib cage, but stay below the diaphragm, and work your way up to your center again just above the bladder. Rinse and repeat. After I have done this with my fingers, I then massage with the heel of my palm, using a down and circular motion. The pattern described looks like the Japanese character "*no*," or an upside-down letter "*e.*"

I once had the flu so badly that I had to lie in bed all night doing this technique, visiting the bathroom every twenty minutes or so for eight hours. After this time, the flu was gone, and I escaped needing to throw up; I had pushed it all through. Even though that night was not pleasant, had I not applied this technique, I would have added vomiting to the list of unpleasantness, as well as doubled my toilet time.

This technique can also be used upon others, and I have performed this many times on students and on spouses. Make sure when doing this on others that you don't press the diaphragm or use too much or too little pressure. Communicate with the other person and make sure that the pressure is just right. Ask the person to breathe deeply and to relax as much as possible. We are trying to encourage their bodies to push out the poison, gas, or other digestive problem, so they need to be in a relaxed state to make this happen. It may take many trial runs of this pattern, so do not be discouraged if the results are not immediate— though they sometimes are. I will often use the heel of my hand, follow the same lines, and give gentle vibrations to the entire abdomen. This will relax the patient and get fluids and juices moving.

Impossible Pain Tolerance

One of the most spectacular things I have ever witnessed in martial arts is when my aikido sensei sat seiza (kneeling) for six hours without moving, changing position, or getting up. After this time, he stood up and simply walked around normally. This feat is impressive by itself because most people can't sit this way for fifteen minutes, let alone for an hour. What is more is that the day before, he severely injured his knee and could not walk down stairs; he had to hop down on one leg. He sat there, with a knee injury, and no one in the room had the slightest idea that he was injured. I had found out by accident that day when I caught him descending the stairs in the dojo. He stood on the stairs, and we had a conversation for about ten minutes. Then he finally said, "Okay, you caught me." And he proceeded to limp down the stairs like a wounded animal. Minutes later, he watched a six-hour aikido test while sitting seiza.

I made the blunder of asking my sensei how he was able to do this feat, and the next private class I had with him, we sat seiza for two hours. My legs and indeed my hips were numb, and I was in terrible agony. I shifted from side to side; I sat up; I massaged my feet and neck. I was stiff all over. He then proceeded to give me what I now call the pain lecture.

"Do you think I don't feel any pain?" he asked us. What followed was a long description about how pain is only in the mind and that we have the ability to choose how we feel about pain. We can complain, we can shift, we can manifest discomfort in our bodies, or we can come to a point of acceptance. It is this acceptance of pain that holds what humans throughout time have viewed as a truly impossible power.

This same sensei once tore ligaments in his right arm, becoming unable to raise it above the waist. This injury lasted many months, but only a handful of people knew about it. He never complained, never made mention of the injury, and never guarded the injury. That is, he wouldn't massage his shoulder; he wouldn't stretch it out and moan. He simply lived his life as though this injury were not present. He filled his mind with positive thoughts and carried his body in such a way as to facilitate the healing process. He always sat upright and always stood tall. He never shifted his weight needlessly and always made sure that his back was in a straight position. This keen attention to posture allowed him to heal more quickly.

During the time of his shoulder injury, he taught a weekend seminar consisting of daylong classes. I saw him throw fifty or more people in a technique that required him to raise his right arm over his head. Not only could he perform the technique without a hitch; he never made it known that raising his arm was incredibly painful. He ignored that pain and raised his hand over his head as if he were completely healthy.

My aikido sensei also told me of a story about a peer he once practiced with when he was a young man. This aikido student got into a contest with a karate practitioner. The karate guy wanted to fight the aikido student, but the aikido student wasn't fully confident in his arts yet—but he did know how to roll. He challenged the karate man to a rolling contest ... on the pavement. The karate guy agreed. The aikido student rolled several miles on the pavement, scratching and bruising arms, legs, hips, and feet, but carrying on despite the pain. The karate guy was injured early and conceded.

The first time I broke my right hand, I thought I sprained something in my wrist. So I kept on fighting during a sparring class. I knew the hand was broken when one of my sparring partners punched my hand and I could feel the bone slip over itself and then back again. This pain was intense, but I think the adrenaline nullified part of it. I kept fighting, and I didn't go to the hospital for hours. Most people would call this stupid, but I think that continuing to practice while injured bestows some benefits. Obviously if you are having cardiac arrest, you should seek medical attention immediately. However, if you just have a broken hand, you can still punch with the other hand and kick with your feet. Knowing your pain limits is important. If you were to break your hand in a real fight, there is no such thing as a time-out. You can't suddenly complain that you are injured and call in the referee for help on the street.

If you sustain an injury while practicing martial arts, try to do an activity in class that you can do. If your hand is in a cast or sling, don't go punching with that hand. Use your other hand. If your foot is broken, don't go kicking with that foot. If it is a medical emergency, you need to have that taken care of immediately. If you are dying of blood loss, don't try to do extra reps of push-ups; go to the hospital. But for minor injuries, take advantage of that time to practice, even if it is just standing there and taking the pain.

I once was sparring full-contact many years ago, and a really fat opponent kicked me in the head. I was surprised that he could kick so high, and that caught me off guard. I managed to raise my left arm up to block, and so I took the full force of his kick on the boney point of my shoulder, a place you should not receive impact on. For the rest of the fight, my left arm was useless. I could not use it to punch, block, or do much of anything other than hold it up with my will alone. I managed to finish the fight without stopping to nurse my injury. I fooled everyone there into believing that I was uninjured. Hiding injuries is a skill one should learn in martial arts. Had I demonstrated how crippled my left arm was in a real fight, my opponent could use that knowledge to cause me significant grief.

Another time in class, I asked a black belt to punch me for the sake of demonstrating a technique. I had assumed that he was going to go slow motion so that I could show the arts I wanted to do. He apparently misunderstood, and struck me as I was looking away from him. I caught the movement out of the corner of my eye, and I managed to put up my left hand to block it in time. Unfortunately in my haste, I managed to also break my hand. I didn't let anyone know, and I proceeded to teach for another hour and a half. Then I chatted with students in my usual manner after class, and only much later did I go to the hospital. Again, people may say this is stupid. But understanding pain is one of those impossible techniques that is incredibly valuable and could save your life sometime.

One need not break bones or tear ligaments to practice how to do the impossible with pain tolerance. The first way we practice pain tolerance is to simply show up to class as much as possible. If you are feeling somewhat ill, if you have a minor injury, then don't let it stop you going to your dojo and practice. Even if you just show up and watch the class, this is better than not showing up. What we need to do as martial artists is develop the idea in our subconscious that we are always training. By having the feeling that we are always training, regardless of our physical condition, we will begin to push away the excuse of being sick or injured. This feeling will then transfer in our daily lives, and as a consequence, we will always feel ready should our arts ever be needed.

Practicing once or twice a week does not help your subconscious feel as though it is always training. Your mind realizes these gaps of time, and when the time comes when your arts are needed, you may not be ready. This is a sort of pain tolerance. Daily practice can be tiresome, and we may crave lying on the couch more than punching and kicking. Get over this by practicing ten minutes each day. Everyone has ten minutes a day for practice, so do not delude yourself into thinking you do not have the time for practice. If you can find the time to brush your teeth, you can find the time to practice. With the ten-minutes-a-day attitude, your subconscious will begin to internalize that you are always practicing; and since the subconscious cannot refuse the thoughts we provide it, you will cultivate a feeling of readiness. This is the first step in mastering impossible pain tolerance.

Another method for developing pain tolerance is to sit seiza for as long as you can without fidgeting or moving. This sort of meditation can be done while watching TV or eating dinner. For beginners, target twenty minutes sitting in this position without shifting or moving whatsoever. If you can distract your mind, like watching TV, this is much easier. For more advanced practitioners, you should be able to sit this way for an hour. During seiza practice, you will feel your legs go numb, starting with your feet, then your calves, then your thighs. The pain actually increases if you shift around because it allows the flow of blood back to your legs, renewing the pain you would otherwise become numb to. So sit still. Acknowledge the pain is happening and know that moving around to avoid the pain will create more pain. Convince yourself that being still is the best remedy. This will allow your mind and your body to relax more. Set a time limit for yourself and stick to that plan. Your mind can relax more if it knows that there is an end in sight. Gradually increase this duration each time you practice this exercise. Take the pain.

If you have bad knees, do not bother with this exercise as this will make knee injuries worse. We are not trying to cripple ourselves; we are trying to develop impossible pain tolerance. Another way to practice this idea is to just stand in horse stance. That is, with your feet double-shoulder-width apart, your feet pointing forward, and your knees bent. This exercise is a physical endurance test, but this sort of pain can be managed as well. Do not move away from the pain by standing up. Move into the pain by relaxing and sinking your weight downward. Again, novices should try to hold this position for twenty minutes, and more advanced people should be capable of holding it for an hour.

I had a student who was seventy years old. He could not bend one of his knees more than 90 degrees due to a severe knee injury he sustained in his thirties. But this man could stand in horse stance for an insanely long time, putting many twenty-year-olds to shame. I asked him many times about his injury, which he received by falling off of a house roof. His knee had developed arthritis and was in constant pain, and yet he was on the mat every day doing this type of practice. He never complained about the knee, even though I could see him limp in and out of class. He would participate in rolling forward and backward, and even could do hard falls (flipping in midair and landing on your side). He did not believe in pain medication, and could ignore pain that would drive most people insane.

All of these stories share one thing in common: they demonstrate that with a mastery mind-set, one can endure any pain. You are not your pain, and your pain should never be the master of you. You are the only one who can control your mental attitude. If you are in the habit of making excuses because of pain, learn to be quiet and figure out what you *can* do, instead of concentrating on what you can't do.

Where to Start?

By now you may be thinking, *Where do I start? How do I begin to increase my internal power? How do I develop unyielding resolve? How do I practice devastating punches and kicks? How can I master pain?* The answer is quite simple. To pursue the mastery mind-set, you must first decide this is what you want for yourself. You must make the conscious decision that you intend to master whatever it is you are seeking to master. Then, you must repeat this affirmation daily; think of it like weight lifting for the mind. Imagine, dream, and create positive pictures in your head. Get emotionally involved in the process of learning and fall in love with studying. It really is that simple, but you must endeavor to do this every day.

Be a Visionary

Now this may sound corny, but all great things started as a vision in someone's mind. Henry Ford imagined the motorcar, and the Wright brothers imagined a flying machine. These people were called crazy by their neighbors, but now history remembers them as great visionaries. All great men and women became successful by first dreaming up something in their minds. So to master your arts, you too must dream. Your subconscious will accept anything you feed it, so feed it positive images of your arts. Do not beat yourself up and tell yourself you are terrible or that certain levels of mastery are unattainable because of this or that reason. Speak to yourself in a tone that cultivates strong personal values.

Use phrases like, "I am strong. I am powerful. I have an unyielding spirit." This will program your mind to get in that mastery mind-set. You don't have to tell others this, as it may seem like you are overconfident or egotistical. Keep it private.

Think Critically

If you practice an art already, ask yourself critical questions while you pursue it. Look at your teacher. If your teacher is amazing, then this is where he or she can lead you. If your teacher is average, then you will only ever become average. If martial arts are a hobby and nothing more to you, then being average may not matter at all. In which case, keep doing what you are doing, but know that you can certainly improve more if you set your sights higher. If you only wish to do martial arts for yourself and never intend to teach them, then you are free to practice anything you choose to get better. My advice is to practice the things you love to do, and then these areas will naturally shine.

If you are truly seeking depth and wisdom from the arts, you have to see things critically. Really see your teacher. Can he or she lead you to where you want to go? If not, maybe it is time to go someplace else. There are plenty of teachers out there in plenty of different styles. Seek out those who can do things that you cannot. Ignore the secretive teachers who hide their arts, as it has been my experience that true masters never hide their arts. The people who hide their arts are those who are insecure about themselves or their arts.

I was once a part of a martial arts organization that had a lot of old-timers in it. The organization was huge, and there were many students and instructors. Out of the hundreds of people in this organization, there were perhaps five individuals who really knew any of the arts. This means that despite everyone's sincere efforts, only a tiny percentage really understood what was going on. People will all love to share their opinions of the arts, but always consider the source. If that person cannot do the things you want to accomplish, then he or she is useless to you in terms of being a good teacher. This may seem unnecessarily harsh, but consider: if you stick with and climb the hierarchy of a "sick" organization for fifty years, what sort of prestige will you attain in an organization that has basically nothing to offer? So you become the king. King of what? King of the fools? Get out, go to seminars, experiment, dig deep, learn, and explore. The alternative is mediocrity. If you are not going forward, you must be going backward, because nothing remains the same.

There are some who would argue that slumps in training are stagnation, keeping you at the same level of skill. I disagree. Slumps are worse than mere stagnation, because they are pulling you away from mastery. Slumps will cause you to backslide to the point where you will eventually quit. Have the courage to reignite your enthusiasm for mastery of the arts. Bob Proctor, a self-help guru, puts this concept well when he says, "You are either creating or you are disintegrating."

With open eyes, you will see opportunities that you may not have seen before. With diligent practice and a critical mind, you will uncover these secrets and develop a powerful self-reliance. Become the teacher that you always wanted. Keep striving for a deeper and bigger purpose, and you will find that power will come to you naturally.

Little by Little

What the mind can conceive and believe, the mind can also achieve.—Napoleon Hill

If you plant an acorn in the ground, you wouldn't expect an oak tree to be there the next day, right? Mental seeds are similar to real seeds in that they require a period of time to germinate within our minds before we understand these things fully. And, just like real seeds, our mental seeds require continual nutrients to grow: practice. You must be persistent in keeping up with diligent and critical practice. Practice proper structure every day. Practice this with a partner every day, even if this is only five minutes at each session. The more you do this, the more you plant that seed in your mind, and the more that seed will grow and grow and grow. If you fail to do this, you will likely meet with failure and then give up when you meet with disappointing results. If you don't work for it, expect to achieve only the same level of skill you already have.

If you truly want to understand internal power and allow your arts to transcend the physical, then you must continually hone your mind. Hold that goal in your conscious mind and see yourself performing these arts flawlessly. If imagining your fists glowing with blue flames of light helps you create a better image for yourself, by all means use this. Imagination is a powerful tool, so why not employ it? Put your imagination to work.

Many martial arts have developed a belt ranking system as a means of goal setting, with a hierarchy of milestones that you must meet along the way. This is a good start, but I would encourage everyone to go far beyond that. Pick something that interests you and excites you, and work on that one skill until you see noticeable improvement. Do not pick something because you assume you should get better at it. If something is cool to you, you will be more likely to see it through. For me, this was the devastating punch and absorbing power. I practiced both relentlessly after first seeing how they were done until I was able to do them myself. Set a goal for yourself that is both fun and achievable. Do a little bit each day toward that goal. If you want a stronger punch but you don't punch every day, how can you expect that goal to come to fruition? Practice each day, and after you complete that goal, set another one. In this way, we reach our destination little by little.

Become Emotionally Involved

You may say to yourself that you would like to develop internal power; you may even believe that to be true. But if you do not become emotionally involved in this endeavor, you will likely quit trying when your results don't change just because you think they should. Becoming emotionally involved with this idea will stimulate your subconscious mind and make you feel enthusiastic. Enthusiasm will generate the necessary energy to motivate you to reach higher and higher goals. Set the goal so high it gives you chills just to think about it.

Get excited about your arts again. You may have been practicing for twenty years and forgotten exactly why it is you are training. If this is you, remember the glory and the wonder that you had when you first started. Have that childlike enthusiasm ignite your passion for arts that have become routine.

At times I demonstrate techniques that I think may be boring. Then a student will gasp with delight, and I see this glow overtake him or her and I suddenly remember that indeed these arts are amazing. Use the enthusiasm of beginners to fuel your own desires and to keep a healthy flow of positive energy in your dojo and within your life.

To help maintain that enthusiasm, I recommend writing out a goal card and keeping it with you at all times. Read the card throughout the day until you have memorized it. Write your goals as though you have already attained them. Your subconscious mind does not have the ability to reject any ideas that we feed it, and so feed it grand and positive messages and soon you will reach that goal.

Example of a Goal Card:

- I am a master of [NAME OF ART]. I have a powerful punch that I can employ with minimal effort. I can absorb any punch or kick to my body without receiving any injury. I have mastered internal power.
- I give back all of the wealth of knowledge that I know, and share freely with my peers and students.

In goal cards, I like having a statement of giving back for what you intend to gain. This flow of energy keeps the wheels of abundance turning. Hoarding knowledge does nothing but make you a librarian. There is no such thing as something for nothing. What are you prepared to give back for all of the internal power you intend to gain?

Form a Mastermind Alliance

Napoleon Hill was a famous self-development author who studied hundreds of successful men to determine what made them so successful. One of the things he found that was common with all of these men was that they had formed mastermind alliances.

A mastermind alliance works on the principle that two or more brains are more powerful than one. If these people work in perfect harmony toward a definite purpose, then they can create a powerful synergy that will yield greater results than if just one brain were doing the work. People like Henry Ford, Thomas Edison, and Andrew Carnegie all formed mastermind alliances with people who had the necessary skill sets that they did not themselves possess. By utilizing this combined brainpower, you will be able to discover things much more quickly than you could on your own.

Martial arts and internal power cannot fully be realized in a book. A book is a reference and perhaps a source of inspiration, but that's about it. To fully develop your arts, you need to be held accountable. If you cannot find a teacher for this, find a sparring partner to help you. Continuous work with a peer will launch both of you closer to your goals. Teamwork can be like a multicelled battery of your minds, the result being more power for all the members of your group.

Even if you have a fantastic teacher, I urge you to form a mastermind alliance with at least one other peer whom you trust so that your combined minds can wrestle with all the wonders that the martial arts world has to offer. By doing so, you will be able to see things clearly that were once invisible to you.

You will not master martial arts inside a box. You will not get better at internal power by yourself. You must seek out its mysteries with others of like mind; test things out on each other, come up with theories, and implement them. You may find that some old techniques that you abandoned will become more useful; likewise, arts that you leaned on before will now be put by the wayside. Chances are you will be reinventing the wheel, but this should not impede you at all. So what if someone else has discovered the truths of a technique or secret to internal power? Discovering it for yourself is far more valuable than having someone simply tell it to you. Moreover, you will retain information that you discover yourself, and assign an emotional attachment to it, like a source of pride, which will help you continue on your pathway to the mastery mind-set.

Train Smarter

There are some who believe that you must train hard each time you work out or it is not really training. This is a young person's mind-set, and for young people, this is true. Train hard and give it 100 percent. When you are young, you heal quickly. You can push your body more than an older person, so take advantage of this opportunity to get more training. For those who are over thirty-five, you should begin to train smarter and not necessarily harder. If you treat yourself like you are twenty when you are fifty, you will constantly become physically worn-down, and more importantly, emotionally worn-down as well. When you are fifty, you don't need to do 10,000 repetitions. You can do five hundred repetitions that have more purpose and are more focused. Your practice is still deliberate and never lazy, but the nature of your arts should change as your body changes.

If you attempt high kicks when over fifty, then you might be risking some serious injury to yourself. Yes, it is possible to kick high when you are fifty, but it's also more probable that you will break or dislocate a hip at that age too. Self-defense isn't just about kicking ass; it's about honoring your own body. Torturing your body or your mind is the opposite of self-defense.

In general, we should avoid activities that will cause us injuries; however, as serious martial artists, we should be tougher than the average Joe on the street. I define an injury as anything that keeps me out of the dojo for more than a week. We are practicing martial arts, and so bruising, scrapes, and minor sprains are not injuries—they are battle wounds! This type of pain is mildly annoying at its worst, so we should not miss class because of a bruise. An injury might be a broken bone, muscle tear, serious sprain, ligament or tendon damage, detached retina, or ruptured eardrum. You should be able to punch each other hard in the chest and receive no injury from it. Bruises will happen, but those go away quickly and don't really interfere with life. A detached retina will really ruin your day.

Know the limits of your own body, and make a conscious effort to train smarter. I once grabbed a few fifty-pound dumbbells and I proceeded to do about two hundred squats. Good workout, right? Oops, I pulled a muscle in my back, and I was out for two weeks. A grandmother could have kicked my butt during that downtime. I had felt that something was wrong during the workout, but I thought I would just power through the pain.

Recognize your pain; sometimes it shouldn't be ignored. Stretching pain, bruising pain, or pinching pain can all be ignored. Yeah, you will have a pink mark the next day, but so what? If you feel a muscle go "pop" or a joint go "crunch," then listen to that and step off the mat for a second. I once demonstrated a wrist-lock technique (*nikkyo*) to someone who wanted to see something "cool." I applied the lock on the man, and he just stood there. Most people fly downward and take a knee from this type of pain. I was surprised, so I did the technique harder. Still zero reaction. *Holy crap,* I thought, *this guy is one tough son of a bitch!* I slammed down on that man's wrist with everything I had. At this point, the man screamed, but still didn't go down.

When I let go, he said, "I was in so much pain, I could not move! Why did you do that two more times? Once was enough." I had no idea it was working on him because I was not reading his body language correctly. Not only should we realize our own limits; we should also sincerely recognize our opponent's limits. Sometimes this is not obvious. I've had flexible women in class whom I could bend in impossible directions, and they would simply not tap out because it felt like nothing to them. Then I've applied the same pins to some men at about 1 percent of normal power, and they start screaming. If you bring yourself more in harmony with your opponent, you can feel this edge of pain more clearly.

I was in class once when a student got kicked in the eye and had his retina detach from the blow. The woman who kicked him did not mean to do this. The man had bent forward from a previous technique, and she kicked him as his head was moving downward. It was clearly an accident, but this sort of thing could have been avoided if both people were paying more attention.

If you are one with your opponent, that is, if you are matching his or her speed and timing, it becomes easier to read his or her level of pain tolerance. People with low pain tolerance guard their bodies and make it obvious when you have applied enough pressure on a given throw. People with a low pain threshold will often try to move away from the pain. When you first encounter this aversion to pain, your application of power is usually enough. Going past this is where injuries occur, especially while throwing.

Get rid of the thought that you have to punch hard, kick hard, and throw hard in order for it to be "real" practice. This is actually doing everyone a disservice. First of all, doing things hard usually means that you are tensing up, and, ironically, this actually makes your techniques weaker. To hit hard, you must relax. To kick hard, you must relax. To throw hard, you must relax. This sounds like a paradox, but it's true. If you tense up, you use only a few muscles, but when you relax, you have your whole body to actuate a counterattack or a throw. The results look impossible, because it takes so little movement from you to create huge results in your opponent.

I discovered this by accident many years ago when I would spar with beginners. I would naturally relax more, because I was not afraid of being injured by a novice, regardless of his or her talent or enthusiasm. I reached out and punched one student in the jaw, and he collapsed unconscious from what I thought was just a tap. This happened with several others, and each time I struck with a relaxed body and mind and I had no intention of knocking anyone unconscious. Granted, they were only out for a few seconds, but these hits were fight stoppers.

My business partner and I faced this odd situation: the more relaxed our technique became, the more we were causing injuries. Both of us broke bones of students, and both of us dropped students with what we thought were light taps. From a business perspective, you shouldn't be injuring your clients. We then stopped this practice and changed the way we demonstrate our techniques so we can hit full-power and not hurt anyone. This is why we do a lot of contact training to the chest; it allows us to understand power in a safe manner.

Many situations will arise in your training that you can learn and benefit from. Each person out there can teach you a valuable lesson. Train with all sorts of people—young, old, fit, thin, and fat. Different people react differently to pain and differently to being struck or thrown. Sometimes their reactions will be exactly opposite to how you anticipate them. The more body types you are familiar with, the greater your ability will be to employ any technique on any person, and therefore the greater your mastery will become.

For Teachers

If you are a teacher, know that you wear many different hats. Knowing how to perform your arts well is not enough. A good teacher will also be a good salesperson, a good businessperson, and a good leader, as well as being skilled in the arts he or she hopes to teach others.

Be Competent at Your Arts

As a teacher of martial arts, we first need to be competent at the arts that we practice. Unlike sports coaches, who can tell their players what to do even if unable to physically do it themselves, we must be able to show people what they must do. Practicing combat arts is a completely different experience from shooting hoops. Make sure you can take a punch from all of your students. This will do many things for you. First, it will demonstrate that you can take a hit and that you have something very real that they can learn from you. Also, it will demonstrate your willingness to do everything that you ask of your students. If you ask your students to do a jump kick, you better be able to do a jump kick. If you ask your students to do a handstand, you should be able to do a handstand yourself. Never ask your students to do an activity that you yourself are not capable of.

Be a Good Salesperson

Secondly, we need to be good at pitching our arts. Being a salesperson doesn't mean you need to get yourself an old sport coat and mustache, and slick back your hair. You have to sell your arts to your students in ways that are interesting and exciting. You must sell yourself if you wish your classes to grow in size. This has absolutely nothing to do with money, but the end result may be more money from having more students. If your students are not sold on a technique by your sales pitch, then you must work on your sales pitch. If you say something like, "Well, I guess you can sort of do this art if you want maybe," then you will not inspire confidence, and your students will wonder why you are showing them this art and wasting their time. Arts that you believe in strongly should be taught with vigor. Try this instead. "This technique is perfect for self-defense because it works regardless of you being scared and it works even if you aren't a master at it." Words like this encourage students to follow you.

Be a Good Businessperson

Being a good businessperson is also a part of the package. If you have a class full of women and you are teaching exclusively hard-style martial arts, you may lose each one of your students. Likewise if you have a group of people who have knee injuries and you insist on doing kicks and strikes to the knees, then you will soon find yourself in an empty dojo. Pay attention to what people want, and guide the classes so that people are getting what they paid for. This has a lot to do with what your students' expectations are. If you walk into a movie expecting an action movie and it turns out to be a romantic comedy, you will be disappointed. I don't care how funny or great the comedy movie is, your first impression will be a poor one. This same feeling applies to class. Know your audience, and make sure they see something that they came to see.

If you are teaching a group of young adults, don't bore them with meditation, but rather teach them how to punch, kick, and throw. Do many repetitions and change the exercises frequently. If you are teaching a group of fifty-year-olds, do not teach them the same way you teach children. You will lose the audience.

I once assisted teaching a large class full of beginners, about forty college-aged students. The instructor taught a class so boring and dull that I was speechless. I was unable to turn the class around because this instructor had in his mind the formula of the class, and he stuck to it, even though none of the students were interested. Ten minutes in, people kept looking at the clock. Twenty minutes in, and people were giving looks to one another, sighing and rubbing their necks. A blind man could have seen what was happening! Out of the forty people who came that day, only one or two returned for the next class. If you do not sell everyone in the room on your ideas and your enthusiasm, you are not doing a good enough job. Learn from your mistakes, pay attention to what people enjoy, and really muster the courage to step outside of the box sometimes and do things a little differently.

Be a Good Leader

> **If you haven't sold everyone on your ideas, this means your presentation is terrible.**—Bob Proctor

When we step into a dojo as a teacher, whether we like it or not, we become a role model. People will begin to imitate you and follow your example. Children especially will absorb even the most minor of behaviors and use them as their own. Be careful, then, what sort of example you are setting for others. We teach people how we want to be treated through our actions and interactions with others. When we teach, we automatically assume a role of responsibility, because people are looking to us for guidance, and we need to be available mentally and emotionally for our students.

Leadership encompasses a large number of skills. As martial artists, we must portray confidence, we must be respectful, we must demonstrate that we have a game plan, we must take responsibility, we must be a role model, and we must be invested in our students' success. When our lives are very busy, we may neglect some of these areas. It is important to always address your own conduct so that you can become a better teacher as well as a better leader.

To portray confidence, we must first be competent at the arts that we teach. Hopefully if you are teaching, this should not be an issue. However, I have seen many talented martial artists shoot themselves in the foot by the words they choose. I once had one teacher who would often preface everything he did by saying, "I'm not very good at this." Do not be the naysayer in your own life. People will know if you are good at something or not; just be yourself and lead the class. As a rule of thumb, you should never ask anyone to do something that you yourself are unable to do. You should be able to demonstrate any art that you wish others to participate in. The exception is if you have been teaching for many decades and can no longer do a young-person's art like spinning kicks. Have a junior instructor demonstrate this if that is the case.

Classes you teach should have cohesion and a main focus for each session. You can plan your classes beforehand, or do what I do and wing it. For me, it is very exciting to not know what I'm going to teach until just the moment before I teach it. This may or may not suit your personality. At any rate, your classes should have a theme to them, rather than a random meandering that will be difficult to follow for some people. A good leader should keep people connected and on task. It's not my goal to show you specific ways to make your class more exciting, but I will say this: if you are bored, your students will be bored. If you cannot lead a group, people will quickly lose faith in you, and again, your classes will be sparse.

Learn to lead people by first understanding what makes an interesting class. This starts with knowing your audience. If your class is not working for some reason, grab the reins and change it. Maybe you have been working on kicks for two hours, and people are either bored or exhausted. Change it up. Do some meditation, or do some slower activity that can match their current speed. You are guiding the ship, and if that ship is going down, you have the power to steer into the wave, around the wave, or anything else.

Often the difference between a good teacher and a bad teacher has little to do with the martial arts skill set that he or she has. You could be the greatest martial artist in the world, but if you cannot connect with people, you will forever be cast aside in favor of the more exciting personality.

A good leader also knows how to inspire enthusiasm in his or her students. If you are not enthusiastic about your arts, then who the hell will be? If you are unable to generate joy and enthusiasm for what you do, how do you believe you will ever develop internal power? How will other people find joy in what you do? If your classes suck, it's probably because your attitude sucks. And if your attitude sucks, I'm guessing your ability to generate internal power is limited.

Practicing enthusiasm generates energy. Become emotionally involved and really sink your soul into the arts that you study, no matter what the arts are. Immerse yourself in them, and experience the joy that will be transferred to everyone around you. If you believe in others, others will believe in you.

Often when I teach, I am challenged by students who ask unexpected questions. These questions make me think of the arts from different angles that I may not have thought of before. Looking at a problem from many angles will improve not only your ability to do that art, but your ability to teach that art. Knowing that you have to teach something automatically increases your retention for ideas that work. If you know you don't need to know something, that knowledge may escape you immediately. Teachers, however, need to remember everything.

As sensei, you should cultivate respect for everyone in the dojo, as all things in martial arts begin and end with respect. This is why we bow to our partners, and at the start and close of class. This should carry over into your attitude toward everyone. Show everyone respect, and respect will then be paid back to you. Slight people, and they will slight you.

Notes on Being an Asshole

Perhaps the first lesson in martial arts, even before awareness, is practicing to be a good person. Good people attract good things in their lives, while bad people attract bad things. The more you practice this law of attraction, the greater your life's success will be.

Think back to high school and of all the cliques that were formed there. The bad crowd smoked, did drugs, and continuously got into trouble with the police or school officials. The good crowd got fine grades, studied together, always went to class, and probably got scholarships for their efforts. This demonstrates that like-minded individuals attract like-minded individuals. The bad crowd can learn to be in the good crowd, and the good crowd can learn to be in the bad crowd, by adopting the mannerisms and practices each side holds. We choose each day what side of the fence we wish to be on.

Moreover, being a good guy and being a douche bag require the same amount of energy. So why not become the good guy? Also, being a dick will one day come back to haunt you. Someone somewhere will take a poke at you someday. Being a good person is by far the best self-defense advice I can ever give anyone. If you are the nicest person in the world, people will defend you with their lives. If you are a jerk, they will watch laughing as you go down drowning.

Be cautious, then, of your attitude toward others. Make light of others, and they will make light of you. Criticize others, and they will criticize you. We must be diligent and always have an even disposition. You cannot make everyone like you, but you can certainly reduce the number of people that loathe you.

An easy way to demonstrate respect is to recognize people's personal power and sense of self-worth. I once had a very formidable bodybuilder join my class; he had an intimidating demeanor as well as physique. He was tough, and I pointed this out many times in class, and as a result I never had a problem with him. I said once, "I need someone very strong for this next demonstration," and then pointed to the bodybuilder, saying, "Could you please help me?" I did this just one time, and the man was happy and engaged with class even when I beat on him. Fill someone like this with rage, and he may tear you to pieces.

Once during a low point in my live-in aikido practice, I found myself in a position where I could have easily pushed my sensei down a flight of stairs—payback for hundreds of torturous classes. How much would his decades of martial arts experience protect him from that? The thought occurred to me, but only in the sense that it was something I would never do. My teacher never gave me a reason to *want* to push him down the stairs. I knew deep down that my teacher only wanted what was absolutely best for me, despite some grueling lessons. So in this spirit, he protected himself from those he taught as well. If you are arrogant, at some point, one of your students will call you out on it, and it might just be when you're at the top of a nasty flight of stairs.

Another time I was in my aikido dojo many years ago, and a student came in and took some swings at one of the junior instructors. The instructor was known for being arrogant and a know-it-all, who would often belittle students through sarcasm. I was in the back room at the time of the attack, so I rushed to the dojo floor to see what was going on. The student had shaved his head and was carrying a skateboard, menacing the teacher, who had his back to the wall. He was obviously distraught. I crossed the mat and walked right between the two men. The student with the shaved head gritted his teeth and tried to head butt me. I dodged the blow, patted his head, and then immediately sat down. Now, at the time, I had no idea why I sat down; it just seemed like the right thing to do.

The man stood over me, puzzled.

"When did you shave your head?" I asked.

He straightened himself up, and we began a long, healthy conversation. This man had come back to the dojo with the intent to pay back the instructor for his mistreatment. That instructor was so arrogant that he had no clue why anyone would attack him, and yet he attracted this to himself. If you are arrogant or a jerk or have the habit of creating bad energy, this will come back to you somehow. Even if you don't get beat up, fighting a student always makes you the loser.

Teach Others How You Wish to Be Treated

I was a class clown growing up. I told stupid jokes, and I was always trying to find funny moments in serious situations. Part of my childhood was rather harsh, and I likely developed this habit in an attempt to make my surroundings more civil. This led to something I did not foresee: when I tried to be serious or if I was angry, people dismissed me and thought I was trying to be funny. This, of course, made the situation worse for me.

I realized much later in life that I taught people how I would like to be treated. I taught them that I was the funny guy and that they should only come to me if they wanted a good laugh. To this day, I still have old friends who want to engage in funny, witty banter even if I am not in the mood to receive it. I created that aura and atmosphere for myself.

I'm glad I've given people joy over the years, and I'm glad I was able to make people laugh in tense and horrible situations, but sometimes I have something else to say, and I've had to work hard to change the way people see me. Taking responsibility for teaching others how you wish to be treated is an important step in changing how you will be treated throughout life.

How we interact with others on a daily basis tells people how we want to be communicated with. Pay close attention to this lesson. If you seek a promotion at work or are trying to attain something higher in life, you will need to start training others on how you wish to be treated. If you want others to compliment you, you must first compliment others. If you want people to respect you, you must first respect others. This translates directly over to practice in the dojo as well, for our partners will come at us with punches, blocks, throws, or whatever in response to how we train with them. Train rudely or dismissively with others, and you might have someone itching for a fight.

This begins with learning to respect everyone you meet, even if you do not like him or her. You will find the good in people if you actively look for it. If you constantly seek the bad in people, you will find the bad instead. If someone rubs you the wrong way, you should find out why, because chances are you rub him or her the wrong way too. So much of the unpleasantness in our relationships comes from assumptions and misunderstandings.

I once worked with a woman who rubbed me the wrong way. She and I clearly did not like each other, and her words to me were biting and nasty. My disdain for her because of this probably gave her the sense that I was an arrogant jerk, escalating each of our emotions. Then one day I decided I would change this relationship we had, and I started complimenting her on her work. At each moment when it was clear her efforts were great, I let her know in a genuine way how much I appreciated her assistance and how much I liked the quality of her work. In just two weeks, she began to praise my work too, and our working relationship was forever fixed by this transformation in my attitude.

If you want others to treat you differently than you are currently being treated, you must change yourself first. Only in this way can others start to see you in a different light. If you want others to treat you with respect, you must demonstrate and show that you deserve respect. If you want others to treat you seriously, you must bring that serious energy with you.

I had several teachers who could muster at a moment's notice an aura of deathly seriousness that I called "the death look." This look was sort of like the look a disapproving parent would give to his or her child after the child was caught doing something he or she should not have been doing. But the death look was much more than that. The death look was mustering the will to kill someone with your eyes. We once had some people come into our dojo who were disruptive while watching class. My sensei was in no mood for it, and he simply walked closer to them and used the death look. He then pointed to the door. Both men left without a word.

The death look is useful when you need to make a point of how serious the situation has become, but be warned: some people react very differently to this approach. Most people will back away, but some people will welcome the invitation to release their aggressive behavioral issues, making things devolve very quickly. Use this death look sparingly.

A much better look to muster is "the wise sage" look. I once had the misfortune of introducing two very powerful masters to each other. They both had a disdain for the other's arts, and one of the masters wanted to challenge the other just to see if the arts worked. This wasn't out of malice or evil, but a sincere curiosity. When these men met, I had visions of all sorts of terrible things happening; I thought there was going to be a fight. I saw no way that this was going to end in a good way. But then something peculiar happened. One of my teachers smiled, shook the other's hand, and mustered his wise sage look. This look does not instill hostility, nor does it encourage people to fight or even back down. This look is one of sincere friendship and admiration and overflows with positive energy. The two masters then spoke Japanese to each other. I had no idea what was being said, but I could tell that the situation was diffused and that there was never going to be a fight.

I felt shame at that moment. I had underestimated this quality in one of the men; he always knew the right thing to say. He was not only a master of martial arts; he was also a master of diplomacy. I did not need to interfere with this fateful meeting. He had long ago made a decision to secure the relationship through the bonds of friendship and mutual respect.

I now feel like the wise sage look is the superior art. You do not strike a wise man, a holy man, or someone of high respect. The death look can still be used in some situations, but there is no denying that the wise sage look has far more weight to it.

We should endeavor to cultivate the wise sage look for our daily lives, as I believe this to promote peace and harmony in all of our relationships. The death look should be used only when it is truly necessary to do so. Masters should endeavor to try diplomacy before punches.

Philosophy

I have often had new students come into the dojo and talk about how the philosophy of martial arts speaks to the core of who they are. I'm perplexed by this, because this philosophy seems to be nebulous in nature and also very different for every single person. The philosophy of martial arts is as diverse in nature as religion and politics.

How do people come to these conclusions, never having practiced martial arts before? Typically people study up about several arts before they go shopping for a dojo, and they find some catch phrases or pop-culture quotes that they use to form a paradigm about what martial arts are. I often hear, "I like the philosophy of karate," or, "I like the philosophy of aikido." Oh? And what would that be exactly?

To me, the philosophy of any of the arts I have studied is to improve oneself.

That's it.

Now, you can coat this in any way, shape, or form, but at the end of the day, it is all about the daily practice. Some people read into the arts deeper than was originally intended. For example, in aikido, it is typical practice to do falling as a part of a warm-up routine. I have heard some say that this is to symbolize that even if we are knocked down, we get up again. This may have some truth in it, or it may be that if you are on the floor and you wish to stand, you should just get up.

I saw one dojo whose sensei had a very bad knee, and he had to wear a brace on it; he walked with a limp. All of his students performed the arts as if they had limps. Each one of them threw as though they had a peg leg and could not bend that leg. This looked very comical from the outside. Sometimes teachers have quirks or injuries, or maybe they felt like doing something weird one day. Be careful not to fixate on the wrong area, or you may end up with peg-leg syndrome.

Once while looking at an online martial arts forum, I found posts from a woman who was very well spoken and quite eloquent. She mentioned many philosophies and cited arts, and it sounded as though she had a lot of experience. The name looked familiar, and about twenty minutes later, I remembered who this person was: it was a woman who came to my class for about eight weeks and then quit. At that time, the most experience she could have had was five months, assuming she joined another dojo. In the brief time I knew her, she was very cerebral and quite intelligent. And yet, because she lived so far removed from her body, it was exceptionally difficult to teach her anything.

In short, her arts were terrible, but this wasn't a bad thing; after all, she only had a few months of practice. However, by looking at her writing on the philosophy of the arts, you would come to the conclusion that she was a master. While I applaud her efforts of mental projection to mastery, sometimes some things are better left unsaid. I think it is great that she was pursuing her passions, but this should also be tempered with the true philosophy of the arts, which is to practice and improve.

I feel that because philosophy is just as diverse as religion or politics, it is best to keep quiet of such things in the dojo. You may have a personal philosophy that differs from my own, but if your philosophy keeps you motivated, then that is not a bad thing. We should not interfere with others' personal beliefs, so long as they are not detrimental to our practice.

If students ask me my opinion on a matter, then I freely share how I feel about these things; however, I believe that too much talk and not enough action creates an odd dojo. I've been to dojo where all they do is talk. They may get up and practice one or two arts each class, but to me this is a waste of time. You cannot intellectualize violence. You must get in there and get your hands dirty. We can talk after class over a beer if you want, but during class, we should just be concentrating on the arts and not "talkido."

Some may believe that striking another person is morally wrong, and this may be a part of their philosophy. Perhaps they are inspired by the peaceful or calm behavior of the masters. But remember this, while we do not actively seek violence, we do practice a violent art, which makes devastating use of punches, kicks, throws, and restraints. If you come to my dojo, you will be punched and thrown, but in a safe way that encourages growth and development. We don't just bash the snot out of each other for no reason. But then again, we are not practicing ballet or lawn bowling. Martial arts have real-world fighting applications, and shying away from this is rather bizarre to me. The peaceful masters' philosophy doesn't see them fighting because they are not able to; they refrain from fighting because they don't want to hurt anyone.

To understand violence, we must, to an extent, engage in violent activity. You can talk all you want about morality and philosophy, but if you cannot block my punch, then your opinion or philosophy on the arts really doesn't mean much. Do you think the bad guy on the street cares what your beliefs are? If, however, you can perform these techniques and more, I am more likely to listen and pay close attention to what you have to say.

Arts Improve by Sharing Them

Whether you are a student or a teacher, you should get in the habit of sharing what you know with people who are interested. Do not squander knowledge or keep secrets from students or peers. Keeping secrets will make you backslide in skill. By freely sharing your knowledge, you will discover different avenues to communicate your ideas. This communication facilitates new images and previously unknown facets to knowledge you already have. This process is crucial in making all of your arts possess higher quality. Demonstrate and communicate, but if your students still cannot do it, you must find another way to teach the same thing. If you can change the mental image someone else has, then it is easy to change your own image.

If you are in the habit of keeping knowledge away from peers or students, stop this behavior right now. Having secrets in martial arts is a stupid way to control others. This sort of secretiveness supposedly came from very old schools, where hiding one's technique might save one's life. Perhaps this had some relevance several hundred years ago, before the Internet, traffic jams, and automatic weapons. Some schools keep hiding their "true" techniques, thinking that this is the most traditional way to carry on the arts. I've seen teachers deliberately show one way of performing an art to their students, which was incorrect, and then perform it differently themselves. These people deliberately kept their students down, and as a result, themselves as well.

Why would you want to maliciously hold your students back? This is the twenty-first century! If we don't like our teachers, we can go across the street and find another one. We can YouTube just about every art out there and find exactly what it is that we're looking for. Hiding things from others is a paranoid delusion and nothing more. This type of thinking demonstrates insecurity. Hiding arts in the beginning of a student's training, just to give it away later as a prize, is a cowardly way to treat people who have been loyal to you for many years. It isn't a gift if it was purposefully concealed.

If you were hiding arts and revealed this to your students, perhaps years later, do you think that they would be grateful—or resentful? Would they praise you or despise you?

My teachers shared everything and hid nothing. This doesn't mean I understood all of their arts right away. In fact, in some cases, it took ten years or more to truly understand the lessons they taught me. But I knew, even when I had that aha moment, that they had not deceived me even remotely. I just wasn't ready to digest the material that was offered to me at that time, and it took me many years to discover it in my own mind. This is much different than deliberately misleading me into a wrong path.

Students must trust their teachers, and we must never destroy this trust. We are sometimes practicing some very dangerous techniques, and everyone needs to trust the others to enjoy the experience, learn from one another, and not cause injuries.

Some may argue that trust is earned or that trust develops over time. I have a different feeling on the subject of trust. I trust everyone with my heart and mind open. I trust everyone until they give me reason *not* to trust them. By openly revealing my trust for others, people will naturally trust me. If you are openly distrustful and wary of others, others will not trust you; in fact, they may become wary of you. This is a horrible way to live. Trust everyone. If someone breaks that trust, throw him or her out of your life and move on.

When we share the wealth of knowledge we know, it will render to us tenfold the riches. I'm not talking about money in the bank; I'm talking about the long-lasting friendships, long-lasting student-teacher relationships, and other knowledge that we learn when we openly and freely give to others everything we know. If you bend over backward for people, they will bend over backward for you. If you do nothing for others, others will do nothing for you.

Share what you know freely, and you will attract to you good people worthy of trust. Let go of the half-baked "tradition" that your arts are secret and sacred. Being secretive and deceptive will naturally attract secretive and deceptive people to your life. This will only further reinforce your paradigm of paranoia. As civilians, we do not need to harbor these feelings. That's right, the vast majority of us are civilians, and martial arts are civilian arts, no matter how much you would like to talk about "the battlefield." I have never been on a battlefield, nor do I care to be. Martial arts are not about warfare; guns, artillery, air strikes, and offshore support do this much more efficiently than do fists and feet. Martial arts are not military arts, so don't treat them as classified information. Also, it took me decades to get where I am, so for someone wanting to steal my arts, it will likely take him or her years to do so. There is no such thing as stealing arts from someone.

Martial arts may never be beneficial in your life in a direct and obvious way because you may never actually get involved in a real fight. This is a good place to be, and I would argue that if you have never been in a real fight, then you have been practicing self-defense very well. Martial arts will improve your life and fill you with purpose. Sharing your arts with others will create strong bonds between you and your students that are difficult to manufacture elsewhere. Your reward for hard training and dedication is enlightenment, and by sharing your wisdom with others, you will help them reach their goals.

We are not warriors because we have no war to fight. Thinking that we must fight to exercise our arts might transform our lives into war if we let it. If we think about peace, we shall have peace in our lives. If we think about struggle, strife, and even antiwar, we will have those negative things attracted to us in our lives.

By continuously sharing positive things with our peers or with our students, we create for ourselves a positive place to live in—a place free from fear, doubt, and paranoia.

Developing the Mastery Mind-Set

Victory is always possible for the person who refuses to stop fighting.—Napoleon Hill

For years I tried to follow the philosophy of developing the "beginner's mind," meaning, always be humble and eager, like a beginner, to learn new skills. I have since changed my mind on what my mental approach is toward my arts. While I agree that one should keep an open mind like a beginner, one should also shoot higher in life. If you aim low, you are likely to hit low. If you aim high, you are definitely going to hit higher than if you were aiming low in life, even if you don't reach the top.

Beginners may have enthusiasm, but they may also carry with them a mind-set or a paradigm brought from somewhere else. Perhaps they loved old kung fu movies, and what they want to learn is movie martial arts. Perhaps they read a book on aikido and want to learn the spiritual side of the arts. Whatever it is, they have come to the dojo with some idea of what it is that they will be doing. These ideas often hold us back, because we cannot accept the truth behind arts that don't fit into our preconceptions. This is why I prefer to develop the mastery mind-set.

The mastery mind-set is one where we constantly reflect on ourselves and our arts, finding new ideas to encourage others as well as ourselves. Mastery is not a fixed point; it is a goal so big and so huge that it takes daily effort over a lifetime to achieve. It is a driving sense that makes us question everything we do, and makes us search for different approaches to familiar problems to develop a deeper understanding of our lives. The benefits and the experiences you will gain during this journey far outweigh any supposed heights of actually *being* a master, as well as achieving minor goals and believing that your work is complete. The journey, then, is the most important aspect.

Beginning Your Journey

I think of competency in martial arts as being measured in decades; however, mastery has to have a beginning point. Commit to having that point be today. Today you must be good, so that tomorrow you can be better. If you say to yourself, "One day I will be good," you will spin your wheels. When will that be exactly? Having a vague goal like this will likely continue to produce vague results in your life. If you look at a map to find a destination, you need two points: where you are and where you are going. If you do not know where you are starting, the map is useless. Likewise, if you do not know what your destination is, the map is useless. The same is true for martial arts. The starting point is today, and mastery is the destination; the route you take is simply the arts you have chosen to practice.

You don't have to be great at everything; start small. Start with mastering your stance work, for example. If you have to adjust your stance here and there to make it perfect, then you have not mastered this stance. Practice with your feet in a natural position, and then step forward into all of your stances. I no longer practice stepping backward in line basics. I feel like stepping back is a very natural response to being attacked, and it doesn't really need to be practiced all that much after you have the basic idea of how to do it. Stepping forward and into danger, however, is not a natural thing to do, so this must be practiced in great depth. Step forward in whatever stance you choose and make sure that you do not have to shift your weight or correct anything. Be solid. Be confident. Psychologically, stepping forward affirms your commitment to the mastery mind-set, because stepping backward in life will only get you the same level of skill with your arts as you have known.

After you have developed stances that are solid, I would recommend finding a handful of techniques that you like, that you are good at, or ones you just think are cool. If you make practicing your arts a choren like doing the dishes, you may just put off practice for another time. You must find your arts interesting and thrilling; then it will be no problem to find time to practice them.

I like having a few "oh shit!" techniques. These are my set of go-to arts that are universal. What I mean about universal is that it doesn't matter how my opponent attacks me; these arts work whether one kicks, punches, or whatever. After all, your opponent is hitting you first with intent to cause harm, and this intention can be received first, and then acted upon. Each martial art has its own set of "oh shit!" techniques; find these, make them your own, and practice them every day. This is a basic building block to create bigger and better things.

What Makes a Master?

All masters started out as students. All masters struggled with techniques and had to learn many hard lessons. All masters hit plateaus in their training, and all masters hit walls, either in their minds or ones that others created before them.

Hopefully you are learning your arts from a master, but even if you are not, you should endeavor to develop the mastery mind-set. The mastery mind-set is one where you project the future into your mind's eye, see the man or woman that you wish to become, and strive with all of your being to get there. Use a mastermind alliance to cultivate and nurture this intention.

When you practice your arts, ask yourself, "What would a master do?" When you teach, ask yourself, "How would a master teach this?" When you conduct yourself outside of the dojo, ask yourself, "How would a master react to this situation?" If you practice a kata and you do not know the application for a particular form, what are you going to do about it? Are you just going to shrug and do something else? Or are you going to attempt to figure it out?

Pay attention to the words you use in daily life. I once took class with a teacher who had been practicing for twenty years, but his self-confidence was so bad that he could barely look people in the face. He would constantly shift from side to side and fidget throughout the class. This man would preface each demonstration with, "I'm not very good at this, but ..."

Is this something that a master would say?

If you find yourself saying things like this, stop immediately. They do nothing to build self-confidence, and have everything to do with why you might be experiencing the poor or mediocre results you are experiencing. When you talk about yourself in your mind, you should use positive words, which in turn will create positive images. Do not limit yourself or put up artificial boundaries. Life can be hard enough as it is, and you do not need to be your own enemy.

In martial arts, we are also seeking wisdom and aspiring to be humble. But in order to be humble, we must recognize the gifts we have and actively promote ourselves in our own minds. This may sound like egotism, but it is nothing of the sort. Being humble comes from understanding, not by self-deprecation.

Masters' calmness comes from their self-confidence. They do not boast of their prowess, but they also do not engage in needless self-defeating practices like telling people, "I'm not very good at this." If you are calm and at ease, people may very well see that you are not good at something, but they will also see earnestness in your body and your eagerness to improve. It is this power that will help bring people along with you.

I met a karate teacher once who did not know as much as I did about the arts. That is, when he punched me, I could absorb his power, and when I punched him, he would fall down to the mat. I'm not boasting of my prowess; I'm commenting on this man's level of understanding of karate. Still, this man had a charming and magnetic personality. When he came in the room, everyone smiled and wanted to shake his hand. It was like he was a celebrity without being famous. He had over two hundred students in his dojo. Two hundred! Do the math on that one, and you will know that there can be a great deal of money in the martial arts if you apply your attitude correctly.

When we bow, we are showing respect to our dojo, to our students, to our fellow practitioners, but most importantly, we are bowing to that inner master—the teacher that lives inside of us who will one day blossom into a master at a ripe old age. Each time you bow, bow to the man or woman you wish to become and honor that person. Recognize your faults and your shortcomings, and actively endeavor to become a better person—not just for yourself, but for all the other people in your life. How do you think your spouse will react to you becoming a better person? Your coworkers? Your friends?

The big goal of our training is to become masters; however, we should never call ourselves masters, as I believe this title is granted to people by their students and not by themselves. I've asked martial art masters about mastery, and they always look uncomfortable about the subject. I do not think they consider themselves as masters yet, even those with over fifty years of experience. This is part of the mastery mind-set. They are continuing to learn far beyond the point of mastery.

Mastery comes only if we continuously dream about the next steps our lives will take. We must climb a higher mountain in our mind and make goals so vast that we may first believe, "That's impossible!" Is it? I used to think some things were impossible, but I know them now to be the truth. What is impossible in your mind? When I go to sleep at night, I have dreams of flying, walking through walls, and casting magical spells from my hands. My waking self dismisses this as dream and impossible in the real world.

But, what is the real world? A world of disbelief? Perhaps all we need is belief to be able to walk through walls. After all, the wall is not solid. The spaces between the wall's atoms create more gaps than actual matter. Besides, matter is energy anyway, just like our bodies. So it may very well be possible to match the vibration of a wall and walk through it.

As a side note, if anyone figures out how to do this, please call me anytime, even in the middle of the night, because I sure would love to be able to do this.

I was sometimes frustrated early in my training because I couldn't perform advanced techniques and my teachers were always showing these arts that in my opinion were way off in left field. I wanted to say, "Dude, teach me how to punch first, so I can worry about this other crap later."

Since then, I see what was really happening. My teachers were striving to do more, to stretch the boundaries of their knowledge and instill their students with inspiration. At the time, part of me thought, *Thanks, Grandpa. Teach me more about punching first!* But the lesson here was that my sensei was working on developing higher levels of the arts, not only the lower tiers of the arts. He often taught dozens of new ideas each time he came to class, because he wanted to move on to the next thing. This is one way you can see mastery: these people do not dwell on what they already know, but they are continuously pushing forward with new ideas and exploring new avenues.

Experimentation Creates Enthusiasm

When I first go to a new city, each road, each highway, and each avenue is an adventure. I stare in wonderment at buildings, architectural oddities, and things that are different from back home. This sort of childlike wonder is infectious, and often the people showing me around remark, "Yeah, you are right. That is cool!"

Remember the time when you were first introduced to martial arts, and remember the awe and wonderment at learning a new art, movement, or technique that really knocked your socks off? You can relive this moment with beginners who are discovering these things for the first time. This enthusiasm spreads like wildfire throughout your dojo and gives everyone energy and power.

As a practitioner or as a teacher, experimenting with the arts is a unique way of learning. Many martial artists frown upon this type of practice because it runs contrary to their school's "tradition." Your art teacher may teach you to paint a certain way; he or she has the best intentions for your education, but his or her vision might not be how you connect with the medium. The only way to find out is through experimentation.

In this way, martial arts are similar to visual art. Our canvas only exists while we practice, because we express ourselves through physical movement. The moment we stop practicing, our canvas disappears from sight. A painter may make a painting, hang it on the wall, and even twenty years later, point to it and say, "See, I'm a painter."

As martial artists, our paintings exist for only a little while and then vanish. This might lead you to think that we need to constantly be "painting" through the repetition of our techniques. This mind-set will make your arts become boring and laborious because we have told ourselves we must do a million punches or a million kicks to get better. Well, if you truly believe that only by practicing something a million times you will get better, this is how long it will take you.

Experimentation, not millions of repetitions, is the key for advanced practitioners to continue to grow in their arts. Become a painter who with your techniques iconoclastically creates great works that speak from your soul, regardless of what came before it. This will generate that childlike enthusiasm required to push you forward. Chances are you will be reinventing the wheel with each movement you "discover," but that's fine. This self-discovery is priceless because it generates a beginner's enthusiasm that will, in turn, cultivate the mind-set of the master, keeping you hungry and looking for more.

Always be hungry for your arts.

Do the Impossible

There was a time when I worried that these mastery secrets would be lost to time forever, in part because many of the masters adhered to old traditions and did not freely share their knowledge. I was fortunate in finding several masters for whom this was not the case. They gifted me with their understanding and knowledge. By sharing these arts with others, our arts will live on and continue to improve. Share all that you know with those who are of similar mind, so that together we may all become masters of the impossible and be able to transmit this knowledge to the next generation.

It is my sincerest desire that all who encounter this text in their pursuit of understanding martial arts take heed of the lessons within and study them thoroughly. Leverage my experience and the lessons found in each chapter to leap ahead and attain more skill on your journey to mastery. Find the topics that speak to you and reread them over and over, making them a part of your daily practice and even way of life. Do not allow a fear of failure, worry, or doubt to sway you on your path. Decide right now that you will become a master of the martial arts—not to indulge your ego or for sinister designs, but simply because you are worthy of it. Have the faith to follow your dream.

All masters had to start somewhere; every mountain climber puts one foot forward at a time until he or she reaches the summit. Steady, forward motion takes place first in your imagination, then in a plan within your mind, and finally in reality—but it never ceases here. The mastery mind-set has us perpetually dreaming and perpetually achieving. By harnessing powerful positive images, we may develop skills that look impossible to the untrained.

The unknown and impossible should not be feared; instead, they should excite and inspire you to a greater scope of everything you do in life—not just martial arts. If we can really wrap our heads around there being limitless dreams to find, then we can surely create the lives we wish to live. Thus, we can project the future and mold the outcomes we desire, be it a devastating punch or a healthy life filled with affirming relationships. True self-defense comes from mastering the mind-set of positive self-worth and respect for others. Endeavor to hold positive designs of your dreams, and you will lead an amazing life.

Have the courage to make the impossible possible.

Special thanks to Elijah Zupancic (far left) and Robert Audette (far right).

Glossary

Age tsuki	Rising punch or uppercut
Aikido	A Japanese martial art derived from samurai battlefield arts
Arts	The word "arts" is used in reference to martial art techniques
Boshiken	Thumb fist strike (thumb tip or thumb knuckle)
Chudan	Stomach level
Dojo	Martial arts studio
Empi uchi	Elbow strike
Forms	A set pattern in karate used for training purposes
Fumikomi	Stomping kick, using the heel
Furi tsuki	Swinging hook punch
Gedan	Groin level
Gedan barai	Downward block
Gyaku tsuki	Reverse or cross punch
Haito uchi	Ridge-hand strike
Hakama	Pleated pants used in some Japanese martial art styles
Hangeki	A preemptive or simultaneous counterattack
Hanmi	Half-facing body position (hips and shoulders are 45 degrees)
Harai uke	Sweeping defense
Hikite	Returning hand
Hiza geri	A kick using the knee to strike an opponent
Ipponken tsuki	One-knuckle fist punch
Jodan	Head level

Judo	A Japanese competition-style martial art derived from jujitsu
Jujitsu	A Japanese martial art using throwing, grappling, and submission holds
Juji uke	"X" or crossed-arm defense
Kagi tsuki	Roundhouse punch
Kake uke	Hook defense
Karate	Originally an Okinawa martial art derived from Chinese martial arts. Karate was once called Tote or Totejutsu
Kara uke	Void defense
Kata	Forms or patterns in karate
Keiko uchi	Chicken-beak strike
Kenjutsu	Japanese swordsmanship
Keri	Kicking techniques
Kiba dachi	Horseback stance
Kihon	Fundamental techniques
Kizame tsuki	Jab
Koken	Arc-fist strike
Koken uke	Arc-fist defense
Kumade	Bear claw strike
Kusshin	A defensive method that incorporates up or down movement of the body
Mae geri keage	Front rising kick, using the heel, the ball of the foot, or the shin
Mae geri kekomi	Front thrust kick, using the heel or the ball of the foot
Ma-hanmi	Side-facing body position (hips and shoulders facing to the side)
Mawashi geri	Roundhouse kick, using the ball of the foot, or shin
Mawashi uke	Roundhouse defense
Mikkatsuki geri	Crescent kick, using the inside or outside edge of the foot

Moto dachi	A short fighting stance
Nagashi uke	Scraping defense
Nami gaeshi	Returning wave kick, using the inside edge of the foot
Nan quan kung fu	Southern style of Chinese martial art
Nekoashi dachi	Cat stance
Nukite	Spearhand strike, used to move off-line
Oi tsuki	Lead-hand punch, performed while moving
Omote ude uke	Outer-arm defense
Ra-ka	A heavy blocking method used to crush an opponent's attacking limb disrupting his or her balance
Ryu-sui	A soft defensive method used to avoid an opponent's attack, simultaneously leading the attacker off balance
Sanchin dachi	"Three battles" stance
Seiken	Closed-fist position
Sesan dachi	A long front stance slightly leaning forward
Shiko dachi	Sumo stance
Shomen	Front-facing body position (hips and shoulders square to the front)
Shotei uchi	Palm-heel strike
Shotei uke	Palm-heel defense
Shuto uchi	Sword-hand strike
Shuto uke	Sword-hand defense
Soto uke	Outside defense
Taisabaki	"Change position." A defensive method that incorporates footwork to avoid an attack
Tap out	A gesture used while training to allow your partner to know that you have been pinned or choked successfully
Tate tsuki	Vertical-fist punch
Tettsui uchi	Hammer-fist strike

Tote	The original name for karate, translated as China hand
Totejutsu	Another name for karate meaning China hand technique
Tsuki	Punching techniques
Tsuki uke	Punching defense
Uchi	Striking techniques
Uchi uke	Inside defense
Uke	Receiving techniques; blocks, parries
Uraken	Backfist strike
Ushiro geri	Back-thrust kick, using the heel
Wushu	Chinese martial arts
Yoko geri kekomi	Side-thrust kick, using the heel
Zenkutsu dachi	A long forward stance
Zu tsuki	Head butt